AMERICAN STUDIES – A MONOGRAPH SERIES
Volume 247

Edited on behalf
of the German Association
for American Studies by
REINHARD R. DOERRIES
GERHARD HOFFMANN
ALFRED HORNUNG

SYLVIA MAYER
ALEXA WEIK VON MOSSNER (Eds.)

The Anticipation of Catastrophe

Environmental Risk in North American Literature and Culture

Universitätsverlag
WINTER
Heidelberg

Bibliografische Information der Deutschen Nationalbibliothek

Die Deutsche Nationalbibliothek verzeichnet diese Publikation
in der Deutschen Nationalbibliografie;
detaillierte bibliografische Daten sind im Internet
über *http://dnb.d-nb.de* abrufbar.

Gedruckt mit Unterstützung
der Fritz Thyssen Stiftung

ISBN 978-3-8253-6334-5

Imprimé en Allemagne · Printed in Germany
Druck: Memminger MedienCentrum, 87700 Memmingen

Gedruckt auf umweltfreundlichem, chlorfrei gebleichtem
und alterungsbeständigem Papier

Den Verlag erreichen Sie im Internet unter:
www.winter-verlag.de

Contents

SYLVIA MAYER, ALEXA WEIK VON MOSSNER

The Anticipation of Catastrophe: Environmental Risk in North American Literature and Culture / Introduction.....7

I Fictionalizing Global Climate Change

SYLVIA MAYER
Explorations of the Controversially Real: Risk, the Climate Change Novel, and the Narrative of Anticipation.....21

AXEL GOODBODY
Risk, Denial and Narrative Form in Climate Change Fiction: Barbara Kingsolver's *Flight Behavior* and Ilija Trojanow's *Melting Ice*.....39

ANTONIA MEHNERT
Things We Didn't See Coming – Riskscapes in Climate Change Fiction.....59

II Representations of Nuclear Risk

HOLGER KERSTEN
"These Rays May Be Helpful or Harmful": The Depiction of Radium in Early 20th Century American Newspapers.....81

ALEXA WEIK VON MOSSNER
The Stuff of Fear: Emotion, Ethics, and the Materiality of Nuclear Risk in *Silkwood* and *The China Syndrome*.....101

ANNA THIEMANN
Nuclear Risk, Domestic Responsibility, and the Uses of Comedy: Elizabeth Stuckey-French's *The Revenge of the Radioactive Lady*.....119

III Environmental Risks Across Media

CHRISTINE GERHARDT
Beyond Climate Refugees:
Nature, Risk and Migration in American Poetry..139

KARIN HÖPKER
A Sense of an Ending – Risk, Catastrophe and Precarious Humanity
in Margaret Atwood's *Oryx and Crake*..161

NICOLE MARUO-SCHRÖDER
"It's theoretically possible": Disaster and Risk
in Contemporary American Film..181

COLIN MILBURN
Green Gaming: Video Games and Environmental Risk..201

Index..221

List of Contributors..225

SYLVIA MAYER AND ALEXA WEIK VON MOSSNER

The Anticipation of Catastrophe: Environmental Risk in North American Literature and Culture / Introduction

Since the 1980s, "risk" has been one of the most productively employed categories of analysis in the social sciences, especially in the disciplines of sociology, cultural anthropology, and psychology. Risk theory and risk research in these disciplines have shown that pervasive risk awareness has increasingly reconfigured societies, politics, and cultures in our period of late modernity. Arguing from different theoretical perspectives, sociologists such as Ulrich Beck (1992 [1986]; 1999; 2009), Anthony Giddens (1991; 2009), Niklas Luhmann (1993 [1991]), or François Ewald (1986; 1991) have pointed out that crucial social, political, and cultural transformations – such as the emergence of new and often transnational political actors and institutions, a re-assessment of the sciences, but also the emergence of new subjectivities and identities – during this period can be understood as responses to risk perception and risk assessment. Risk, suggests Beck, "represents the perceptual and cognitive schema in accordance with which a society mobilizes itself when it is confronted with the openness, uncertainties and obstructions of a self-created future" (*World at Risk*, 4). It is therefore a concept that centrally involves perceptual, affective, evaluative, and imaginative processes. Rather than an "objective" hazard that threatens us, risk denotes the imagination of a future hazard. As Beck puts it, "Risk is *not* synonymous with catastrophe. Risk means the *anticipation* of the catastrophe" (*World at Risk*, 9). It is these imaginative and anticipatory qualities of risk that turn it into an important category for the analysis of cultural texts that explore the actual or potential consequences of anthropogenic transformations of various local environments and of our planet as a whole.[1]

Historically, the concept of risk has referred to a whole spectrum of notions, ranging from chance and probability to loss and threat. Etymologically, the word "risk" has been traced to Greek, Latin, and Arabic roots. Renaissance Latin "riscum" signals the economic – that is, capitalist – context of the early modern period when risk referred to the calculation of profits and losses, esp. in maritime trade enterprises and when the emergence

[1] For an introductory survey of the development of risk research in the social sciences see Arnoldi 2009 and Lupton 2013.

of mathematical probability theory and statistics marked the rise of our contemporary insurance industry. This (early) modern notion of risk focused on "natural" environmental risks, that is storms, floods, or epidemics, and often attributed the resulting calamities to divine providence. Scholars such as Beck have therefore insisted on a form of premodern "fatalism" that disregarded the human dimensions of such risks. However, as for instance historian Arwen Mohun has shown, this assessment underestimates the complexity of early conceptualizations of particularly environmental risk: "While many expressions of fatalism can be found in the historical record," Mohun explains, "premodern people also recognized the importance of human agency. They might not have been able to do anything about *preventing* natural calamities, but they routinely assigned human responsibility for limiting the negative consequences of these events" (7-8, emphasis added; see also Arnoldi 20-28). Such assignment of responsibility implies the rationalist conviction that adverse consequences of such events, or of a decision taken, can be calculated, minimized, or even avoided in order to protect communities from harm or turn the risky venture into an economic success. This rationalist conviction, with its emphasis on human agency and trust in the calculability of risk, has marked the modern period until the 20th century. In late modernity, however, especially since the last decades of the 20th century, the meaning of the concept of risk has changed. What Jakob Arnoldi labels a "crisis of risk" (36) refers to the fact that due to an increasing awareness of unintended side effects of contemporary technologies, "belief in the ability to calculate, to objectify, potential dangers as risk has … waned" (35). Risk today is strongly defined by a sense of uncertainty, threat, or danger. Arnoldi therefore concludes: "Rather than believing that all risks can be accurately known, assessed and managed, the conception is now that in many cases uncertainty remains and that some risks should therefore not be taken" (34).

In the history of the United States, the focus of Mohun's study, environmental risks have played a particularly prominent role. Mohun reminds us that "in early America, fire, disease, weather and animals presented the most important dangers to property and human life" (3). The vast expanse of the North American continent is particularly prone to all kinds of "natural" disasters – be they earthquakes, draughts, wildfires, tornadoes, or hurricanes – and so the European settlers who wanted to build their lives there somehow had to deal with these risks. However, only very rarely did this mean that they consciously tried to avoid them. As the environmental historian Ted Steinberg has shown, Americans exhibit a remarkable tendency to ignore the fact that "natural calamities frequently do not just happen; they are produced through a chain of human choices and natural occurrences" (xxi). The result of such thinking has been large settlements in high risk areas such as deserts and certain coastal regions. In *Ecology of Fear*, Mike Davis reminds us of "the obvious fact that Los Angeles has deliberately put itself in harm's way" because "[f]or generations, market-driven urbanization has transgressed environmental common sense" (9). In spite of this long history of deliberately ignoring the potentially devastating consequences of environmental risk for the sake of development and profit, however, US citizens have become increasingly obsessed with the idea of security. Making the case for a "distinctive American risk society" (8), Mohun argues that "over time, Americans have significantly increased the resources dedicated to controlling risk. Whether experts or members of the public, most people expect that something can and should be done to control risk at a level unimaginable to our ancestors" (258).

This trend has risen steeply in the post-World War Two period, and it most frequently has been associated with the uneasy combination of technological and environmental risks. Reflecting the "crisis of risk" of late modernity, the association of risk with threat has also begun to dominate general public discourse in the US. Central to this shift of meaning has been the impact of scientific and technological modernization in various areas. Nuclear technology, but also developments in chemistry and biology have been met by strong public skepticism and resistance and have led to the emergence of social, including environmentalist, movements. In the United States, the publication of Rachel Carson's *Silent Spring* in 1962 marked the beginning of a self-conscious modern environmental movement that sought to raise awareness of the environmental consequences of human actions. The fictitious "Fable for Tomorrow" that opens Carson's nonfiction book describes a pastoral idyll of "checkerboard prosperous farms, with fields of grain and hillsides of orchards" which is threatened by "a strange blight that cre[eps] over the area" (21). The evocation of an "evil spell" and a "shadow of death" seems to hint at divine intervention, but it is soon clarified that "No witchcraft … had silenced the rebirth of new life in a stricken world. The people had done it themselves" (22) because they ignored the risks associated with the use of pesticides such as DDT. At this point, then, another kind of interaction between environmental risk and human agency had moved into the center of attention: rather than failing to avoid natural risks, Americans were increasingly *producing* environmental risks on an unprecedented scale.

Notably, the impact of such anthropogenic environmental risks was not shared by all Americans equally. Beginning with the early 1980s, the environmental justice movement brought attention to the fact that in the United States poor people and minorities were disproportionably exposed to the risks associated with toxic landfills and other environmental hazards. As Joni Adamson, Mei Mei Evans, and Rachel Stein point out in their Introduction to *The Environmental Justice Reader*, the "disparate distribution of wealth and power often leads to … the unequal distribution of environmental degradation and/or toxicity" that may result from such risks (5).

Over the past few decades, civil society organizations in the US and elsewhere have continued to draw attention to the risks that accompany technological innovation, warning against nuclear and chemical risks, risks related to genetic engineering or nanotechnology, or the risks inherent in anthropogenic global warming. And they have increasingly become aware of the large temporal and spatial scales of some of these environmental risks. As Rob Nixon reminds us in *Slow Violence and the Environmentalism of the Poor*, disenfranchised communities around the world "experience environmental threat not as a planetary abstraction but as a set of inhabited risks, some imminent, others obscurely long-term" (4). The inhabitants of a low-lying atoll in the central Pacific may only have a vague understanding of the fact that the rising ocean that threatens their home is a result of carbon emissions elsewhere. Nevertheless, they are constantly at risk to experience a form of "slow violence" that is perpetrated by people who are themselves only dimly aware of their involvement in such violence.

Perhaps unsurprisingly, the unprecedented scale and complexity of man-made global environmental risks such as climate change has also played a central role in much of recent risk theory and risk research. Global environmental risks can be regarded as a qualitatively new type of risk that is defined, for instance, by the fact that it tends to elude traditional forms of human experience and knowledge production. Both Beck, in his model of the "world risk society," and Giddens, in his concept of a "risk culture," point toward a widespread inability to perceive and assess several current global risks "directly" – with the exception of those moments when such risks are, as Nixon puts it, concretely "inhabited" by an individual or a community. Due to the difficulty of assessing the large-scale, and often global, causes of such risks, we are often forced to rely on "secondhand experience" (or even, according to Beck, "secondhand non-experience"), a fact that more often than not leads to an increasing lack of trust in social and political institutions. The difference between local and global environmental risks, explains Mohun, is that the latter involve "man-made, global threats such as environmental degradation or nuclear war that individuals can do nothing about" (8). The same is true for climate change and its complicated politics which, as Giddens reminds us, "is all about risk and how to manage it" (*Politics*, 7). Ultimately, this new type of risk thus marks the experience and impact of an unprecedented degree of danger or threat, revealing that scientific knowledge production in our period of late modernity always involves a dimension of not-knowing and that the consequences of technological innovation cannot be fully calculated.

This experience of radical uncertainty brings us back to the point that both risk perception and risk assessment necessarily involve imaginative and affective processes. Cognitive psychologists such as Paul Slovic (2002, 2010) have drawn attention to the fact "that feelings serve as an important cue for risk/benefit judgments and decisions" (*Feeling*, xxi), and together with the imaginative dimension of risk perception this has important repercussions for the analysis of cultural texts such as literature and film. In a jointly written essay entitled "Numbers and Nerves: Toward an Affective Apprehension of Environmental Risk," Paul Slovic and the ecocritic Scott Slovic point to the ways in which literary texts help us understand otherwise inconceivable threats to the environment through storytelling. Both social science and environmental literature, they argue, have placed an emphasis "on emotion and the language of story in the apprehension and communication of risk" (80). At the same time, they tend to be conscious of the social and contextual factors that influence such individual apprehensions of risk. As Paul Slovic explains, the psychometric paradigm assumes that "risk is subjectively defined by individuals who may be influenced by a wide array of psychological, social, institutional, and cultural factors" (xxv). This insight pays tribute to the results of risk research in the field of cultural anthropology which, in the tradition of Mary Douglas and Aaron Wildavsky, has focused on identifying the socio-cultural dynamics and moral functions that are involved in the identification of risks. They have shown that risk perception relies on worldviews and cultural biases emerging from specific social contexts, as a result of which risk perception in different cultures can differ considerably. This is why the essays assembled in this collection focus on North American perceptions of risk specifically, and on the ways such perceptions have been imagined and framed in cultural texts.

The Cultural Perception of Risk: North American Perspectives

Only very recently has the analytical category of risk also entered literary and cultural studies in a more sustained way. It has done so in the field of ecocriticism, environmentally oriented literary and cultural studies. In 2001, Lawrence Buell's *Writing for an Endangered World* established a relationship between Beck's notion of the risk society and what he calls "toxic discourse": the "expressed anxiety arising from perceived threat of environmental hazard due to chemical modification by human agency" (31). Calling Ulrich Beck "the Rachel Carson of contemporary social theory" (*Future* 5), Buell has repeatedly insisted that the environmental imagination includes the evocation of risk scenarios and that literary criticism must draw on relevant social theory in order to develop approaches that allow for the analysis of such imaginaries.

Frederick Buell's *From Apocalypse to Way of Life* sought to provide such analysis for North American cultural texts, arguing that a continuous "dwelling" (199) in risk and uncertainty has led to the emergence of two markedly different cultural responses in American literature and film, which either "attempt to escape from embodiment and embeddedness in a difficult time" or invite readers and viewers to "come into [their] senses" in order to "face the problems involved in dwelling in deepening environmental and environmental-social crisis" (208).[2] Tracing American cultural responses from the anxious voicing of concern to an acceptance of the status quo, Buell's analysis rings painfully true given the United States' continued apathy in the face of climate change and other global environmental risks. For the most extensive and insightful engagement with risk theory, however, we must turn to the work of Ursula Heise. Her study *Sense of Place and Sense of Planet* (2008) and several essays (2002, 2009) investigate how specific environmental risks are articulated in literature, film, and other kinds of art by drawing on insights of risk research in the social sciences.

Heise rests her argument on two basic premises: First, risks are always mediated, which is why the study of risk also needs a focus on textual representation and communication. "Narrative genres," she argues, "provide important cultural tools for organizing information about risks into intelligible and meaningful stories" (*Sense* 138). Second, literary texts as well as fictional texts that come in other media participate in the discourse of environmental risk communication, which cannot be reduced to a discourse of scientific expertise or political decision making. Heise thus understands literary and other fictional media texts as one form of many ways in which environmental risk can be *staged*. Beck argues that "the distinction between risk as anticipated catastrophe and the actual catastrophe forces us … to take the role of *staging* seriously. For only by imagining and staging world risk does the future catastrophe become present" (*World at Risk* 10, emphasis added). Such imagining and staging of world risk – and specifically environmental world risk – can happen in multiple ways in various kinds of media.[3] Literary texts and films, however, address and communicate risks in very specific ways: in contrast to scientific texts, they explore the complexity of *individual* risk experiences – their cultural, social, political, economic, or psychological dimensions – and they engage their readers imaginatively, intellectually, and emotionally through storytelling.

---

2 Buell calls the first group of cultural responses the "culture of hyperexuberance," which accepts "as its foundation … that people [are] already beyond their limits, out of balance and in disequilibrium with nature" but seeks "to alchemize [these premises] into possibilities, not horrors" (216). In his view, this category includes novels such as William Gibson's *Neuromancer* (1984) and films such as Ridley Scott's *Blade Runner* (1982). The second group of cultural responses, which offer a more sincere engagement with the dwelling in environmental risk and crisis, includes novels like Don DeLillo's *White Noise* (1985) and Octavia Butler's *Parable of the Sower* (1993) and films such as Terry Gillam's *Twelve Monkeys* (1995).

3 For an analysis of how environmental risk has been staged in the news and other popular media formats, see Stuart Allan, Barbara Adam and Cynthia Carter's edited volume *Environmental Risks and the Media* (2000).

The Essays in this Volume

This volume picks up on the innovative work done by Frederick and Lawrence Buell, Heise and others, assembling essays that engage with predominantly fictional contributions to North American environmental risk discourses.[4] The ten essays examine the representation of various environmental risks across genres and media. They are grouped into three sections. The first section focuses on representations of the risk of global climate change in several climate change novels; the second section concentrates on the representation of the nuclear risk in non-fictional and fictional texts as well as in film; the third section draws particular attention to the relevance of genre in the representation of a variety of environmental risks, genres ranging from poetry to posthuman fiction to Hollywood disaster movies and video games.

The contributions in the first section of the book are devoted to climate change, perhaps the vastest and most unpredictable global environmental risk that we face today. In "Explorations of the Controversially Real: Risk, the Climate Change Novel, and the Narrative of Anticipation," Sylvia Mayer engages with the question of how to define the emerging genre of the climate change novel. Drawing on sociological risk theory, she reads the climate change novel as risk narrative and develops a genre-defining distinction between two types of narratives: the narrative of anticipation and the narrative of catastrophe. While the narrative of catastrophe explores the risk of climate change by creating a future fictional world when climate collapse has already occurred, the narrative of anticipation focuses on the present moment when climate collapse can still be avoided, when it is still a risk scenario that needs to be fully grasped in order to be averted. Her readings of Barbara Kingsolver's *Flight Behavior* and Kim Stanley Robinson's Science in the Capital trilogy, the novels *Forty Signs of Rain*, *Fifty Degrees Below*, and *Sixty Days and Counting*, then concentrate on the climate change novel as risk narrative of anticipation and point out in detail its central narrative strategies, techniques, and functions.

Axel Goodbody's contribution "Risk, Denial and Narrative Form in Climate Change Fiction" also looks at the issue of genre, but does so from a comparative perspective, investigating how Barbara Kingsolver's *Flight Behavior* and Ilja Tronajow's German novel *EisTau* adapt well-established genres, narratives and images to their representations of the risk involved in global warming. Drawing on the work of sociologist Kari Norgaard, Goodbody further explores to what extent these climate novels represent the public response to climate change in terms which bear out the conception of denial

[4] For a discussion of risk theory in the context of contemporary American fiction, see also Susan Mizruchi's "Risk Theory and the Contemporary American Novel" (2009).

as an active process. He also looks at how they reflect Norgaard's distinction between outright denial of climate change and more qualified denial of its risk implications, suggesting that an analysis of the two novels can yield insights which complement sociological and psychological studies of denial. Writing and reading literary narratives about global environmental risks such as climate change, argues Goodbody, are likely to have repercussions beyond the immediate reading process not only because they contribute to the public's critical awareness of arguments about environmental risks, but also because they create a sense of the feasibility of change and the need for it through the power of literary imagination.

Climate risk also plays the central role in Antonia Mehnert's exploration of Steven Amsterdam's *Things We Didn't See Coming* in her essay on "Riskscapes in Climate Change Fiction." The somewhat disjointed form of Amsterdam's novel, argues Mehnert, as well as its thematic focus on place attachment, constitute an innovative narrative format for representing the deterritorializing effects of climate change. Building on the work of Arjun Appaduarai, she develops the concept of the 'riskscape' which she sees as characterized by the experience of ubiquitous crisis. Territorial distinctions, she argues, necessarily decline in importance within such a riskscape and socio-cultural practices become disembedded from place. Applying the notion of the riskscape to *Things We Didn't See Coming* allows Mehnert to capture the constantly shifting meanings of place and place attachment within the narrative while also drawing attention to the fact that climate risks are not geographically confined. In such conditions both inhabitation and re-inhabitation become precarious. As a result, the characters of Amsterdam's novel are forced into continuous movement while adaptability and the constant renegotiation of the self become necessary preconditions for survival.

The second group of essays looks at the representation of nuclear risk in different media and in vastly different stylistic registers. In "'These Rays May Be Helpful or Harmful': The Depiction of Radium in Early 20th Century American Newspapers," Holger Kersten reminds us of the fate of the so-called "Radium Girls," a group of female workers who, in the 1920s, became victims of radium poisoning in a factory that produced luminous watch dials. Examining the record preserved in the newspaper coverage between 1900 and 1925, Kersten's essay explores how the excitement and enthusiasm about a scientific novelty can overshadow the evidence of risk. Both radium research and radium applications were represented in overwhelmingly positive terms in the American press, he demonstrates, while the risks involved in the usage of radium were generally ignored. Kersten traces this blind optimism back to a deep trust in science and progress and to a lack of adequate modes of risk assessment, a trust that was thrown into question only in 1925, when the widely-reported deaths of the "Radium Girls" finally turned the dangers of radium exposure into a topic of national debate.

Alexa Weik von Mossner's "The Stuff of Fear: Emotion, Ethics, and the Materiality of Nuclear Risk in *Silkwood* and *The China Syndrome*" focuses on the ways in which Hollywood films have represented the material and emotional dimensions of nuclear risk and on how these representations engage viewers. James Bridges's *The China Syndrome* and Mike Nichols's *Silkwood* both frame their representation of risk as suspense-driven political thrillers and in both cases the fictional drama is heightened by the films' relationships to real-world risks and events. While the invisibility of radiation raises representational problems, both films use their viewers' pre-existing risk perceptions to engage them in plotlines that are driven by the *anticipation* of catastrophes rather than by the catastrophes themselves. By telling melodramatic stories about courageous individuals who struggle to uncover the truth about nuclear risk, argues Weik von Mossner, the films not only illustrate Ulrich Beck's claim that the determination of risk is a form of ethics; they also demonstrate that emotional processes such as fear are vital components of ethical decision making in the face of unpredictable material agencies and the environmental risks they pose.

Anna Thiemann's contribution, entitled "Nuclear Risk, Domestic Responsibility, and the Uses of Comedy: Elizabeth Stuckey-French's *The Revenge of the Radioactive Lady*," explores a very different emotional register by looking at the way in which absurd humor and comedy can convey and negotiate the epistemological and ethical challenges of environmental risk. *The Revenge of the Radioactive Lady*, argues Thiemann, moves beyond the American black humor tradition of the 1960s and illustrates the comic mode's critical and transformative potential through its foregrounding of the correlation between (ir)responsibility, risk, and comedy. Drawing on Ulrich Beck's sociological deliberations on the relationship between late modern risk society and the Kafkaesque "comedy of the absurd" and applying his insights to Stuckey-French's novel, Thiemann addresses a deficit in the emerging field of literary risk criticism, which has not yet given enough attention to the role of comedy in literary explorations of risk society. Her contribution to the volume enriches the existing debate by reminding us that the literary representation of environmental risk must not necessarily be fear-inducing in order to be effective or successful.

The third section opens with Christine Gerhardt's essay "Beyond Climate Refugees: Nature, Risk and Migration in American Poetry." This essay draws attention to a literary genre whose contribution to contemporary environmental risk discourse has not yet received the sustained scholarly attention it certainly deserves, the genre of poetry. Gerhardt analyses poems by Morton Marcus, Nicole Cooley, W.S. Merwin, Amy Clampitt, Margaret Atwood, and Teresa Palomo Acosta that engage a cultural moment characterized by growing risk awareness in a context of global environmental transformation and intensifying migration within and across national borders. The poems, she shows, develop complex perspectives on how the natural environment, risk, and migration intersect in the cultural imagination of North America. Gerhardt distinguishes between three kinds of poems: poems that address migration as causing environmental risks; poems that explore migration as an integral and risky part of human and non-human existence; and poems that investigate the destabilization of frames of reference that marks the migration experience, including frames of reference defining the human-nature relationship. Her readings ultimately demonstrate that migration can be considered a significant parameter in contemporary literary conceptualizations of environmental risk.

Karin Höpker's essay "A Sense of an Ending – Risk, Catastrophe and Precarious Humanity in Margaret Atwood's *Oryx and Crake*" demonstrates the specific capabilities of posthuman fiction to radically expose the excesses and shortcomings of our current world risk society and to question, and replace, current humanist notions of subjectivity. The postapocalyptic setting of the novel and its envisioning of a future in which the human species has been largely extinguished, allows it to look back at a past – our present – in which an anthropocentric, purely economically driven logic of risk has led to catastrophe. Höpker, in particular, draws on work by Niklas Luhmann and Giorgio Agamben to show how the novel presents its explorations of the posthuman world and of a posthumanist subjectivity. She uses Luhmann's concept of the *Katastrophenschwelle*, or "disaster threshold," to show how *Oryx and Crake* criticizes a pre-collapse society that acknowledges and deals with the existence of risk only in a reductionist, actuarial way that ignores the fundamental systemic openness of the future. Agamben's concept of *intimate caesura* then serves to show how the novel problematizes and overcomes humanist subjectivity.

In her essay "It's theoretically possible": Disaster and Risk in Contemporary American Film," Nicole Maruo-Schröder addresses a genre of visual culture that can be regarded as one of the most influential narrative templates dealing with risk and thereby shaping its audiences' perception of it, the disaster movie. Maruo-Schröder argues that this type of movie does not simply focus on disaster, but also on risk and risk management, and she studies the narrative and visual patterns used to represent risk scenarios that turn into a catastrophe and ways in which risks are assessed and dealt with. Referring to a whole array of disaster movies which have been released since the 1990s, she points out their typical patterns of risk representation. Most significant in this respect may be the combination of two different risk narratives: narratives that present risk scenarios as manifestations of a future catastrophe, usually largely set in the realm of nature, run parallel to narratives of (successful) risk management, usually in the realm of culture and technology. This parallelism allows for a re-affirmation of the self-healing powers of both nature and culture, a feature that marks the conservatism of the genre's discussion of and illustrates its close link to the jeermiad. This conservatism is only highlighted in Maruo-Schröder's discussion of Steven Soderbergh's *Contagion*, a rare example of a disaster movie that refuses to comply with these generic patterns and that presents risk as ultimately uncontrollable.

Colin Milburn, finally, in "Green Gaming: Video Games and Environmental Risk," focuses on yet another medium and its engagement with environmental risk, video games. He is centrally interested in finding out whether video games can contribute to the creation of ecological awareness, and, even more importantly, whether they can raise awareness of gaming's own complicity in creating environmental risks. Milburn introduces video games as an environmentally contested technology, which in its production and consumption relies heavily on energy and other resources. This reliance often spells environmental, but also social, political, and humanitarian problems. Milburn then moves on to analyse and compare a number of games that concentrate on coping with environmental threats. He discusses their narrative organization and the ways they position the gamer ethically. Ultimately, he establishes a typology of three types of games that promote ecological thought in different ways: games of environmental discipline, games of environmental control, and games of environmental responsibility. Only the last type of games draws the gamer's attention to his or her own involvement in the environmentally and socially problematic activity of gaming. These games, Milburn argues, are essentially ironic undertakings and present a kind of green counter-gaming, a gaming against itself.

Works Cited

Arnoldi, Jakob. *Risk. An Introduction*. Cambridge: Polity Press, 2009. Print.

Beck, Ulrich. *Risk Society. Towards a New Modernity*. London: Sage, 1992. [*Risikogesellschaft. Auf dem Weg in eine andere Moderne*. 1986. Frankfurt: Suhrkamp, 2003] Print.

---. *World Risk Society*. Cambridge: Polity Press, 1999. Print.

---. *World at Risk*. Cambridge: Polity Press, 2009. Print.

Buell, Frederick. *From Apocalypse to Way of Life: Environmental Crisis in the American Century*. London and New York: Routledge, 2003. Print.

Buell, Lawrence. *Writing for an Endangered World: Literature, Culture, and Environment in the U.S. and Beyond*. Cambridge, Mass, and London: Belknap Press, 2001. Print.

---. *The Future of Environmental Criticism: Environmental Crisis and Literary Imagination*. Malden and Oxford: Blackwell Publishing, 2005. Print.

Carson, Rachel. *Silent Spring*. 1962. New York: Penguin Classics, 2000. Print.

Davis, Mike. *Ecology of Fear: Los Angeles and the Imagination of Disaster*. New York: Vintage, 1998. Print.

Douglas, Mary and Aaron Wildavsky. *Risk and Culture: An Essay on the Selection of Technological and Environmental Dangers*. Berkeley, CA: University of California Press, 1982. Print.

Ewald, Francois. "Insurance and Risk." *The Foucault Effect. Studies in Governmentality*. Ed. Graham Burchell, Colin Gordon and Peter Miller. Chicago: University of Chicago Press, 1991. 197-210. Print.

---. *L'Etat providence*. Paris: Grasset, 1986. Print.

Giddens, Anthony. *Modernity and Self-Identity: Self and Society in the Late Modern Age*. Stanford: Stanford University Press, 1991. Print.

---. *The Politics of Climate Change*. Cambridge and Malden: Polity Press, 2009. Print.

Heise, Ursula K. "Cultures of Risk and the Aesthetic of Uncertainty." *Scientific Cultures – Technological Challenges. A Transatlantic Perspective*. Ed. Klaus Benesch and Meike Zwingenberger. Heidelberg: Winter, 2009. 17-44. Print.

---. *Sense of Place and Sense of Planet. The Environmental Imagination of the Global*. Oxford: Oxford University Press, 2008. Print.

---. "Toxins, Drugs, and Global Systems: Risk and Narrative in the Contemporary Novel." *American Literature* 74.4 (2002): 747-78. Print.

Luhmann, Niklas. *Risk: A Sociological Theory*. New York: de Gruyter, 1993. [dt.: *Soziologie des Risikos*. Berlin: De Gruyter, 1991] Print.

Lupton, Deborah. *Risk*. 2nd ed. London: Routledge, 2013. Print.

Mizruchi, Susan "Risk Theory and the Contemporary American Novel." *American Literary History* 22.1 (2009): 109–135. Print.

Mohun, Arwen P. *Risk: Negotiating Safety in American Culture*. Baltimore: Johns Hopkins University Press, 2013. Print.

Nixon, Rob. *Slow Violence and the Environmentalism of the Poor*. Cambridge, MA: Harvard University Press, 2012. Print.

Perrow, Charles. *Normal Accidents: Living with High-Risk Technologies*. 1984. Princeton: Princeton University Press, 1999. Print.

Slovic, Paul. *The Perception of Risk*. 2000. London: Earthscan, 2002. Print.

---. *The Feeling of Risk: New Perspectives on Risk Perception*. London and Washington, DC: Earthscan, 2010. Print.

Slovic, Scott and Paul Slovic. "Numbers and Nerves: Toward an Affective Apprehension of Environmental Risk." *The Feeling of Risk: New Perspectives on Risk Perception*. Ed. Paul Slovic. London and Washington, DC: Earthscan, 2010. 79-84. Print.

Steinberg, Ted. *Acts of God: The Unnatural History of Natural Disaster in America*. New York: Oxford University Press, 2000. Print.

Stuart, Allan, Barbara Adam, and Cynthia Carter. *Environmental Risk and the Media*. London and New York: Routledge, 2000. Print.

I

Fictionalizing Global Climate Change

Sylvia Mayer

Explorations of the Controversially Real: Risk, the Climate Change Novel, and the Narrative of Anticipation

One of the major global risks we are confronted with today is the risk of climate change. After decades of research into – and controversial debate about – the causes of global warming, climate science today overwhelmingly agrees that current climatic changes have anthropogenic causes. The authors of the IPCC report 2013, for instance, claim that it is "extremely likely that human influence has been the dominant cause of the observed warming since the mid-20th century" ("Summary" 12), and some scientists go as far as to proclaim the advent of a new geologic age that is characterized by historically sustained human intervention into the planetary ecosphere, by the notion of humanity as a geological force: the anthropocene.[1] Global climate change refers to the fact that the planet's atmosphere has undergone a process of warming up, caused by a carbon-based, fossil fuel economy whose rate of greenhouse gas emissions has, since the beginnings of industrialization, rapidly grown thereby transforming ecological systems on a global scale. Climate change modeling envisions drastic ecosystemic changes that involve a variety of far-reaching geographical and biological transformations across the world. Global warming causes the melting of the polar ice caps and of glaciers in other parts of the world as a result of which rising sea levels threaten to inundate coast lines worldwide and extreme weather phenomena such as heavy storms, flooding, heat waves and droughts become more commonplace. Such large-scale ecological changes obviously imply dramatic transformations of established economic, social, political, and cultural orders.

Politics and public opinion in countries around the globe by now predominantly acknowledge the existence of the risk of anthropogenic climate change. The development of policies, technologies, and economic practices that aim at curbing greenhouse gas emissions or replacing fossil energies entirely to at least slow down the process of global warming is a clear sign for this acknowledgement. However, the obvious failure to achieve

---

1 The concept of the anthropocene was introduced by Paul J. Crutzen and Eugene F. Stoermer; on its relevance for the humanities, and in particular for the discipline of history, see Chakrabarty (2009).

extensive results – to restructure both national economies and the global economy as a whole on a more sustainable energy basis – indicates that engagement with the specific threats climate change poses has of today been inadequate. There are several valid explanations for the fact that the knowledge climate science has accumulated has as yet not led to a more adequate response, among which the following three seem to be of particular relevance. First, prediction of future scenarios that illustrate the results of a changed climate is difficult. Scientific computer models of climate change, for instance, are only approximations of developments that occur on a global scale and manifest themselves locally or regionally in very different ways. Scientific uncertainty thus remains a major source for hesitation or even reluctance concerning the development and implementation of policies that would curb greenhouse gas emissions more effectively (Hulme 72-108). Secondly, climate change can to a certain extent be considered intangible as it is, for instance, not possible to attribute single, specific destructive weather events to the impact of global warming. This impossibility indicates the more general difficulty of linking individual, local experience with processes of global ecological transformation that usually occur over a longer period of time. Climate change thus for many turns into a distant and impersonal issue, whose effects are expected to occur only in the (far) future. Thirdly, communication about the risk of climate change has revealed acute shortcomings. Neither reliance on the expert languages of science nor reliance on a "fear appeal" (O'Neill and Nicholson-Cole) in reporting about the various threats climate change entails have been able to communicate its present manifestations and possible future developments in ways that would arouse a more powerful engagement with the problem. Instead, the predominance of information presented either in a language inaccessible to non-scientists or by means of an alarmist rhetoric and the invoking of apocalyptic future scenarios may have generated a sense of "disempowerment, apathy and skepticism" (Hulme 348).

Explanations like these suggest to the literary and cultural studies critic that anthropogenic climate change has only insufficiently been recognized, and analyzed, as a cultural issue.[2] To be sure, work on environmental risks in cultural anthropology and cognitive psychology has by now firmly established that risk perception and risk assessment must be considered as deeply entrenched in patterns of thought and moral evaluation particular to specific social groups – and can, therefore, differ considerably.[3] Human

---

[2] The scholar pointing out this deficit particularly clearly and pioneering the study of environmental risks in literary and cultural criticism in general is Ursula K. Heise (2002 "Risk and Narrative", 2002 "Toxins", 2008, 2009).

[3] Central to studies of environmental risks in cultural anthropology has been the work of Mary Douglas (esp. Douglas/Wildavsky 1982; Douglas 1992). Her influence, for instance, strongly figures in the volume *Risk and Morality*, edited by R.V. Ericson and A. Doyle, a collection of essays which unites contributions from various disciplines in

geographer Mike Hulme thus acknowledges that "[t]he idea of climate exists as much in the human mind and in the matrices of cultural practices as it exists as an independent and objective physical category. The multiple meanings of climate . . . are an essential part of making sense of what is happening around us today in our climate change discourses" (28). Anthropological and psychological studies have, however, not taken into account the contribution of fictional texts to these discourses, most notably films and literary texts that address the risk of climate change. These fictional texts introduce the issue to a much wider audience than the one reached by scientific accounts, and they contribute to the discourses of climate change in a very specific way. Due to their essentially infinite imaginative and formal range they can explore the complexity, and diversity, of individual and collective risk experience worldwide in ways that work with and at the same time transcend factual, scientific representation. The intellectual and emotional appeal fictional texts can develop may, moreover, succeed in making the various cultural, social, political, economic, and psychological factors that figure in specific experiences of the climate change risk more easily perceptible, intelligible, and concrete.

As Adam Trexler and Adeline Johns-Putra have pointed out, Anglophone climate change fiction can be regarded as a genre that appeared only in the 1990s and has slowly grown in terms of the number of texts published since the year 2000 (186).[4] Outlining especially what can be called the emergence of the "climate change novel," they draw attention to the strong impact that science fiction and the dystopian mode of narration have had on the current novelistic production. And indeed, it seems that the envisioning of future scenarios of a devastated planet after total climate collapse dominates the fictional imagination of the risk of climate change. Novels such as Stephen Amsterdam's *Things We Didn't See Coming*, Margaret Atwood's *Oryx and Crake*, *The Year of the Flood*, and *MaddAddam*, T.C. Boyle's *A Friend of the Earth*, Octavia Butler's *Parable of the Sower* and *Parable of the Talents*, or Dale Pendell's *The Great Bay. Chronicles of the Collapse* all present a world in which climate change has caused dramatic and devastating changes in the global ecosystemic, economic, social, political, and cultural orders.

This essay, however, concentrates on a different group of novels that also characterizes the current Anglophone literary response to anthropogenic climate change. It looks at four American novels that do not focus on future scenarios of global climate collapse, planetary devastation, and the (near)

---

the social sciences. For the contribution in the field of cognitive psychology see, for instance, Slovic 2002.

4 Trexler and Johns-Putra's essay is one of a still very small body of work on climate change fiction. While this situation seems to be gradually changing – in this volume alone three essays address literary climate change fiction – it seems to be a fact that the issue of climate change does not lend itself easily to fictionalization (see, for instance, the discussion of this point in Heise 2008, 205-10).

extinction of the human species and that do not predominantly rely on the dystopian mode of representation. Resisting the "fear appeal," the alarmist rhetoric, of risk communication which is transported by this mode, they instead focus on the present moment, which is, first and foremost, characterized by a strong sense of uncertainty and controversy about how to respond to the various threats – and probable first signs – of the global environmental risk of climate change. I approach these novels by regarding them as "risk narratives," a concept that draws on insights of risk theory in the social sciences, especially in sociology[5]. Moreover, in order to better account for the specific thematic and formal features that distinguish this particular group of climate change novels I propose a generic distinction between two types of risk narratives, the distinction between "narratives of catastrophe" and "narratives of anticipation." In contrast to the dystopian novels just mentioned, which I regard as narratives of catastrophe as they explore the risk of climate change by focusing on a future marked by climate collapse, the novels at stake in this essay can be categorized as risk narratives of anticipation. Taken together, I argue, these two types of risk narratives define the currently emerging genre of the climate change novel.

The novels to be discussed in the following are Barbara Kingsolver's *Flight Behavior* and Kim Stanley Robinson's Science in the Capital trilogy, that is, the novels *Forty Signs of Rain*, *Fifty Degrees Below*, and *Sixty Days and Counting*. Before turning to the analysis of the novels, however, I will develop a more precise definition of the two types of risk narrative I introduce, a definition that rests on sociologist Ulrich Beck's concept of risk and his model of the world risk society.

The World Risk Society and the Anticipation of Catastrophe

For Ulrich Beck, the key category that allows us to identify, analyze and adequately understand the current phase of modernity is the category of risk. Beck regards risk as a transformative force, which "represents the perceptual and cognitive schema in accordance with which a society mobilizes itself when it is confronted with the openness, uncertainties and obstructions of a self-created future . . ." (2009, 4). The category of the risk society, Beck argues, "designates a developmental phase of modern society in which the social, political, economic and individual risks increasingly tend to escape the institutions for monitoring and protection in industrial society" (1994, 5), which is to say the institutions of government, industry, and science. This latest developmental phase of modern society in which the risk society and the world risk society have emerged Beck calls "reflexive modernity" – a

5 In her study of "illness narratives", Ann Jurecic also uses the term and defines risk narratives as "autobiographical and literary explorations of the meanings of risk" (19).

modernity, that is, which keeps responding to the forces of modernization, to the "unforeseen consequences" or "side-effects" of the scientific and technological successes of an earlier modernity, industrial modernity. In our period of reflexive modernity "the very idea of controllability, certainty or security," Beck argues, "collapses" (1999, 2). As a result we can observe the transformation of social structures and political processes of decision making.

Beck introduced the concept of the risk society in the mid-1980s. Since then he has expanded the concept considerably, acknowledging, most significantly, the impact of globalization.[6] In *World at Risk*, his most recent book publication on the world risk society, he identifies three key global risks: global economic threats, the threat of global terrorism, and global environmental threats – most prominently, the risk of global, anthropogenic climate change. Moreover, in *World at Risk* Beck introduces a distinction between risk and catastrophe that is directly relevant to my distinction of the two types of risk narratives, to the distinction between narratives of anticipation and narratives of catastrophe. Beck argues:

> Risk is *not* synonymous with catastrophe. Risk means the *anticipation* of the catastrophe. Risks concern the possibility of future occurrences and developments . . . Whereas any catastrophe is spatially, temporally and socially determined, the anticipation of catastrophe lacks any spatio-temporal or social concreteness. Thus the category of risk signifies the controversial reality of the possible . . . Risks are always *future* events that *may* occur, that *threaten* us. But because this constant danger shapes our expectations, lodges in our heads and guides our actions, it becomes a political force that transforms the world. (9-10, emphasis in the original)

The reality of risks, their influence on our subjectivities and on our personal and collective notions of self, thus strongly relies on anticipation and on the controversial. It is risk *scenarios* in which the anticipation of a possible future catastrophe expresses itself, scenarios developed, for instance, by scientific modeling – or in works of fiction. Risk scenarios are marked by controversy, by differences in risk perception and risk assessment that reflect the impact of a variety of cultural factors. As comparative risk research has shown, risk perception depends on the specific social, economic, cultural and geographic position of individuals and social groups, and differences can be found both within a society and between societies. What is perceived as a major risk in one group or society may be regarded as a small one, as a perfectly calculable phenomenon, in another.

---

[6] Moreover, in the development of his theorizing about the (world) risk society, Beck has also responded to the criticism leveled against specific elements of his concept. For a recent summary of this criticism see Sørensen and Christiansen 123-40.

The reality of risks, moreover, depends on what Beck in *World at Risk* calls the "staging" (10) of risk. It needs the representation and communication of risks to make them real, to create awareness of an imminent threat that might result in catastrophe. Risks are thus not simply objectively measurable phenomena, but subjective or collective cultural constructions. Only if represented and communicated is the "controversially real," the anticipated, turned into a shaping force in the realms of the personal, the political, the social, the economic, and the cultural. Obviously, this argument is important for literary and cultural studies. If risks emerge and become effective through representation and communication, risk research can certainly benefit from the study of fictional risk narratives which have participated in the various risk discourses of the last decades. The creation of fictional risk narratives has run parallel to the creation of scientific risk scenarios – making use of the latter's scientific findings, but also of other kinds of knowledge that mark the diversity of human experiences of risk.

"Risk means the *anticipation* of the catastrophe" – here Beck's definition draws attention to two elements that centrally define risk: a state of anticipation and an awareness of a future scenario of catastrophe. It is from this definition that I develop the distinction between risk narratives of anticipation and risk narratives of catastrophe. While both types of risk narrative need the awareness of possible catastrophe as a point of reference, they differ in their choice of focus. The narrative of anticipation, on the one hand, concentrates on the state of anticipation, on the moment of uncertainty in the present when awareness of the risk figures prominently and controversially in a culture, but has not yet led to catastrophe. The narrative of catastrophe, on the other hand, concentrates on the future when a risk scenario has materialized in a catastrophe; the period that precedes this future, the stage of anticipation, is also introduced, for instance by means of flashbacks that delineate the characters' world before the onset of catastrophe, but it is usually given less narrative space. In the case of the climate change novel, the narrative of catastrophe explores the consequences of a collapse of ecosystems in the future that is ultimately global in scope and involves the breakdown of social, economic, political, and cultural structures. It relies heavily on the dystopian mode of representation; life in these narratives is marked by dramatic experiences of displacement, toxic pollution, and species extinction. The narrative of anticipation, in contrast, does not present global climate collapse, but focuses on the exploration of the strong sense of uncertainty and controversy that marks the perception and assessment of global warming in the present. Large-scale catastrophe is envisioned, if at all, only as a possibility, usually signaled by the representation of weather anomalies and their socio-economic consequences that indicate the impact of global warming. In this, also the narrative of anticipation has to rely on the dystopian mode. This mode of representation, however, does not dominate the novels.

The Climate Change Novel as Risk Narrative of Anticipation

Barbara Kingsolver's novel *Flight Behavior* and Kim Stanley Robinson's Science in the Capital trilogy, the novels *Forty Signs of Rain*, *Fifty Degrees Below*, and *Sixty Days and Counting*, explore the risk of climate change in ways that turn them into risk narratives of anticipation. As the following discussion will show, these climate change novels share the central features of this type of risk narrative: first, the temporal setting in the present or the very near future; second, the thematic focus on the risk of climate change as a controversial reality, as an indication of a widespread sense of uncertainty, and as a global problem; and, third, the employment of a spectrum of narrative modes and genre conventions that goes beyond the reliance on the dystopian mode.

Set in Southern Appalachia, in contemporary Tennessee, Kingsolver's *Flight Behavior* tells the story of twenty-eight-year old Dellarobia Turnbow and her family. The novel uses heterodiegetic narration, but relies on Dellarobia as single focalizer. The risk narrative is thus presented from her perspective: the thematic focus on climate change as a controversial reality, as an indication of a strong sense of uncertainty, and as a global problem is represented through this protagonist's experiences and development. This narrative strategy thus draws attention to one particular type of subjectivity that emerges in the world risk society, thereby making the global risk of climate change concrete and tangible.

The Turnbows are sheep farmers, members of the local Christian community of Feathertown, and – as are their neighbors – preoccupied with making ends meet, even battling poverty. The novel can be categorized as a climate change novel because it is centrally concerned with manifestations of a changing climate and its ecological, economic, and social consequences. Most importantly, it addresses the appearance of millions of monarch butterflies on a mountainside owned by the Turnbow family and located in the vicinity of their homes. It turns out that the animals have changed their usual migratory route to accommodate climatic changes wrought by global warming on their usual winter roosting sites in Michoacán, Mexico. They have migrated further North, probably too far, though, since in Tennessee they face the danger of too low temperatures and are thus exposed to the threat of extinction. In the course of the novel it becomes, moreover, clear that the ecological transformation indicated by the butterflies' changed migratory route is accompanied by dramatic economic and social transformation. Shortly after the discovery of the butterflies, Dellarobia meets a Mexican family, the Delgados, who lived in the region where the animals used to roost. From their story she learns that the ecological changes that occurred there have turned them into climate refugees: substantial landslides in the region destroyed not only the mountainsides where the butterflies used to roost, but also the economy that had developed around the phenomenon of the butterflies. Like the animals, the Delgados had to leave their home, in search for a new place that provides them a chance of economic and social survival.

Manifestations of climate change are, moreover, indicated by what the local characters perceive as increasingly irritating weather aberrations, especially continuous rainfall and unusual seasonal temperatures. By November, the time the events start to unfold in the novel, large amounts of rain have fallen all through the preceding summer and fall and have caused considerable damage in the forests, fields, and orchards of the region. These damaging weather conditions culminate in the flooding of the region at the end of the novel. Together they mark the use of the dystopian mode – whose major function does not lie in representing total climate change collapse, but in foreshadowing, that is, in anticipating, the danger of a larger, ultimately global catastrophe in the future.

The characters' present is marked by "flight behavior." This *leitmotif* of the novel refers both to the activity of flying and to acts of involuntary and voluntary escape. At stake are the unusual flight behavior of the monarch butterflies, the enforced flight behavior of the climate refugees, but also the flight behavior Dellarobia reveals, especially in the opening pages, but also towards the end of the novel. In the opening pages of *Flight Behavior* she plans to escape from a life which she finds unbearable. She feels trapped in her life as wife, mother, and daughter-in-law, as someone who is caught up in a dead-end situation, in the meaningless routines of her daily life. In a moment of frustration she decides to run away with another man. The meeting point they choose is on the mountain where the butterflies have begun to roost. Unaware of this fact, Dellarobia climbs the mountainside, inwardly debating her decision to abandon her life and family. In the course of her reflections, she suddenly becomes aware of "the dark uncertainty of the trail" (14) she is following. The metaphor of uncertainty, thus introduced on the first pages of the novel, here refers to her personal situation. But it is soon linked to the uncertainty that marks the ecology and economy of her home to which she is, after encountering the mass of butterflies, returning. This uncertainty is, due to the environmental forces at work, ultimately global in scope.

The encounter with the butterflies becomes a turning point in Dellarobia's life that from then on offers her the chance to ease what seems to be an essential part of her sense of frustration: an "unemployed mind" (6). In the weeks and months that follow the discovery of the butterflies, her world and mind expand dramatically. Once the news about the appearance of the butterflies spreads, she becomes centrally involved in the question of what to do with the forest where the butterflies roost. Learning to put long-term ecological considerations over short-term economic ones, Dellarobia successfully opposes her father-in-law who is about to sell the trees to a lumber company, in order to better their desperate economic situation.

Moreover, she starts to meet various kinds of people that come to their place to visit the butterfly site, among them media people, environmentalists from all over the world, and, most significantly, scientists, the entomologist Ovid Byron and his research team. Dellarobia becomes part of the team and is introduced to scientific work thereby gradually resuming her formal education, which ended when she became pregnant at age seventeen. In her work and in the many conversations she has with the scientists, but also with the diverse groups of environmentalists and with the local people, she gradually becomes aware of the controversial scope of meanings the appearance of the butterflies on the mountainside entails.

While it is clear to the scientists that the changed migratory route of the butterflies is a "bizarre alteration of a previously stable pattern" which indicates a "continental ecosystem breaking down," most likely "due to climate change" (228), other characters reject any such interpretation, either by bringing up opposing scientific voices or by insisting that the phenomenon must be seen as an isolated act of God that does not point to environmental risk, but must rather be understood as a reflection of the power and beauty of divine creation. The latter response is that of the majority of the townspeople. They reject the results of climate science and show a general distrust of any form of environmentalism. By employing a protagonist who moves within and between both worlds, the world of the scientists and the world of the townspeople, the novel sheds light on the variety of subjectivities that exist in the world risk society and on the controversial character of climate change discourse. Moreover, in her encounter with representatives of the various groups of people, Dellarobia realizes that it is their respective socio-economic situation and cultural background that motivate their stance toward climate change. Most importantly, she recognizes that an environmentalist stance, as valid as its goals may be, often goes hand in hand with an unacknowledged privileged socioeconomic status, and that the response to environmental problems of poorer people is to a large extent motivated by socioeconomic insecurity and fear. She explains the reluctance of the townspeople to acknowledge the risk of climate change to Ovid Byron and his team and argues: "I think people are scared to face up to a bad outcome" (231). Here, the novel introduces the issue of environmental justice and complicates any simplistic notion of climate change denial, the stance that has been identified as one of the crucial obstacles to developing and implementing efficient remedial measures against global warming.[7]

In its attempt to develop a risk scenario that anticipates climate catastrophe in the future and still focuses on the present situation, *Flight Behavior* has in part to rely on the dystopian mode. As mentioned before, the

[7] For a comprehensive discussion of the phenomenon of climate change denial in *Flight Behavior* see Axel Goodbody's essay in this volume.

descriptions of the damaging weather conditions that have marked the recent past and the present of the Turnbows and their neighbors make the ominous impact of climate change, its environmental, but also its socio-economic consequences, concrete. They challenge any notion of a pastoral existence that the novel hints at in various ways – most conspicuously, perhaps, in its introduction of the Turnbow family as sheep farmers. As a risk narrative of anticipation, however, the novel also relies strongly on the employment of further genre conventions and modes of representation in order to put emphasis on the experience of uncertainty and suggest a more open outcome in terms of projecting future climate development. *Flight Behavior*, most importantly, makes use of elements of the *bildungsroman* and of the mode of irony.

With the choice of a protagonist who, through a dramatic expansion of her social contacts, undergoes a process of intellectual, emotional, and moral growth the novel draws on conventions of the *bildungsroman*. This formal choice suggests openness for her personal future and, metaphorically, openness in terms of future developments of global warming. Dellarobia in the end gains new options for her life and the life of her children. She separates from her husband, negotiates an arrangement with him concerning the children, and, learning about the opportunity work-study programs provide, is about to move to the nearest college town and start a college education. While there is no guarantee that she will succeed in her plans – as the last pages of the novel in which she watches the flooding of the region indicate, her future remains uncertain – her actions still suggest a more promising and satisfying future. Dellarobia's decision to pursue an education that will ultimately turn her into "a vet" or "[s]ome kind of scientist" (426) puts emphasis on the role of education, and in particular on gaining further scientific knowledge. This signals a rather strong confidence in the power of climate science to at least mitigate the negative impact of global warming in the future.

The choice of Dellarobia as single focalizer, finally, accounts for the effective use of irony in the novel. Right from the beginning it becomes clear that one of her central strategies to battle frustration and despair has been the employment of irony. Her descriptions of and comments on the attitudes and daily practices of her family, friends, and neighbors, on the ignorance of elitist environmentalists and scientists, on the calculated ignorance of journalists and the media, but also on her own, sometimes misguided, actions and motives reveal a large mental capacity for irony – including, very significantly, also a rather high degree of self-irony. This capacity permeates the novel, it lightens its tone and mood considerably, and it provides a counter-weight to the didacticism that almost unavoidably accompanies the process of her intellectual, emotional, and moral growth. *Flight Behavior* thus balances dystopian and ironic, sometimes even comic, modes of representation thereby putting emphasis on uncertainty and openness. In this context, even the ending of the novel, the flooding of the region, can be ambiguously read: either as a sign of destruction, or as a sign of cleansing and renewal.

Kim Stanley Robinson's Science in the Capital trilogy, *Forty Signs of Rain*, *Fifty Degrees Below*, and *Sixty Days and Counting*, differs from Kingsolver's novel in various ways: in its urban setting – the novels are predominantly set in Washington, D.C. (hence the trilogy's name); in its cast of characters – the protagonists are a group of well-educated, middle-class male and female scientists; and in its focus on the realms of science and politics – the novels explore the "complex matrix of institutional forces that lie at the heart of the American political machine," "contradictory forces," as Roger Luckhurst points out, that drive the "social and ecological relations" (172) in the United States. And yet, the trilogy and *Flight Behavior* share several central thematic and formal features as risk narratives of anticipation. Robinson's novels are set in a very near future when climate change shows increasingly destructive symptoms, first and foremost in terms of weather anomalies, but also in terms of the economic, social, and political consequences that result from them. The risk of climate change, moreover, again emerges as controversial reality, as indicating a strong sense of uncertainty, and as an ultimately global problem. Finally, Robinson's novels also only partly rely on the dystopian mode, balancing its impact by employing further genre conventions and modes of representation. This strategy again puts emphasis on uncertainty and openness of the future as features that define the experience of living in the world risk society.

The trilogy covers a period of about two years in which several severe weather irregularities, culminating in a temporary stalling of the North Atlantic Gulf current, transform the personal lives of the major characters as well as US and international environmental politics. *Forty Signs of Rain* ends with a large-scale flooding of Washington; *Fifty Degrees Below* traces the impact of very unusual seasonal temperatures, especially a severe winter, that are at least in part linked to the stalling of the Gulf current; and *Sixty Days and Counting* focuses on the massive political, economic, and scientific-technological efforts undertaken to fight against the continuing threat of changing weather patterns – ultimately on a global scale. The fictional world Robinson develops revolves around the probable effects of "abrupt climate change." This scientific risk scenario postulates the possibility that the effects of global warming might show much more rapidly than what is assumed by the majority of climate science studies. The scenario of abrupt climate change allows Robinson to create a near-future setting that is plausibly interlinked with the present moment and thus particularly capable of making the contemporary risk experience concrete.[8]

---

[8] Abrupt climate change is the risk scenario that was popularized by the blockbuster movie *The Day After Tomorrow*. In contrast to the movie, however, Robinson's trilogy

Robinson's novels work with a cast of characters that consists, with few, though important, exceptions, of scientists, science administrators, politicians, or scientific political consultants. The three protagonists of the novels are Frank Vanderwal and Anna and Charlie Quibler. Frank and Anna are scientists and initially work as colleagues at the National Science Foundation in Washington, a central national research funding organization; Anna's husband Charlie works as a science consultant for the liberal senator Phil Chase, who in the third novel has become president of the United States and begins major restructurings of national and international environmental politics, trying to establish what Luckhurst calls a "productive, ecologised capitalism" (172). The three characters are the major focalizers of the novel, and it is thus largely through their perceptions and experiences that the reader can trace the controversy surrounding the risk of climate change, its controversial reality and global reach, especially in the political realm. Frank, Anna, and Charlie, moreover, like Dellarobia Turnbow in *Flight Behavior*, represent subjectivities that emerge in the world risk society. Tracing their experiences, the reader learns how risk, in the words of Ulrich Beck, shapes their expectations, lodges in their heads, and guides their actions – ultimately illustrating the claim that global risk has become a political force that transforms the world.

The controversial reality of climate change becomes immediately visible in Charlie Quibler's experiences as science consultant for Phil Chase. During one of Chase's terms as senator, Charlie helps him push climate change legislation that would curb greenhouse gas emissions. In this context, he is confronted with a federal administration that insists on the inconclusiveness of climate science – despite overwhelming scientific agreement that global warming is real and needs to be urgently addressed – and thus refuses to implement any mitigating measures. In a conversation with the president and his head science advisor Charlie's arguments are ultimately denounced as "alarmist talk" (*Forty Signs* 165). Later on, when Phil Chase has become president and Charlie is part of his White House staff, contributing to attempts to implement new environmental policies that involve major economic changes, Charlie still has to battle old opponents whose economic philosophy continues to be environmentally short-sighted. In a meeting with representatives of the World Bank, he realizes that "they were still exteriorizing costs without even noticing

---

does not present the reader with the rapid onset of a new ice age, it does not develop a risk narrative of catastrophe. Instead, it shows that the international community – led by the American president Phil Chase – is able to coordinate a major rescue effort to re-energize the Gulf current. An enormous, international fleet of tankers transports salt to the Arctic and drops it there, thereby setting the Gulf current in motion again. It is not at all clear whether this will help permanently; the climatic future remains uncertain. But the point the novels try to make here is that international political cooperation might, eventually, be able to make a difference. On the central function of abrupt climate change in the trilogy see also Prettyman 190f.

it or acknowledging such exteriorization had been conclusively demonstrated to falsify accounts of profits and losses" (*Sixty Days* 202).

Controversy about climate change and its global dimension, but also the complexity that characterizes living in the world risk society, becomes most conspicuous in the development of Frank Vanderwal. Frank can be regarded as the central character of the trilogy, not only since he undergoes a personal identity crisis that teaches him to develop a sense of self that integrates scientific rationality and spirituality, but also since he encounters and gets involved with a diversity of people that mark the novels' "social totality, a matrix of power that fully intertwines science, society and politics" (Luckhurst 175). Frank used to be a researcher at the University of California, San Diego before joining the staff of the NSF in Washington. He has close contacts to a group of scientists who work in a California bio-tech company, financed by venture capital. In Washington, he becomes friends with the Quibler family, but also with a group of Buddhist monks that come to Washington to lobby for support of their home, the island of Khembalung in the Indian Ocean that is threatened by rising sea levels caused by global warming. Eventually the island is flooded, and its population turned into climate refugees. Frank also befriends a group of homeless war veterans and a counter culture community of "fregans," people without permanent homes that try to live outside the money economy by staying in abandoned houses and living of, more often than not high-quality, leftovers of a materially saturated society. In a love story sub-plot, moreover, Frank becomes the target of illegal surveillance by a political group that tries to undermine the American democratic system. Finally, he moves with Diane Chang, in the first two novels head of the NSF, to the White House to contribute to the new president's efforts to restructure international environmental policies. In his encounters with such a variety of people and milieus, in his involvement with a diversity of economic and political institutions and organizations, and in his travels to various locations in the U.S. and abroad, Frank becomes the character that introduces the reader most comprehensively to the controversial complexity and global reach of the risk of climate change.

Like *Flight Behavior*, Robinson's Science in the Capital trilogy uses the dystopian mode, especially in its representation of severe weather anomalies and their accompanying socio-economic and political consequences that mark the impact of climate change. As risk narratives of anticipation, however, the novels also rely heavily on other modes and genre conventions in order to put emphasis on the experience of uncertainty and an ultimately open future that continue to characterize the fictional present even after such major destructive manifestations of climate change as the temporary stalling of the Gulf current. The novels, most importantly, draw on the comic mode and on a variety of genre conventions, most significantly, perhaps, of the domestic novel, the picaresque novel, and the political thriller. By doing so they even create what has been identified as a utopian quality.

Roger Luckhurst has argued that in the trilogy "there is surprisingly little catastrophe on display" (170). He points towards the trust in technological and bio-engineering solutions the novels envision as adequate and potentially successful responses to climate change, towards the "democratic victory" in U.S. politics that is signaled by Phil Chase's presidency, and to the "triple marriage" at the end of the third novel to argue that the trilogy presents a "traditional, human scale comedy" (170) in which various conflicting issues are resolved. Moreover, he draws on Joseph Meeker's arguments in *The Comedy of Survival* to claim that Robinson's novels ultimately develop a "comic ecological vision," that is a vision that relies on socio-economic and cultural "compromise formations, mitigations that will restore an equilibrium between culture and nature" (179). Gib Prettyman, moreover, in his wide-ranging analysis of the modification and functionalization of various genres in the trilogy, sees the latter as another manifestation of Robinson's goal as a writer to "inspire critical theories of utopian thought" (182). Most significantly in the context of this essay, he regards the novels as representative of what he calls the "fortunate crisis genre," a genre that presents crisis – here the sense of crisis created by an awareness of the risk of global climate change – as a chance for improvement and that therefore insists on an open future. The fortunate crisis genre, according to Prettyman, serves the following functions: "it liberates people from their ordinary habits and modes of thought; it reminds people of the ecological big picture; it shows the ultimate contingency and vulnerability of the present order of things; it causes people to reassess their true needs . . . it serves as a catalyst for experiment and for adoption of new habits" (192).

The arguably most important genres the novels draw on in order to achieve this kind of catalytic or even utopian effect may well be the genres of domestic novel, picaresque novel, and political thriller. The impact of the domestic novel figures in the essential role of the motif of community building in the novels. First and foremost the centrality of the Quibler family, but also the large Buddhist community from Khembalung that has to resettle in the U.S, the homeless war veterans and the ferals, the three couples that get married in the end, and the international community of countries that begin to finally cooperate in environmental matters, point towards the central cultural work the domestic novel performs: to address critically socially relevant issues and to develop new values and practices by means of envisioning the core units of a society, single families or communities, engaging with these issues. In Robinson's novels, it is the impact of the risk of climate change that these families and communities engage with; they struggle to come to terms with the question of how to respond more adequately to conditions of living in a world that is increasingly transformed by the effects of global warming.

Frank Vanderwal, finally, can be read as a *picaro* figure that signals the impact of the picaresque novel, but also of the political thriller on the trilogy's attempts to point toward uncertainty and an ultimately open future as characteristics of a world impacted by the global risk of climate change. Frank is a traveler, both literally and spiritually. He not only develops a more complex understanding of doing science, but in his restless movement from one home to another – from an ordinary apartment to a self-built tree house in a former city park to a room which he shares with a Buddhist monk – he becomes the *picaro* who encounters and provides insights into how different individuals and social groups assess and cope with the social, economic, political, and cultural meanings the risk of climate change entails. In his travels, moreover, he has to deal with and overcome the criminal maneuverings of a politically subversive group that tries to manipulate the American political system and the world markets. When the novels here employ genre conventions of the political thriller, they on the one hand draw attention to the fragility and corruptness of the political and economic system; on the other hand, however, this fragility can also be read as flexibility that allows for transformation that would accommodate environmentally necessary political and economic measures.

Narrating Climate Change: The Cultural Functions of Risk Narratives

In her study *Illness as Narrative*, an investigation of autobiographical and fictional risk narratives, Ann Jurecic reflects on the pervasiveness of the risk experience in late modernity. She points out that "[b]eing 'at risk' constitutes a newly recognized social, cultural, and psychological position that must be made meaningful in order to be endured" (29). In her summary of the functions of these narratives she argues that they are able to personalize, and to an extent also normalize, the risk experience by going beyond statistically founded general risk assessment. It is in particular the employment of literary means that make a more adequate representation of the personal risk experience possible. Ultimately, she argues, risk narratives "must balance the responsibility to remain true to a scientific view of the world with the desire to give meaning to lives lived in uncertainty" (42).

The literary explorations of environmental risk undertaken by the emerging genre of the climate change novel equally reveal that it is indispensable to go beyond the knowledge provided by scientific scenarios and statistical, probabilistic risk assessments in order to capture and express facets of the complex, diverse, and controversial reality of living with the risk of climate change. Similar to the illness narratives Jurecic analyses, climate change novels as risk narratives insist that identities and subjectivities in late modernity, in the world risk society, are crucially inflected, to use Ulrich Beck's words once again, by the openness, uncertainties and obstructions of our self-created future. To articulate this experience in a meaningful and more accessible way, climate change novels develop narrative structures that often draw on existing formal conventions and shape them in ways that fit their particular purposes.

The type of risk narrative this essay has focused on in its discussion of the novels by Kingsolver and Robinson, the risk narrative of anticipation, is one specific narrative form that is able to capture the complex, diverse, and controversial experience of climate change and what Hulme has called the multiple meanings of climate. Its specific contribution to contemporary climate change discourse can be seen in its focus on the present moment, which is not yet characterized by full-blown climate catastrophe, but by the anticipation of catastrophe. This moment needs glimpses of a possible catastrophic future to create awareness of the environmental threats our contemporary socio-economic and cultural systems may ultimately bring about. More importantly, however, it needs exploration of exactly these socio-economic and cultural systems of the present in order to clarify how they translate into ethical concepts and psychological and emotional dispositions that underlie the various kinds of human engagement with their environment. By engaging the controversially real experience of climate change in the present, the risk narrative of anticipation sheds light on, and makes more easily perceptible and intelligible, what may be called an environmentally precarious, certainly indeterminate and unstable cultural moment.

Works Cited

Beck, Ulrich. "The Reinvention of Politics: Towards a Theory of Reflexive Modernization." *Reflexive Modernization: Politics, Tradition and Aesthetics in the Modern Social Order.* Ulrich Beck, Anthony Giddens, Scott Lash. Cambridge: Polity Press, 1994. 1-55. Print.

---. *World at Risk.* Cambridge: Polity Press, 2009. Print.

---. *World Risk Society.* Cambridge: Polity Press, 1999. Print.

Chakrabarty, Dipesh. "The Climate of History: Four Theses." *Critical Inquiry* 35 (2009): 197-222. Print.

Douglas, Mary. *Risk and Blame: Essays in Cultural Theory.* London: Routledge, 1992. Print.

--- and Aaron Wildavsky. *Risk and Culture: An Essay on the Selection of Technological and Environmental Dangers.* Berkeley, CA: University of California Press, 1982. Print.

Ericson, R.V. and A. Doyle, eds. *Risk and Morality.* Toronto: University of Toronto Press, 2003. Print.

Heise, Ursula K. "Cultures of Risk and the Aesthetic of Uncertainty." *Scientific Cultures – Technological Challenges. A Transatlantic Perspective.* Ed. Klaus Benesch and Meike Zwingenberger. Heidelberg: Winter, 2009. 17-44. Print.

---. "Risk and Narrative at Love Canal." *Literature and Linguistics: Approaches, Models, and Applications. Essays in Honor of Jon Erickson.* Ed. Marion Gymnich et al. Trier: wvt, 2002. 77-99. Print.

---. *Sense of Place and Sense of Planet. The Environmental Imagination of the Global.* Oxford: Oxford University Press, 2008. Print.

---. “Toxins, Drugs and Global Systems: Risk and Narrative in the Contemporary Novel.” *American Literature* 74 (December 2002): 747-78. Print.

Hulme, Mike. *Why We Disagree About Climate Change. Understanding Controversy, Inaction and Opportunity.* Cambridge: Cambridge University Press, 2009. Print.

Jurecic, Ann. *Illness as Narrative*. Pittsburg: University of Pittsburg Press, 2012. Print.

Kingsolver, Barbara. *Flight Behavior*. New York: Harper Collins, 2012. Print.

Luckhurst, Roger. “The Politics of the Network: The Science in the Capital Trilogy.“ *Kim Stanley Robinson Maps the Unimaginable. Critical Essays.* Ed. William J. Burling. Jefferson, NC: McFarland, 2009. 170-80. Print.

O’Neill, Saffron and Sophie Nicholson-Cole. “’Fear Won’t Do It’: Promoting Positive Engagement with Climate Change through Visual and Iconic Representation.” *Future Climate Change. Critical Concepts in the Environment. Vol. IV. Framing the Debate.* Ed. Mark Maslin and Samuel Randalls. London: Routledge, 2012. 415-36. Print.

Prettyman, Gib. “Living Thought: Genes, Genres and Utopia in the Science in the Capital Trilogy.” *Kim Stanley Robinson Maps the Unimaginable. Critical Essays.* Ed. William J. Burling. Jefferson, NC: McFarland, 2009. 181-203. Print.

Robinson, Kim Stanley. *Fifty Degrees Below*. 2005. New York: Bantam Books, 2007. Print.

---. *Forty Signs of Rain*. 2004. New York: Bantam Books, 2005. Print.

---. *Sixty Days and Counting*. New York: Bantam Books, 2007. Print.

Slovic, Paul. *The Perception of Risk*. London: Earthscan, 2000. Print.

Sørensen, Mads P. and Allan Christiansen. *Ulrich Beck. An Introduction to the Theory of Second Modernity and the Risk Society.* London: Routledge, 2013. Print.

“Summary for Policy Makers.” Working Group I Contribution to the IPCC Fifth Assessment Report Climate Change 2013: The Physical Science Basis. 27 September 2013. <http://www.climatechange2013.org/images/uploads/WGIAR5 SPM_Approved27Sep2013.pdf>.

Trexler, Adam and Adeline Johns-Putra. “Climate Change in Literature and Literary Criticism.” *Wires. Climate Change* 2 (2012): 185-200. Print.

Axel Goodbody

Risk, Denial and Narrative Form in Climate Change Fiction: Barbara Kingsolver's *Flight Behavior* and Ilija Trojanow's *Melting Ice*

Changing attitudes: how can cultural risk theory help meet the challenge of climate change?

As the scientific evidence has accumulated over the last few decades, the likely impact of anthropogenic global warming has been shown to be widespread and potentially catastrophic in the longer term: water shortages and the spread of diseases will lead to decreased agricultural productivity, while the rise in sea level, increased seasonal flooding, and extreme weather events will endanger coastal conurbations.[1] The projected increase in global average temperature by the end of the century, unless far-reaching measures are adopted to limit carbon emissions, lies between 2 and 6 degrees centigrade,[2] and the internationally recognised goal of climate policy of keeping the temperature rise to a maximum of 2 degrees could already be exceeded in just a few decades. Radical change would appear necessary if famine, mass migration and armed conflict over resources are to be avoided in the current century.[3] Yet, even in countries where there is a high level of public support for the environmental movement and widespread awareness of the risk associated with climate change, everyday life goes on almost as if it does not exist, few people spend much time thinking about it, and as yet little social action is being taken.

There are some obvious reasons for the discrepancy between the perception of the risk from global warming among experts and the general public. The factors involved in the phenomenon are complex and the scenarios for the future fraught with uncertainty: for some time after scientists first expressed concern over anthropogenic climate change in the 1950s, individual researchers such as Stephen Schneider proposed that

1 See "IPPC, 2007: Summary for Policymakers."

2 See "IPCC, 2007: Synthesis Report."

3 See for instance Harald Welzer, *Klimakriege*, or Rahmstorf and Schellnhuber's more optimistic introduction to climate change in the 'C.H. Beck Wissen' series, *Der Klimawandel*.

human impact would lead to cooling rather than warming. (This theory has since been discredited.) In Northern Europe there is also ironically the danger of an abrupt drop in temperature resulting from interruption of the Gulf Stream, which currently maintains a mild winter climate. Above all, climate change is singularly intangible and abstract in nature. Public concern tends to be driven by unusually hot summers, mild winters, early springs, drought, and extreme weather occurrences such as hurricanes. These cannot individually be directly attributed to global warming. And while a rise of half a degree centigrade in the global average temperature over a decade may be hugely significant, it is not detectable by the individual. It is difficult to either grasp the current impact or imagine the future consequences of something whose manifestations in our daily life are sporadic and which principally affects others in far-away countries.

For these and other reasons, people in industrialised countries are reluctant to accept the necessity for rapid transition from the fossil energy-based economy to post-fossil sustainability, and to embrace the changes in lifestyle which mitigating global warming demands. In consequence, the traditional information deficit model of science communication, which relies on simply conveying factual information to change people's awareness and behavior, is not working. This paper examines how public perception of the risks from climate change is represented in two recent novels, Barbara Kingsolver's *Flight Behavior* (2012) and Ilija Trojanow's *EisTau* (Melting Ice, 2011). My argument that climate change fiction deserves serious attention is based on the premise that the mechanisms through which risk is perceived must be examined as well as the bare facts of risk, and that strategies must be developed for engaging with these mechanisms. Climate change is a 'superwicked' problem,[4] and in-depth understanding of how dangers from it are perceived by the public and why is a precondition for the communicative and psychological work to promote a more appropriate response which must accompany the pursuit of technical solutions.

The study of risk perception mechanisms necessitates multi-disciplinary work in cultural risk theory, including, as something of a late-comer, literary studies. Ursula Heise has provided a helpful summary of the development of risk theory in her study *Sense of Place and Sense of Planet*.[5] Research into how environmental risks are perceived started in the late 1960s, and developed in the disciplines of cognitive psychology, sociology, and anthropology. Since the 1990s, researchers in political science and economics have also been increasingly concerned with environmental risk

---

4 The term 'superwicked' denotes highly complex problems for which there is an urgent need for extensive change, but no clear solution. See Levin et al., "Playing it Forward."

5 See Chapter 4, "Narrative in the World Risk Society," especially pp. 124-136, "Theories of Risk Perception: Science, Culture, Narrative." I am also indebted to Chapter 6, "The Things We Fear", of Mike Hulme's book, *Why We Disagree About Climate Change*.

perception. Understanding of risk was revolutionised by the cultural risk theory first formulated by the anthropologist Mary Douglas and the sociologist Aaron Wildavsky in 1982, in their study *Risk and Culture: An Essay on the Selection of Technological and Environmental Dangers*. Prior to this, research focused on differences between expert and lay perceptions: objective, statistical considerations were seen to shape the former, while the latter were curiously indifferent to them. Until the early 1980s, it was assumed that lay risk perception was the product of a combination of the characteristics of the risks themselves and individuals' cognitive behavior, with the latter needing to be explained and ultimately corrected.

Noting that in a given community only some risks are selected for conscious awareness and given social and cultural significance, Douglas and Wildavsky drew attention to the 'cultural' factors involved in risk assessment. Worldview, collective thought patterns, and values were, they argued, as important as models of individual cognition for the construction, perception and ranking of risks. Research on the cultural dimension of risk has focused mainly on the role played by broad social, cultural and political attitudes in shaping risk perception.[6] It is now widely accepted that risk perception includes affective, social and cultural factors as well as cognitive ones. The predominantly realist assumptions of the 1970s have been replaced by increasingly nuanced analyses of the social and cultural frameworks that shape non-expert risk assessments.

Social and cultural factors would appear to play a particularly important role in cases of environmental risk, whose assessment relies on dimensions which are hard to quantify, such as uncertain consequences, long-term futures, and the intrinsic value of nature. Drawing on research by the anthropologist Michael Thompson, Mike Hulme has shown how cultural risk theory can be mapped onto different ways of regarding nature (for instance as benign, ephemeral, perverse/ tolerant, and capricious) (186-90), and he has further explored the emotional and cultural factors involved in the perception of climate risks.[7] Hulme discusses at some length the ability of narratives, metaphors and symbols to amplify (or attenuate) the perception of climate risks and their manageability, citing the coupling of climate change with the language of global terrorism after 09/11, the introduction of the idea of 'tipping points' (which shifted public perception of the crisis from

---

[6] Hulme reviews research suggesting that individuals, social groups and entire societies can be placed in the framework of a fourfold classification of "fatalists", "hierarchists", "individualists," and "egalitarians," depending on whether they are group-oriented or individual-oriented, and the extent to which they believe rules are needed to control behavior.

[7] Hulme presents for instance the findings of an empirical study by the psychologist Tony Leiserowitz which demonstrated that environmental risk perception in the United States is greatly influenced by emotional and affective factors on the one hand, and by underlying values and worldviews on the other.

the prospect of slow incremental change to large, rapid dislocation of the climate system), and links with cultural pessimism as examples of the cultural (re-)construction of risk perception.

In the following, I am concerned with the implications of cultural risk theory for the study of literature and the part it plays in public debate and cultural change. *Flight Behavior* and *EisTau* provide a basis for examination of key genres, narratives and images which contemporary authors are retrieving from literary tradition and adapting to their representations of the risk involved in global warming.[8] Both Kingsolver and Trojanow have made clear in interviews their intention to alert the public to the risks posed by climate change through their writing.[9] By personalising the experience of global warming and dramatising its consequences, they seek to bring it alive and help readers imagine the future.

My discussion is focused on two questions. The first is to what extent these climate novels represent the public response to climate change in terms which bear out an understanding of denial as an active process. Sociologist Kari Norgaard has recently developed an active conception of climate denial as a response involving the use of cultural "tools" in order to manage emotions. Secondly, I discuss how Kingsolver and Trojanow draw on the historical archive of genres, narratives and images in order to challenge and destabilise hegemonic systems of perception, attention and morality. I show how Norgaard's distinction between outright denial of climate change and more qualified denial of its risk implications is reflected in the two novels, and suggest that literary analysis of texts such as these can yield insights which complement sociological and psychological studies of denial. Finally, I argue that telling and listening to, writing and reading stories about environmental risks and our attitudes towards them can facilitate a change of attitudes and action, both by contributing to the public's critical awareness of arguments about environmental risks, and by creating a sense of the feasibility of change and the need for it through the power of literary imagination.

Climate denial 1: how do sociological and psychological studies of denial explain the public failure to respond to climate change?

Kari Norgaard's study of public attitudes towards climate change in Norway and the United States, *Living in Denial: Climate Change, Emotions, and Everyday Life*, throws new light on the ways in which social and cultural

8 Page references to the two novels are given in brackets in the running text. *EisTau* has yet to appear in English: the translations are my own.

9 See Bryan Walsh, "Barbara Kingsolver on *Flight Behavior*," and Stefan Gmünder, "Ilija Trojanow: Vor der Katastrophe."

factors affect the perception of environmental risk by combining ethnographic fieldwork and interviews with media analysis. Her main focus of interest is the disjuncture between the collectively constructed sense of normal everyday life and the troubling knowledge of climate change and our contribution to it. She describes a mental landscape wherein the possibility of climate change is both deeply disturbing and almost completely submerged, common knowledge, yet unimaginable (p. xix).

Norgaard starts by distinguishing between three different forms of denial of environmental risk: literal denial of the existence of climate change (climate skepticism), interpretive denial (framing the change in such a way as to make it appear positive), and implicatory denial (denial of its political, social and moral implications). Denial is a product of at least four different factors: it is a matter of the political and economic circumstances, a consequence of the work of lobby groups and the media, a product of social norms and a matter of individual psychology. Norgaard does not regard the media or political party interests as principally responsible for climate apathy in the US. Nor does she hold, contrary to the view of many contemporaries, that the underlying cause is today's pervasive individualism, selfishness and greed, or an irreversible process of moral degeneration. Rather, she argues that we block the topic from our minds in order to avoid feelings of fear, guilt and helplessness. Climate denial is a form of evasion, through frequently unconscious organisation of information about global warming in such a way that it remains outside the sphere of everyday reality.

The information we receive from climate scientists challenges the basics of contemporary social organisation. Climate change is therefore a daunting and depressing subject. It engenders fear of the severity of consequences and their implications for our future life, guilt over our own actions and failure to take action, and feelings of helplessness and inefficacy. These threaten individuals' sense of how the world is and the meaning of life, and their faith in progress. They also undermine conceptions of individual and national identity. We block information in order to maintain coherent meaning systems, desirable emotional states, and a sense of our ability to control our lives. Norgaard examines denial as a socially organised process by which individuals collectively distance themselves from information, through adherence to social norms and use of a repertoire of means provided by their culture. On the one hand this cultural dimension of climate perception and denial consists of norms of attention, perspective, emotion and conversation. On the other it involves the use of received worldviews and their articulation in symbols, stories and rituals.[10]

[10] See Norgaard, Chapter 4, "The Cultural Toolkit, Part One: Cultural Norms of Attention, Emotion, and Conversation," and Chapter 5, "The Cultural Toolkit, Part Two: Telling Stories of Mythic Nations."

In everyday life, Norgaard observed cultural scripts which supported individual acts of turning away from climate change. She identified three common displacement strategies, by means of which problems such as climate change are screened out, so as to avoid being overwhelmed by guilt and despair: (1) changing the topic to something less difficult and troubling, (2) focusing on an aspect about which action can be taken, and (3) treating the subject with humor, in a way which releases the pressure associated with the uncomfortable emotions raised by taboo topics. At the same time, she found that the media tended to write of climate change in subtly reassuring ways, e.g. presenting untoward events as unique, stressing things were going fine, smoothing over troublesome questions, appealing to people's sense of their own toughness. Attention was often directed to local happenings and the past – making it difficult for readers to think in terms of the scales of time and space needed to conceptualise climate change.

Of particular relevance for the student of literature is the concept of the 'cultural toolkit,' which Norgaard borrows from the sociologist Ann Swidler. Swidler suggests that culture influences action less (as originally assumed in cultural risk theory) by providing the values towards which action is oriented than by placing a repertoire or toolkit of "chunks of culture" (283) (stories, rituals, symbols and worldviews) at people's disposal for solving problems. Publicly available meanings facilitate certain patterns of action, while discouraging others. Denial is thus carried out through a cultural stock of strategies and social narratives, with the aim of achieving 'thought prevention,' 'perspectival selectivity,' and 'selective interpretation' (Norgaard 94).

For Norgaard, ignoring climate change is an active process, in which understanding of the science and care about the consequences are muted, in order to protect individual identity and sense of self-efficacy, and to maintain culturally produced conceptions of reality. She observed how selective attention to issues and perspectival selection were achieved in Norway by focusing on the past and the local (norms of time and space), through codes of desirable behavior such as toughness (norms of emotion) and through permissible patterns of social interaction (restricting the conversational spaces in which concern over climate change could be freely expressed). Discourses of self-understanding as a nation also played a role. In the USA, Norgaard highlights the respective implications of the traditions of individualism (which has the effect of disempowering people in the face of climate change by undermining their confidence in the efficacy of collective action and the ability of the political system to deliver a solution), anti-intellectualism (making it difficult to engage with science), and exceptionalism (implying Americans are allowed to be different because they spread democracy).

Climate denial 2: how can ecocritics enhance this understanding of denial by showing how debates on climate change are framed by conventions of narrative, form and image?

The importance which an environmental sociologist such as Norgaard attaches to cultural traditions, constructions of identity, and the symbols, stories and rituals through which they are conveyed, as factors shaping the perception of risk from climate change, supports the claim of literary, art and film critics to have a special contribution to make to risk theory. It is important, however, to distinguish between broad sociological definitions of culture as "the publicly available symbolic forms through which people experience and express meaning," and "symbolic vehicles of meaning, including beliefs, ritual practices, art forms, and ceremonies, as well as informal cultural practices such as language, gossip, stories, and rituals of daily life" (Swidler 273), and the much narrower understanding of the term in cultural studies (literature, film, art, music, fashion, popular culture). Swidler and Norgaard do not distinguish between the meanings and beliefs in a culture and the cultural products encoding them: Swidler writes of the toolkit as consisting of "symbols, stories, rituals, and worldviews" (273), and elsewhere of the "tacit culture" of "habits, skills, and styles" (273, 281). Norgaard includes in her cultural toolkit "features of everyday life from emotion norms to cultural narratives" (215). I am here concerned with the narrower question of the role of genres, narrative patterns and metaphors in articulating the conceptions of nature, self and environmental risk which underlie texts.[11] Perceptions of global warming and other risks are shaped by and filtered through narrative templates, and visual images can come to function as shorthand for particular dangers and crises. Modes of writing utilising particular rhetorical tropes and genres are among the most important means of "organising information about risks into intelligible and meaningful stories" (Heise 138).

Apocalypse, or the perception of an inexorable worsening of the situation until a climax of destruction is reached, which may facilitate a fresh start for survivors, has been one of the most influential modes of risk communication in the environmental movement. An equally influential mode of writing is the pastoral, today normally found in the form of elegiac lament over the loss of a world in which harmonious relations with nature supposedly once prevailed in holistic, small-scale communities. Important genre models in accounts of risk are the detective story (which evaluates clues and eyewitness accounts, discovers and exposes the criminal), the *bildungsroman* (in which the protagonist comes to recognise the dangers from environmental change), tragedy (which depicts fateful events which individuals are only partly in

[11] See the section "Risk and Narrative" in Heise's *Sense of Place and Sense of Planet* (136-43).

control of), and epic (in which the planetary implications of risks are experienced). As Heise has commented, understanding how these rhetorical and genre traditions filter and shape information about risk so as to postulate certain causal consequences, make some scenarios plausible and others less so, make some appear more threatening than others, and outline likely future courses of events, is an aspect of risk theory to which ecocritics have a significant contribution to make (139). Alongside this 'pathological' practice of discourse analysis, examination of the potential of tropes and genres, narrative structures and metaphors to enrich and enhance arguments may throw light on the mobilising potential of literary texts as resources which can be drawn on in addressing climate apathy.

Genres and narratives as framing templates in Flight Behavior *and* Melting Ice

Flight Behavior combines elements of different narrative genres (narrative of conversion, *bildungsroman*) and modes of writing (sublime, apocalypse, pastoral). The book opens with what appears at first sight to be a religious experience. Dellarobia Turnbow, the central figure, is a farmer's wife in the southern Appalachians. A bright and attractive 28-year-old with a gentle, passive and unambitious husband, she is trapped in claustrophobic rural poverty and the drudgery of life as a mother of two small children. Breaking out in desperation from her unfulfilling everyday existence, she is on her way to an illicit assignation with a young telegraph engineer in a hunting hut on the mountainside above the farm. The would-be adulterer is stopped in her tracks by the sight of a forested valley seemingly alight with a cold orange flame. Dellarobia's experience is described in terms bordering on the miraculous:

> The forest blazed with its own internal flame. "Jesus," she said, not calling for help, she and Jesus weren't that close, but putting her voice in the world because nothing else present made sense. The sun slipped out by another degree, passing its warmth across the land, and the mountain seemed to explode with light. Brightness of a new intensity moved up the valley in a rippling wave, like the disturbed surface of a lake. Every bough glowed with an orange blaze. (*FB* 14)

Though not a religious person, Dellarobia decides that the strange explosion of light must be some sort of warning, like the burning bush in which the Lord confronted Moses: "Unearthly beauty had appeared to her, a vision of glory to stop her in the road. [...] It had to mean something." (15-16) It jolts her out of the rut of frustration and escapist fantasies, at the very moment when she was about to jeopardise her future, and that of her family, since nothing remains secret for long in small-town Tennessee. Her impulse to commit an act of blind self-destruction is transformed into determination to live differently. "I was going to run out on our marriage in a stupid way", she later confesses to her husband. "It was like I had to come back and do the right thing." (384) "Flung from complacency as if from a car crash" (23), Dellarobia descends the mountain, imbued with a new self-confidence, and impatient with the pettiness of everyday affairs like Moses after receiving the Ten Commandments.

Doubt is, however, simultaneously cast on the implication of divine intervention present in the biblical echoes of the description of Dellarobia's encounter with the "fierce and wondrous", seemingly burning forest. Its mysteriousness is largely due to her vanity: wishing to make a good impression on the lover she is rendezvousing with, she has left her glasses behind and cannot see properly. We soon learn that the "lake of fire" (16) consists of millions of bright orange Monarch butterflies, and that their arrival is a consequence of global warming. Everyone in *Flight Behavior*, from religious fundamentalists to environmentalists and the ratings-conscious media, frames the phenomenon to suit their own interests. A local newspaper, which presents Dellarobia as "Our Lady of the Butterflies" (77), her husband Cub, and, after some hesitation, also her mother-in-law interpret her 'vision' as a sign of divine grace, and Dellarobia is initially tempted to believe it herself.

However, the arrival of the entomologist Ovid Byron and a team of researchers soon acquaints her with the sober scientific facts. Changes on the Mexican mountainsides where they normally overwinter, drought affecting the plants they eat, an increase in pesticide spraying because global warming has brought in new mosquitos, changes in weather patterns, the northward spread of fire ants, and higher infection rates from parasites which limit their flying ability are climate-related factors responsible for disrupting the butterflies' normal migration pattern. Here in the Appalachian mountains they are faced with extinction, for, exposed to sub-zero temperatures, they will be lucky to survive the winter. Dellarobia learns that their presence is a symptom of damage to the earth's fragile ecosystems, and to understand it as part of a broader picture of change including "weird weather" (84, 260), and "unrelenting" rain (49), which are resulting in trees being uprooted, rising groundwater, floods and landslides. Byron explains:

> "We are seeing a bizarre alteration of a previously stable pattern [...]. A continental ecosystem breaking down. Most likely, this is due to climate change. Really I can tell you I'm sure of that. Climate change has disrupted this system. For the scientific record, we want to get to the bottom of that as best we can, before events of this winter destroy a beautiful species and the chain of evidence we might use for tracking its demise. It's not a happy scenario." (228-29)

Byron is driven by grief over the prospect of the extinction of the species, and by frustration and anger at the lack of public concern over climate change. "It will only take a few degrees of change, global average, to knock our kind out of the running," he notes grimly (279), but: "Humans are in love with the idea of our persisting" (282). However, in Dellarobia's world of "little hopes" and thankfulness when short-term targets are reached, there is no room for Byron's bouts of pessimism (283). Our attention is directed towards Dellarobia's perception of environmental risk, and towards the blend of cognitive knowledge, ethical commitment to future generations, and faith in the ability of people to change things which she comes to acquire.

Flight Behavior ends with a dramatic sweeping away of the Turnbows' house by floods, whose advent has been hinted at throughout the novel. However, as the story unfolds, it turns out to owe less to the cultural conventions of the sublime, the apocalyptic, or even the pastoral (which is evoked in passing in passages marking respect for Dellarobia's mother-in-law Hester's knowledge of local plants and the needs and behavior of the animals on the farm), than to the *bildungsroman*, or narrative of an individual's awakening to environmental risk and simultaneous realisation of their potential as an active member of society.[12] Dellarobia undergoes an inner journey from ignorance and absence of concern to scientific understanding of the processes and risks from anthropogenic climate change. This combines with an urge to change her life which is triggered, as noted above, by the butterflies. She eventually leaves her husband to start a new, independent life. At the uplifting end of the book, Dellarobia tells her son that they will move out and share an apartment with her friend Dovey. The children will have to learn to accept their parents' separation, and money will be tight, but she has the prospect of a job, thanks to Byron, which will enable her to pay her way through college. Ecological enlightenment is thus mapped onto female emancipation.

Melting Ice also combines elements of different narrative conventions. In terms of genre, it is structured as a diary: the greater part of the text consists of entries in the diary of Zeno Hintermeier, a former glaciologist who is now working as an academic tour guide on a cruise ship in the Antarctic. Zeno switches to and fro in a stream of consciousness between his account of events on the cruise, passages of travel writing, and autobiographical reflections. The principal mode of writing of Trojanow's novel is, however, to use Heise's term, the "disrupted pastoral" (139). Lyrical passages

---

[12] Whereas the traditional *bildungsroman* is a story of the formation and education of a young person, focusing on their psychological and moral growth from youth to adulthood, and their integration into society, the characteristic narrative structure of the 'Green Bildungsroman' has been identified by Bill Niven as an *unravelling* of the fabric of this integration into the established social and moral order, and the protagonist's reorientation towards an ecological set of values. See Niven, "The Green *Bildungsroman*."

celebrating the beauty of the Antarctic alternate with others lamenting its pollution and desecration by human exploitation and the impact of global warming (10, 64-5). The predominant tone is one of elegy over the passing of the Earth's last pure and pristine wilderness, a place of silence where nature is present in all its fullness (77-8), and creation is visible in unaccustomed clarity (81).

As in *Flight Behavior*, parts of the novel are written in the comic mode. These alleviate the intensity of the pathos and afford relief from the book's gloomy message of man's incompatibility with nature. However, here it is the (male) scientist rather than a (female) member of the general public who is the centre of attention. Zeno's world has fallen apart after a glacier in the Alps whose shrinking he has been studying for decades finally breaks up and melts. Approaching retirement and recovering from illness, he has resigned from his chair at the University of Munich, and taken on a job which reconciles him at least temporarily with the loss of his beloved glacier. But Zeno becomes increasingly embittered in the face of the public's indifference to environmental damage in general and climate change in particular. His diary includes caustic remarks on the consumer society (69-73), greed (79), and the instrumental use of natural resources (83), and records a growing tendency to predictions of the demise of humanity. He fantasises about natural disasters, recalling seeing traces of the great earthquake of 1755 on a trip to Lisbon (121-3), and the thrill he felt watching on television as a mountain village was swept away by an avalanche (118).

At the end of Melting Ice, Zeno highjacks the cruise ship which he is working on, and steams off into the southern Atlantic, leaving the passengers and crew stranded. He lets himself overboard to drown in the icy waters. However, his desperate gesture of protest goes unheeded: the passengers are saved in time by other ships in the vicinity, and reports of the event in the news are drowned out by media babble and advertising, giving us to understand that society maintains its current course unchanged. In contrast with Kingsolver's feelgood tale, this ending appears profoundly pessimistic. Unless, that is, the book is read as a critique of environmentalist apocalypticism. For Zeno would appear to be deliberately constructed as an ambivalent figure. On the one hand, comments such as that he is tired "of being a human being" (154), that the only way to save the human race is to cast it down from its pedestal, and that he is comforted by the thought that one day the only trace of human life to remain will be their faeces (167) indicate a degree of misanthropy. His suicide can also hardly be intended as a model for constructive action. On the other, he attracts our sympathy as a sensitive individual responding with integrity in a situation which we should probably all be experiencing as intolerable. His behavior as a "crank with convictions" (140) is endorsed inasmuch as it draws attention to the public's blindness to our impact on the planet, and appeals to readers' moral conscience. In a key passage, he speaks of being misanthropic in a positive sense, and insists that love of nature does not necessarily mean violence against humanity. It is rather absence of love of nature which leads to violence, including violence against our fellow men (MI 159). Refusing to go along with the shallow optimism of the day, Zeno seeks to open the eyes of the cruise passengers (and the public in general) to the risks from climate change. The fact that the only way of doing so which he can envisage involves committing suicide and putting the lives of others in danger must be understood as a challenge to Trojanow's readers to envisage an alternative.

"Queens of de-Nile": representations of climate denial and responses to it

Both authors then write out of a sense of frustration with the inadequacy of the public response to the risks of global warming, but *Flight Behavior* presents a particularly detailed portrait of climate denial. Kingsolver pulls no punches in exposing the "blindness" of Appalachian farmers and small town communities in America's Bible Belt to the dangers of anthropogenic global warming. She nevertheless depicts their mental world with sympathy and understanding. Political and commercial interests are present in the background, but rather than making the machinations of lobby groups responsible for environmental apathy, or even the media, she focuses on the everyday worries of people without higher education, bordering on poverty. This corresponds closely to the findings of sociological studies summarised by Kari Norgaard: disbelief in the existence of anthropogenic climate change certainly exists in the United States, where well-organised, corporate-funded campaigns under the George W. Bush administration have left a legacy challenging the legitimacy of science in the public sphere. But even in America climate skepticism would appear to be socially less significant than failure to integrate the general cognitive knowledge of climate change and acknowledgement of its seriousness into everyday life action, and to translate it into political action.

Trapped by poor harvests and the repayments on loans they took out before the recession hit, the people of Feathertown are "boxed in" (208). The temptation to liquidate assets is great: logging appears to offer a solution (174), and clearcutting is the preferred method, because it yields greater profits than selective felling. The danger of causing landslides from exposed mountain slopes is ignored. Behind the current recession-driven financial situation of Dellarobia's family lies a long-term economic trend. Her father, a cabinetmaker, and her mother, a seamstress, both lost their jobs to cheap mass production and the import of foreign clothes and furniture (cf. 151, 157f.).

In a world over which they have little control, these people have delegated the responsibility for making decisions to media opinion formers: "Nobody truly decided for themselves. There was too much information. What they actually did was scope around, decide who was looking out for their clan, and sign on for the memos on a wide array of topics." (166) The men are typically overweight and lazy: Dellarobia muses that her husband's first response to a crisis is to take a nap (39). He spends his leisure time drinking beer and channel-surfing TV. Flicking from one channel to another, referred to scathingly by Dellarobia as "ADHD TV" (112), is a mark of the "persistent inattention" (65) of people reluctant to be mentally challenged: "If people played their channels right, they could be spared from disagreement for the length of their natural lives. Finally she got it. The need for so many channels." (258) Living a life of constant distraction, without coherence or focus, they avoid confrontation with inconvenient truths.

The media are of course also not free of blame. Kingsolver acknowledges that they are responding to public demand, but castigates them for doing so without moral principles, inasmuch as they encourage sceptical rejection of scientifically established truth. Rather than collecting information, they seek to shore up the prevailing view of their audience and sponsors. "The official view of a major demographic," as the postdoc Pete comments, "is that we aren't sure about climate change. It's too confusing. So every environmental impact story has to be made into something else. Sex it up if possible, that's what your news people drove out here for. It's what sells." (230) Johnny Midgeon, whose radio show is Cub's prime source of information and opinion, makes fun of global warming whenever a winter storm comes through, with the line: "Al Gore can come toast his buns on this." (260) Dellarobia learns to recognise how the media "archly twisted comedy with news" (187), deflecting attention from the seriousness of issues, and how they sensationalise, manipulate, simplify and invade individuals' privacy in pursuit of stories with popular appeal.

Dellarobia's own initial response to mention of global warming is one of extreme caution ("Climate change: she knew to be wary of that", 147), exemplifying Norgaard's category of interpretive denial in the face of climate risk. Wanting to save trees for trees' sake (44) or to protect species because they are "endangered" arouses suspicion in her community because it hinders farmers' freedom of action (53). Global warming and state programmes to preserve "the ecology" are issues "for them" (the affluent urban middle class) and not "for us". The nation is divided: "The teams are picked, and then the beliefs get handed around," Dellarobia comments (321). Within the last fifteen years, in the US at least, "the environment got assigned to the other team. Worries like that are not for people like us." (322) Kingsolver shows how the self-image of a community used to hunting and logging and driving gas-guzzling 4x4s, and suspicious of interference in their lives by urban intellectuals and the state, militates against their acceptance of climate change: "If you've been called the bad girl all your life, you figure you're already paying the price, you should go on and use the tickets. If I'm the redneck in the pickup, let me just go burn up some gas." (323) Echoing Kari Norgaard's findings on how facts and concerns which are not consonant with the identities and self-understandings of the local or national community are filtered from their consciousness, Byron's wife, the folklorist Juliet, comments: "Once you're talking identity, you can't just lecture that out of people. The condescension of outsiders won't diminish it." (395) The crux of climate denial is addressed in a conversation between Dellarobia and Byron. When she says she just can't see the presence of the beautiful butterflies as "all that bad," he comments that refusing to look at the evidence is a popular form of behavior. She retorts: "It's not that we're all just lazy-minded. [...] People can only see things they already recognise. [...] They'll see it if they know it." "How do they see the end of the world?," Byron asks. Her reply: "They know it's impossible" (282-3) is a shocking recognition for him.

Kingsolver makes extensive use of analogy as a structuring device in the novel. Blindness to environmental change, referred to as "looking without seeing" (52), is multiply paralleled by Dellarobia's suppression of her grief over the loss of her first pregnancy, her mother-in-law's life of quiet desperation and denial (which as we learn at the end of the book derives from having had to give her first, illegitimate child up for adoption in order to be accepted by her husband), and public refusal to face up to the consequences of smoking. "I think people are scared to face up to a bad outcome. That's just human. Like not going to the doctor when you've found a lump" (231), Dellarobia comments at one point, remarking more drily at another that not picturing the crash landing in the cancer ward is a strategy which "works for some" (196). False, ostrich-like optimism and avoidance of difficult topics in everyday life are depicted in ways which correspond closely to Norgaard's conception of individual and social mechanisms managing emotions, suppressing feelings of fear, guilt and powerlessness. As Dellarobia remarks: "The human person cannot face up to a bad outcome, that's just the deal. We're all Cleopatra, like that Pam Tillis song. Cruising down that river in Egypt. Queens of de-Nile" (196).

That Dellarobia succeeds in giving up smoking is a sign of her managing to extricate herself from a life of denial on other levels, including not facing up to the fact that she cannot be happy in a marriage in which, starved of self-realisation and self-respect at the beck and call of her children and husband, she has fantasised about suicide (41). She learns to accept change and to overcome her fear of moving on. That she develops awareness of the unsustainability of the American way of life and a wish to play a part in understanding climate change is thanks largely to her curiosity and her willingness to read and learn. Byron and the other scientists who dedicate their lives to painstakingly building up knowledge of the processes of change are her role models. However, her wildness and defiance also play a role in the process, just as these qualities are shown to be an integral part of the environmental movement, through depiction of groups who arrive to protect the butterflies such as the Californian teenagers from (the real) 350.org and the British members of (the seemingly fictional) WOMYN, who are described as "knitting the earth together" (339), and as "citizens of their own cheerful universe despite their full awareness of its unravelling" (341).

Religion emerges as a form of denial. In an increasingly secular, materialist and individualistic society, the people of Feathertown, suspicious of outsiders and everything foreign (96, 130, 140), cling to traditional values, e.g. the view that "a wife working outside the home is a reflection on the husband." Their most readily adopted explanation for climate change is also a religious one. A conceivable response to the diversion of the butterflies from their accustomed migration routes, and the resultant threat to their survival, would be to interpret it as the potential loss of a part of God's creation. However, that of the local people is rather to trust blindly in providence: weather is "the Lord's business" (261). They ignore the news that the butterflies' presence is at best temporary, and may lead to their extinction, preferring to believe that He has given them the butterflies, either as a reward for good deeds (intending them to derive financial profit from tourism, for instance by opening a theme park, 255), or as a token of redemption and forgiveness for their sins (302). Dellarobia conforms to social expectation by going to the local church on Sunday, but maintains a rebellious stance of sceptical detachment. We are told that she views the church "as a complicated pyramid scheme of moral debt and credit resting ultimately on the shoulders of the Lord, but rife with middle managers" (21). While acknowledging the emotional needs it satisfies, she identifies it as part of the problem of our blindness to climate change.

Climate denial is similarly a leitmotif in Melting Ice. Zeno describes his Bavarian neighbors as "defending their little idyll with every means of blindness" (104). Sleepwalkers (116), anaesthetised by an omnipresent backdrop of light music (66), and drugged by consumption (126), they fail to recognise the environmental risk. Platitudes such as "don't take it to heart", "take a more relaxed view", "turn a blind eye", "it won't turn out so bad", and "things aren't as bad as they seem" serve to placate guilty consciences and play down the seriousness of the situation (83). Zeno castigates his contemporaries' "expedient optimism" (88), false innocence, and laziness. The thought of an empty wallet, he comments, is more disturbing than that of the extinction of the human race (159). However, his angry outbursts disrupting the tacit agreement to act as if all were well contravene the social norms of attention, conversation and emotion. When he expounds his theory of "warmth-idiocy" (an inversion of the delusion experienced by sufferers from hypothermia, whereby the warmer the planet gets the more we want to heat it) to a sympathetic passenger, he only succeeds in filling her with consternation, since he has made it impossible for her to avoid feelings of guilt and helplessness (102).

The position of religious feeling in the mental economy of our relationship with nature also differs from that in *Flight Behavior*. Here the environmental activist is motivated by religious as well as ethical and aesthetic factors. The glacier in the Alps which Zeno's father first brought him to see as a child fascinated him with its chapel-like caverns and ice formations resembling sculptures (36). One day when visiting it as a student, we learn, Zeno was overcome by an urge to pray – to the Gaian earth spirit of diversity and fullness (90). The glacier and, later, Antarctic icebergs are anthropomorphised, or more precisely, theriomorphised: Zeno describes them as vast female animals (51, 65, 87) which possess an erotic attraction for him. That Trojanow as author appears to share this relationship with nature of his protagonist's, rather than hinting at its problematic potential, might be seen as a further dimension in his delineation betraying a lack of critical self-reflection. Zeno's awareness of the risks to humanity associated with climate change is in any case driven by emotions and a sense of moral justice rather than by the scientific rationalism which Kingsolver ultimately champions. If scientists are engaged in a battle against climate denial in *Flight Behavior*, in Melting Ice the majority have become "brokers of destruction" (116). Prophecy is therefore called for, not scientific projections (127). A conversation reminding Zeno that his calls to fellow scientists have gone unheeded in the past finally leads him to seek to shake the public out of their sleep with his suicidal stunt.

Images and metaphors

Moving on from genres, narratives and characterization to visual imagery, the difference between the focus and writing strategies in the two novels is reflected in the metaphors present in their titles. Kingsolver's book is concerned with the changed flight behavior of butterflies as a disturbing symptom of global warming, but at the same time it is a study of human 'flight behavior,' alluding to the public's flight before reality, in denying the necessity to change patterns of production and consumption in response to climate change-related environmental risks and hazards: "If fight or flight is the choice, it's way easier to fly" (231). Trojanow uses perhaps the most familiar visible consequence of a rise in temperature, the transition from solid ice to liquid water, as a symbol of global warming. Our nightmares, Zeno muses, are possibly the most revealing features of the age we live in: whereas his father used to dream of freezing to death, his own nightmares are of ice melting in his hands and water running down his legs (43). Glaciers, which used to be markers of the eternal and the sublime, have become signs of our gross negligence (98). Ice and snow, traditionally associated with the majestic otherness of Alpine peaks, purity, courage, simple living, and nobleness of spirit,[13] are dissolving into shapeless, soiled, vulgar banality. The title, Melting Ice, like the book as a whole, thus enlists readers' aesthetic and moral preferences in support of opposition to climate change, suggesting that with the melting of polar ice and glaciers a process of physical and moral degeneration has begun.

In both books, however, these are only the most prominent among a host of other structural metaphors and images, many of them rich in associations from cultural tradition, through which climate change is brought closer to the reader. Some of those in *Flight Behavior*, such as logging and smoking, have already been touched on. Among the others, blindness/ seeing and the butterfly play a particularly prominent role. Blindness giving way to seeing is a recurring motif. Asked by her husband what she does working for Byron, Dellarobia says: "I see new things." (258) She realises with a start that the old-fashioned receiver shape of her little girl's toy telephone reflects a tendency to see the world as it used to be rather than as it is, since everyone now uses cell phones (134). Looking down from the fields above her home in winter, Dellarobia notes that in summer, the leaves obscure the topography of the farm, and the narrow drainage towards their house which is later responsible for disaster: "With all those reassuring walls of green, a person could not see to the end of anything. Summer was the season of denial." (257) Sitting in the car in a parking lot in the pouring rain, she reflects that the blurred outline of things through the windscreen must be like her father's diminished vision when he had cataracts, brought on by some trauma she had never understood: this "seeing without seeing" is associated with her husband Cub's refusal to talk about the past, to acknowledge the mistakes they made and to consider the alternatives to their present lives (381-2).

Butterflies are of course the central symbol in the novel. *Flight Behavior* celebrates the beauty of the Monarch species (Danaus plexippus) and expresses admiration for the extraordinary intricacy and sophistication of the instincts which enable it to migrate annually over thousands of miles between Mexico and Canada. The individual butterflies die on average after 6 weeks, but they pass on their genes to descendants, who complete the journey northwards. Others again fly back south and congregate at their winter gathering place in Mexican Angangueo. In the first instance, the bright orange butterflies, which are reproduced (albeit in abstract form, as small golden leaf shapes swarming above bare treetops) on the book's dustcover, symbolise the fragile, transient beauty of nature and the risk from global warming. However, their association in folk belief with the souls of dead children is also referred to at several points (e.g. 359). The threat to their survival thus serves as a poignant reminder of the fate of future human generations facing the consequences of climate change. In the final pages of

[13] See for instance Eric Rentschler, "Mountains and Modernity: Relocating the Bergfilm" (139-140).

Flight Behavior, the belated arrival of spring triggers a snowmelt which engulfs Dellarobia's home, in a scene reminiscent of the Biblical flood, suggesting divine punishment. However, the onset of the exodus of the surviving butterflies merges flood and flame in a reprise of the opening scene of the book, suggesting that violent change may also bring rebirth (420).

Trojanow uses a more limited range of images to make climate change resonate in our lives and to help us imagine the future. But here too marital breakdown and cancer are markers of what is wrong with society: the demise of "his" glacier coincides with the breakup of Zeno's marriage and the discovery that he has cancer (105), a disease which he relates to his former "hypocritical everyday life" (161). Just as genres and narratives serve as framing templates in *Flight Behavior* and Melting Ice, both novels thus reveal a consciously organised patterning of imagery so as to connect perceptions of and responses to environmental risk with familiar instances of inadequate or detrimental behavior, and relate them more generally to social values.

In conclusion: the contribution of literary analysis to discourses of risk perception, and the ability of climate fiction to enhance public response to environmental risk

My discussion of the two novels has sought to demonstrate two things. First, that textual analysis using the concepts and methods of literary criticism can complement sociological and psychological studies of seemingly illogical public responses to environmental risk, by giving insight into the role which formal and thematic cultural conventions play in shaping popular perceptions. It has indicated that literary representations of risk denial are consonant with Norgaard's understanding of it as an active process involving the use of cultural tools. And secondly, I have sought to show that writers make a positive contribution to public debates on environmental risk, by drawing on the cultural archive, adapting and experimenting with specific genres, narratives and images. If, Norgaard argues in the conclusion to her book, we are to overcome climate denial, we must go beyond merely providing information and conventional environmental education programmes. But how? She cites as particularly valuable Susanne Moser's calls for communicators to engage with and support individuals and communities, to create a sense of feasibility, collectivity, and urgency, arising from fact, experience, common sense and moral responsibility.[14] This can be done most effectively by tapping into people's desires for a better future, social identities and aspirations, and cultural values.

[14] See Susanne Moser and Lisa Dilling, "Communicating Climate Change."

If literature can play a part in this process, it is perhaps above all by helping the public imagine climate change and related risks. Novelists retrieve, interrogate, and experiment with the assembly of cultural tools relevant to debates on climate change risk, thereby enhancing their readers' competence in assessing and facing the challenge it poses. Globalisation has magnified the challenge of maintaining a sense of citizenship, empowerment, and commitment to a moral community. Fiction can help us imagine how our lives are connected to those of people already affected directly by climate change, and to see how our values are threatened by the problems they face. The two novels examined draw attention to our fragmented awareness of the danger, our failure to recognise the impact of our actions, and the psychic numbing in our everyday lives. Trojanow seeks, despite the weaknesses his book reveals, to reinvigorate the sociological imagination with a narrative which challenges readers to think beyond positions of apathy and misanthropy, while Kingsolver's tale suggests that crossing the threshold into awareness and becoming politically engaged can be a liberating and exhilarating experience, creating a new sense of integrity between self and world.

Works Cited

Buell, Lawrence. *Writing for an Endangered World: Literature, Culture, and Environment in the US and Beyond.* Boston, Mass.: Harvard University Press, 2001. Print.

Douglas, Mary and Aaron Wildavsky. *Risk and Culture: An Essay on the Selection of Technological and Environmental Dangers*. Berkeley, CA: University of California Press, 1982. Print.

Gmünder, Stefan. "Ilija Trojanow: Vor der Katastrophe." *Der Standard*, 27/28 August 2011. Print.

Heise, Ursula K. *Sense of Place and Sense of Planet. The Environmental Imagination of the Global.* Oxford: Oxford University Press, 2008. Print.

Hulme, Mike. *Why We Disagree About Climate Change. Understanding Controversy, Inaction and Opportunity*. Cambridge: Cambridge University Press, 2009. Print.

"IPPC, 2007: Summary for Policymakers." In *Climate Change 2007: Impacts, Adaptation and Vulnerability. Contribution of Working Group II to the Fourth Assessment Report of the Intergovernmental Panel on Climate Change*. Ed. M.L. Parry, O.F. Canziani, J.P. Palutikof, P.J. van der Linden and C.E. Hanson, Cambridge: Cambridge University Press, 2007. 7-22. <http://www.ipcc.ch/pdf/assessment-report/ar4/wg2/ar4-wg2-spm.pdf >.

"IPCC, 2007: Synthesis Report." In *Climate Change 2007: Synthesis Report. Contribution of Working Groups I, II and III to the Fourth Assessment Report of the Intergovernmental Panel on Climate Change*. Ed. Core Writing Team, R.K. Pachauri and A. Reisinger. Geneva: IPCC, 2007. <http://www.ipcc.ch/publications_and_data/publications_ipcc_fourth_assessment_report_synthesis_report.htm>.

Kingsolver, Barbara. *Flight Behavior. A Novel.* New York: Harper Collins, 2012. Print.

Levin, Kelly, Benjamin Cashore, Steven Bernstein and Graeme Auld. "Playing it Forward: Path Dependency, Progressive Incrementalism, and the 'Super Wicked' Problem of Global Climate Change." <http://environment.research.yale.edu/documents/downloads/09/2010_super_wicked_levin_cashore_bernstein_auld.pdf>.

Leiserowitz, Anthony A. "Climate Change Risk Perception and Policy Preferences: The Role of Affect, Imagery, and Values." *Climatic Change* 77 (2006): 45-72. Print.

Moser, Susanne C. and Lisa Dilling. "Communicating Climate Change: Closing the Science-Action Gap." In *Oxford Handbook of Climate Change and Society*. Ed. John S. Dryzek, Richard B. Norgaard and David Schlosberg. Oxford: Oxford University Press, 2011. 161-76. Print.

Niven, Bill. "The Green *Bildungsroman.*" In *Green Thought in German Culture. Historical and Contemporary Perspectives*. Ed. Colin Riordan, Cardiff: University of Wales Press, 1997. 198-209. Print.

Norgaard, Kari Marie. *Living in Denial. Climate Change, Emotions, and Everyday Life*. Cambridge, MA and London: MIT Press, 2011. Print.

Rahmstorf, Stefan and Hans Joachim Schellnhuber. *Der Klimawandel. Diagnose, Prognose, Therapie*, 7th ed., revised and updated, Munich: CH Beck, 2012. Print.

Rentschler, Eric. "Mountains and Modernity: Relocating the Bergfilm." *New German Critique* 51 (1990). 137–61. Print.

Swidler, Ann. "Culture in Action: Symbols and Strategies." *American Sociological Review* 51 (April1986): 273-286. Print.

Trojanow, Ilija. *EisTau. Roman*. Munich: Hanser, 2011. Print.

Walsh, Bryan. "Barbara Kingsolver on *Flight Behavior* and Why Climate Change Is Part of Her Story." *Time Magazine*, 8 November 2012. <http://entertainment.time.com/2012/11/08/barbara-kingsolver-on-flight-behavior-climate-change-and-the-end-of-doubt/>.

Welzer, Harald. *Klimakriege. Wofür im 21. Jahrhundert getötet wird.* 3rd ed., Frankfurt am Main: S. Fischer, 2012. Print.

ANTONIA MEHNERT

Things We Didn't See Coming – Riskscapes in Climate Change Fiction

Climate change is the epitome of a deterritorialized environmental crisis. It is thus a crisis caused by forces that transcend the local and can only be adequately understood from a perspective that considers the impact of processes of globalization. While the effects of global warming—such as sea level rise, weather extremes, and an increase in tropical cyclones—can be observed in specific places, the sources of these events, which lead to greenhouse gases accumulating in the atmosphere, are global in scope. Burning fossil fuels and large-scale deforestation are more broadly defined causes for the increase in average global temperature. However, these global phenomena do not immediately reveal the numerous underlying individual actions and lifestyle choices nor the global production and consumption cycles causing them. Environmental campaigns calling for less consumption of meat further confuse cause-and-effect chains and, as Timothy Clark criticizes, endorse "a bizarre derangement of scales" (136). As a consequence of its global scale, diffuse relationship between cause and effect, latency, and slow development, climate change eludes our perception while being simultaneously omnipresent.

For a large percentage of the population, climate risks exist mainly as ominous graphs of future climate projections, but "the most commonly cited figure in climate change debates—change in the average global temperature—has no correlate in anyone's actual living conditions" (Edwards 33). Since individual lived experience cannot serve as the basis for policy judgments that affect society, reliance on scientific projections such as climate scenarios becomes central in the decision-making process. These scientific scenarios, however, reveal a certain problematic in today's "risk society," which is confronting the time-delayed hazards of its own globalized production processes.[1] As Ulrich Beck has argued, in modern societies "risk

[1] The term "risk society," as coined by Ulrich Beck, describes the development in industrial society, in which "the social, political, economic and individual risks increasingly tend to escape the institutions for monitoring and protections" ("The Reinvention" 5). As Beck emphasizes, "the transition from the industrial to the risk period of modernity occurs undesired, unseen and compulsively in the wake of the

awareness is not based on 'second-hand experience,' but on 'second-hand non-experience,'" because "ultimately *no one* can know of risks if knowing means having consciously experienced them" (*Risk Society* 96). Even though the anticipation of crisis includes a prognostic aspect, it nevertheless needs to be taken seriously. Contrary to historian of science Paul Edwards, who considers the scientific work on climate change as the only knowledge basis to create public awareness and understanding of global warming, I argue that the high level of abstraction of scientific scenarios may hinder us from seeing ourselves simultaneously as actors, initiators, and victims of climate change risks. Instead, other important and effective means, such as novels or films, can help communicate the risks climate change presents. It is worth then taking a closer look at climate change fiction in order to explore the ways in which it engages with the anticipation of global crisis and provides an imaginary realm to depict a deterritorialized phenomenon such as climate change.

Especially when dealing with complex issues, reading literary texts alongside scientific writing provides new insights: they reveal the intimate aspects of the experience of environmental risks and the human struggles that are linked to it, thereby bringing formerly unacknowledged perspectives to attention. As literary scholar Ursula Heise discusses in her seminal work *Sense of Place and Sense of Planet*, literature "provides important cultural tools for organizing information about risks into intelligible and meaningful stories" (138). Climate change fiction, for instance, draws the missing link needed to translate scientific scenarios into the life worlds (*Lebenswelten*) they depict. Furthermore, as Jennifer Gabrys and Kathrin Yusoff emphasize, aesthetic practices function as "a way to materialize and articulate what would otherwise be un-sayable and un-thinkable" (17). The prominent and 'unthinkable' aspect of climate change that this essay examines is the complexity of its spatial dimension, particularly the impact of global risks on our conception of locality and place.

Thinking beyond the local is paramount in the face of the global scale of the climate change crisis. This implies not only an awareness of how one's own lifestyle choices affect distant places ("think globally, act locally") but also a consideration of the ways in which global climate change may transform the perception of one's own local environment. As Heise has argued, "risk scenarios contribute to deterritorialization processes as they prompt individuals and communities to reconfigure their practices of inhabitation in relation to these larger sociospatial scales" (152). She adds that, as a consequence, risk perception may either lead to a dislodging from place after one's conscious or subconscious assessment of the dangers that this place poses or to a strengthening of one's ties to this particular place in

autonomized dynamism of modernization, following the pattern of latent side effects" (ibid.).

the struggle for its preservation (ibid.). However, in the case of global climate risks, this strengthening of local ties may be futile since global processes already pervade localities.

One recent work of climate change fiction, Steven Amsterdam's *Things We Didn't See Coming*, is informative in this context—not only because it provides an innovative narrative format for representing the deterritorializing effects of climate change, but also because it deals with the ways global climate risks challenge attachments to places and ways of belonging and inhabitation. As this essay will demonstrate, Amsterdam's novel depicts the climatically changed world of tomorrow as what I call—following Arjun Appaduarai's work on globalization—a "riskscape."[2]

In "Disjuncture and Difference," Appadurai distinguishes between five different "cultural flows" representing the deterritorialized state of the world: ethnoscapes, finanscapes, mediascapes, technoscapes, and ideoscapes.[3] He uses the notion of *-scapes* not only to describe how globalization has transformed and shaped our experience of time and space, but also to show how these five dimensions are interconnected and continuously in flux (296). Reading Appadurai's work along Ulrich Beck's elaborations on the "risk society," one could add another dimension to Appadurai's framework: the "riskscape."

Accordingly, riskscapes can be characterized by the anticipation and the experience of a ubiquitous crisis, in which territorial distinctions decline in importance and socio-cultural practices are disembedded from place. Applying the term 'riskscape' to Amsterdam's *Things We Didn't See Coming* effectively captures the volatility and constantly shifting meanings of places in the novel. Furthermore, it powerfully demonstrates that climate risks are not geographically confined. The characters in Amsterdam's novel inhabit hazardous riskscapes, and, as a result, are forced into continuous movement. Since these riskscapes impede any form of re-inhabitation, adaptability and constant renegotiation of the self become key to survival.

---

2 The term "riskscape" was first introduced by geographer Susan Cutter (1996, 2006) who has used it in order to describe the complex interaction between environment, technology and society in the production of specific hazardous landscapes. Pointing out the particular vulnerabilities of a place, Cutter refers with the term to very specific and closely defined geographic areas. My employment of the term and reading of it alongside globalization theory, however, aims to go beyond the specificities of place in order to show how climate change creates global riskscapes.

3 In order to emphasize that 'culture' in a globalized world is not confined to one particular place, but rather takes shape in a multitude of interconnected transnational flows, Appadurai uses the idea of '–scapes.' Ethnoscapes decribe the deterritorialized spaces in which people, often migrants, move and live between different countries. Technoscapes, such as the internet, allow for global technological connectivity, and stand in close relation to financescapes which designate the global flow of capital. Mediascapes describe the dissemination of information, which construct 'narratives' beyond the nation state and are similar to ideoscapes, which promote political ideas and perspectives about how we perceive the world through images and texts.

Literature and the Spatial Dimension of Climate Risks

While climate change is forcing us to rethink our relationship to the global, representational means of grasping the spatial dimension of climate risks have yet to be explored in depth. As ecocritic Timothy Clark explains, "The relative absence in ecocriticism of its most serious issue seems more to do with the novelty and scope of the problem than with personal failing, a measure of how starkly climate change eludes inherited ways of thinking" (11).[4] Clark therefore concurs with Heise's argument, pointing out that so far ecocritical discussions have relied too heavily on an 'ethics of proximity' and thus on the idea that there exists a 'natural' connection to one's local environment. Heise convincingly argues that environmentalists' emphasis on localism and their insistence on the need to reconnect with local places has by and large ignored the ongoing discourse of "how experiences of place change under the influence of modernization and globalization processes" (51). Instead, she argues, engaging with two key concepts from globalization studies—deterritorialization and cosmopolitanism—may provide a helpful point of departure for ecocritical analyses, particularly for the analysis of representations of global risks.[5]

While the concept of deterritorialization has been widely discussed by scholars from various disciplines (such as Deleuze and Guattari, Appadurai, Canclini, and Tomlinson), their discussions generally agree on a definition of the term as referring to a detachment of socio-cultural practices from place, or more specifically, from geographical territories. Of particular relevance for this essay is the connection Heise draws between risk theory and Tomlinson's discussion of deterritorialization. She emphasizes that the global dimension of today's risks underlines Tomlinson's argument that

> globalization promotes much more physical mobility than before, but the key to its cultural impact is in the transformation of localities themselves . . . This is in

---

4 Contrary to Clark's argument, I would point out that this scholarly absence is also a result of the 'crisis of the imagination' which has for a long time affected authors and artists alike in representing anthropogenic climate change. Climate change fiction has only slowly emerged since the 1990s. Today, looking beyond generic definitions and categorizations of 'high' and 'low' literature, one can find various textual manifestations that address climate change, both fictional and non-fictional. Among them are science fiction novels, thrillers, but also scientific texts outlining risk scenarios or environmentalist pamphlets that engage with this gradual, individual yet at the same time global phenomenon (see also Trexler and Johns-Putra's survey of Anglophone climate change fiction).

5 Departing from a planetary understanding, Heise ultimately proposes a new approach to ecocritical analysis, which she calls eco-cosmopolitanism. Eco-cosmopolitanism proposes an understanding of the interconnectedness and mutual conditioning of human and non-human, natural and cultural places worldwide. For the purpose of this analysis, I will, however, focus on the concept of deterritorialization.

many ways a troubling phenomenon, involving the simultaneous penetration of local worlds by distant forces, and the dislodging of everyday meanings from their 'anchors' in the local environment. (Tomlinson 29)

Accordingly, global risk scenarios, such as climate change, intensify processes of deterritorialization as people increasingly find themselves confronted with the transformation of localities and begin to question the value of certain places that have come to be endangered. In the face of global risks, it becomes difficult to identify any risk-free spaces at all. Inhabitation and place attachment thus become increasingly futile since one can never be sure how long a given place will remain safe. The result is increased mobility, which in turn leads to the disembedding of social-cultural practices.[6]

In her brief analysis of climate change fiction at the end of *Sense of Place and Sense of Planet*, Heise points out that most literary representations fall short of illustrating the magnitude of such a planetary transformation and of envisioning "less territorially defined forms of inhabitation" (207). She gives credit to David Brin's *Earth* as the only successful example of engagement with a global environmental understanding. Heise reads Brin's fractured and postmodern writing techniques as well as the novel's prominent engagement with digital connectedness as characteristics of a commitment to a multivocal, multicultural perspective and thus as an effective means of narrativizing *global* risks. Mike Ziser, meanwhile, critically examines Heise's line of thought and insists that the range of representational means should be extended. He notes that "understanding climate change and peak oil requires us to acknowledge the ways in which our best critical paradigms, avant- and derriere-garde alike, reflect rather than contest our overconsumption of petroleum and the overemission of carbon dioxide and other greenhouse gases" (187). He, moreover, argues that with increasing weather extremes as well as rising oil prices, the global network is likely to lose in importance. The ways in which societies will interact in a climatically changed post–peak oil world are difficult to imagine, but Ziser's observation is helpful because it illustrates a perspective on the future which acknowledges possible material limitations. It may also serve as an explanation as to why technological connectivity does not play a prominent role in many climate change novels. As the following discussion will show, the ways of representing the global climate change risks are indeed manifold and do not necessarily adhere to any presupposed narrative templates.

---

6 While uprootedness and mobility may be a consequence of risk perception, this does not necessarily imply an emotional detachment from place. On the contrary, as has been widely discussed in postcolonial discourse (see, for instance, Rushdie's *Imaginary Homelands*), imposed exile often rather intensifies the nostalgic attachment to home and results in an elegiac mourning for the home that has been lost.

Amsterdam's novel *Things We Didn't See Coming* is especially interesting in its analysis of the spatial representation of risks because it illustrates the deterritorializing process whereby everyday meaning becomes detached from local environments in a climatically changed world of tomorrow. In the course of the novel, disruptive weather patterns lead to the creation of riskscapes, in which socio-political territorial distinctions have lost as much value as individual attachments to places due to constantly emerging climatic risks. Places are thus no longer recognizable as what has been called an "anthropological place"—that is, a place that "provides cultural identity and memory, binding its inhabitants to the history of the locale through the daily repetitions of 'organic' social interactions" (Tomlinson 109).[7] This is also emphasized by the namelessness of places and of most of the characters in the novel.

Riskscapes also resonate with what anthropologist Marc Augé has termed 'non-places'. He explains, "If a place can be defined as relational, historical and concerned with identity, then a space which cannot be defined as relational or historical or concerned with identity will be a non-place" (77-8). While for Augé these non-places in "supermodernity" are created for a particular purpose—as his examples of the airport, the shopping mall, or highways demonstrate—, they remain spaces of transit and are thus deprived of meaningful communicative practices or relations.[8] Furthermore, he argues that a world dominated by non-places has "surrendered to solitary individuality, to the fleeting, the temporary and ephemeral" (78). Reigned by actuality, demarcated by ideograms and instructions (such as "take right-hand lanes"), non-places are entered and exited but never dwelled in. A key figure in Augé's discussion of non-places is thus the passenger—the person who moves through the world of transit places. Entering these spaces of anonymity, she/he never stays long enough to fill the place with routines or social interactions. Instead, every encounter is superficial, converting these non-places into "places of solitude (even in the presence of others), silence, anonymity, alienation and impermanence" (Tomlinson 110), providing no comfort to the passenger.[9]

---

7 Tomlinson summarizes here key aspects of Marc Augé's work and refers to the anthropologist's opposition between 'anthropological places' and 'non-places'. Augé's 'anthropological place' does not imply that this place is 'naturally' created, but the author acknowledges that this space is also symbolically constructed and functions on various scales (Augé 51-52).

8 Augé characterizes the term 'supermodernity' with "three figures of excess: overabundance of events, spatial overabundance and the individualization of references" (109).

9 While Augé refers to the person passing through transit places and being determined by his destination as a passenger, Tomlinson points out that Augé's analysis relies in itself on the standpoint of a passenger. Explaining that the perception of places as non-places is dependent on perspective, Tomlinson claims that Augé himself is the "eternal

Amsterdam's novel illustrates how supermodernity's unintended consequences have led to the creation of riskscapes in the future world affected by climate change. In these riskscapes, non-places are no longer confined to particular places (for instance, the airport), but are omnipresent and impede any dwelling at all. The figure of the passenger, who in Augé's work is defined by his final destination and able to freely enter and exit the non-places he passes through, is no longer able to navigate freely while moving through climate riskscapes in *Things We Didn't See Coming*. He is thus turned into an *eternal* passenger. After a brief discussion of the particularity of Amsterdam's writing project and the textual manifestations of risks, the remainder of this essay focuses on how place, pervaded by global risks, increasingly loses its "relational value" and thereby figures as a non-place in riskscapes.

Riskscapes in *Things We Didn't See Coming*: Narrative Structure and Genre

Amsterdam's climate change novel offers glimpses into the life of a nameless protagonist and his struggle for survival in a world that is characterized by weather extremes fluctuating between heavy precipitation and severe periods of drought, battles over scarce resources, and an increasing un-inhabitability of places. These changing climatic conditions, indicated to be anthropogenic in nature, force the protagonist as well as the other characters in the novel to continuously re-evaluate their living situations. The title of the novel, *Things We Didn't See Coming*, already alludes to the overarching theme of riskscapes that influences narrative structure and content alike: It refers to disruptions of narrative structure, the reading process, and characters' lives.

Emphasizing this notion of disruption, Amsterdam's work follows a stop-start pattern: Instead of weaving a linear storyline in Aristotelian fashion—chronologically presenting set-up, conflict and resolution—the nine chapters of the novel are disconnected and could be read independently.[10] Impeding closure, each chapter elaborates a novel idea in a new setting, involving different characters. Hence, just as the protagonist is continuously confronted by newly arising environmental disasters, which make it impossible for him to plan his next steps, the reader is unable to anticipate setting or plot of the next chapter. Readers' expectations are thus constantly

passenger, always viewing locals as one passing through them—on trains, in cars, on planes" (Tomlinson 111).

[10] The "stop-start pattern" is a narrative technique used for nonlinear narratives. However, there does not yet exist a fixed definition of the term. In Amsterdam's case, the stop-start pattern emphasizes disruption and the protagonist's own mobility and displacements.

challenged, as she or he is never certain what the next turn in the storyline will bring, or where and in what company the narrator will be found. Because of these repeated narrative displacements, the book requires an attentive reader, who with every new chapter is forced to realize what she/he didn't see coming. However, as collage-like and self-directed as the chapters are, they nevertheless are connected—on the micro level because if read chronologically they form the life story of the narrator, starting at the turn of the millennium when the homodiegetic narrator is still a young boy and ending with the closing of his eyes, and thus presumably his death, about 40 years later. On the macro level, the chapters connect because as a sum they represent a world transformed by climate change—or, as Amsterdam writes in his final chapter, "the itinerary you all signed up for" (185).

The author's narrative technique is innovative in rendering risk scenarios intelligible, as it relies neither on dominant environmentalist discourse models as defined by Buell nor on the genre models that Heise discusses for risk narratives. Instead, it blurs generic boundaries.[11] While employing elements of the coming-of-age story and resonating with elements of the picaresque novel, the narration of *Things We Didn't See Coming* is disrupted to such an extent that generic closure is never really provided. In contrast to the picaresque novel, in which the picaro's heroic act ultimately lies in his resistance against the hypocrisies of the society he lives in, Amsterdam's climate risk fiction does not develop binary good vs. bad moral patterns – which also distinguishes the novel from apocalyptic narratives.

As a recurring theme in environmentalist discourse, apocalypse—the final destruction of the world—is employed to call attention to the urgency of environmental issues.[12] Heise acknowledges that secular forms of apocalyptic discourse may be understood as a form of risk narrative, but points to the nuances which distinguish the two: whereas apocalyptic scenarios often posit a global disaster situation in which destruction may be averted in the hope of restoring a pastoral ideal, risk scenarios emphasize "uncertainties, unintended consequences, and necessary trade-offs" (141). Moreover, they present a world, in which the return to a 'risk-free' future is no longer possible. Amsterdam's novel thus must be categorized as risk narrative since the key to survival in its manifold riskscapes is adaptability to a constantly changing environment. Each chapter focuses on the protagonist's careful considerations of which risks to take and which ones to

---

[11] In his article "Toxic Discourse" Buell identifies four rhetorical templates in the representation of toxic risks. These include 'the disrupted pastoral,' 'total toxic dispersion,' 'David vs. Goliath scenario,' and 'the gothic.' Heise further elaborates that risk scenarios also often rely on genre models such as the detective story, tragedy, or epic (*Sense of Planet* 139).

[12] Killingsworth and Palmer's article "The Apocalyptic Narrative from *Silent Spring* to Global Warming" even argues for an upsurge in apocalyptic rhetoric in recent years, especially with regard to climate change discourse.

avoid, as the riskscapes he moves through are not temporary but "permanent" (Amsterdam 101) in their dangerous changeability. In this context, Frederick Buell's discussion in *From Apocalypse to Way of Life* proves insightful. Buell argues that environmental discourse has shifted away from apocalypse as "crisis has become domesticated into daily life" (186). Amsterdam's novel underlines his assumption that crisis has become part of everyday life, a "slow process of increasing ecological and ecosocial immiseration and rising ecological and ecosocial risk" (186). Instead of proposing an end-of-time scenario, the novel thus depicts future climatic riskscapes in which society, aware of the risk of future catastrophes, increasingly "dwells in crisis." Since there is no means of escape and no clear-cut solution to the given problem, the protagonist in *Things We Didn't See Coming* tries to continuously adapt to—or in Buell's words to domesticate—the riskscapes he moves through, which impacts his experience of space and place.

Riskscapes in *Things We Didn't See Coming*: Narrating Space and Place

Amsterdam's novel investigates in detail the deterritorializing process whereby everyday meaning becomes detached from place and from local environments. Places are often understood not only as territorially defined spaces but as "centers of felt value" (Tuan 4) that play a crucial role in people's subject formation. Emphasis on locality and place as the source of environmental awareness and self-awareness thus often take center stage in ecocritical discourse. However, as elaborated above, this presupposes a rather static understanding of place and neglects the ways in which localities have already been transformed by processes of globalization, thereby becoming increasingly "phantasmagoric" (Giddens), and disembedded from their original socio-cultural context. In contrast to the practice of reassurance that Lawrence Buell sees in our tendency to convert "abstract space into familiar place" (*Environmental* 261), Amsterdam's novel discusses the effects of what happens if such conversion is no longer possible.

Even though in the opening of the novel, safe *places*—comfort zones of familiar encounters, rituals, and comforting memories—still exist, they are not carefree spaces since risks are already starting to pervade them. Fearing a major computer server breakdown at the turn of the millennium, the narrator's father urges his family to leave the nameless city he lives in to seek refuge at his grandparents' house in the countryside. However, once the family has arrived, the harmonious atmosphere is disturbed by quarrels over a road accident, causing the family to spend New Year's Eve in different places. While mother and grandparents stay by the stove inside the house, son and father meet up at the "safest place in the world" (Amsterdam 18)—a spot not far away from a hiking trail in which three trees have fallen down into a triangle. Supposedly still protected in this space by nature, the protagonist's father starts to describe the future disaster scenarios of "breakdowns that can't be fixed" (23). When asked by his young son how to best prepare for such a situation, the father realizes that he does not know the answer. Instead, "he just keeps rocking, telling me he's sorry and hugging me as tight as he can to hold the world still" (24), as the narrator describes. This scene powerfully mirrors how even the supposedly safest place in the world is suddenly pervaded by risks, by the anticipation of a major global breakdown. And even the father, who has supposedly taken all necessary precautions is not prepared enough "for everything to fall from interdependence" (12), nor is he able to explain how to prepare for the changes and disruptions to come. This introductory chapter illustrates that risks already constitute a dominant aspect of the protagonist's life from the beginning on. Moreover, it alludes to the problem of imagining protective action against global risks. As the father comes to realize, no place—especially not this countryside retreat—can keep his son safe from the global disasters to come. While chapter one of Amsterdam's novel describes an awareness of risks that are more technological in nature, in contrast to later chapters that deal with climate risks, it already suggests the multiple reverberations and global scale that risks may have and challenges the very notion of safe places.

The second chapter of Amsterdam's book, entitled "The Theft that Got Me Here," is set in the near future when climate change is already having a noticeable impact on the protagonist's young adult life. The Central, an unspecified government institution, first reacts to changing climatic conditions by dividing human living spaces into urban and rural areas. At this point in the narrative, space is still clearly demarcated, since "everybody had to choose, urban or rural" and thus suburbia, for example, has become an empty, "dry" and "decaying" (33) space. While barricades and special IDs territorially and politically define the urban space the protagonist inhabits, the "city" nevertheless is turned into an empty signifier, because it is deprived of the socio-cultural practices reviving it. The protagonist explains that the city's streets remain empty, dusty, and devoid of interaction since "no one's exactly getting dressed up for a Sunday drive" (26). In this environment, humans become the mirror of the environments they inhabit: shadow figures, like the narrator's grandmother who has been "off the map for six years" (that is, mentally absent due to Alzheimer's), or the protagonist himself who "is lying there decimated, slowed down to a piss puddle of [his] former self" (27), because his only means of dealing with the situation is to sedate himself with drugs.

These deterritorializing tendencies are challenged when all of a sudden the narrator's grandmother is lucid again and attempts to re-territorialize place. Deciding to go on a Sunday drive to the countryside, the family has to face political reality as it is stopped at the barricade demarcating city territory. Yet, the grandmother successfully convinces the patrol officer to let them pass by ultimately restoring meaning to the 'countryside' that lies behind the barricade: In vivid terms, she describes not only her former home and lifestyle there, thereby reterritorializing the place, but also frees the city of its usually socially sterile atmosphere by drawing a personal relationship between herself and the officer. She points out: "Anything named Central doesn't even know what you look like. I do, and I'm watching you to see that you make the right decision here" (33). The officer then waves the family through.

However, the countryside they encounter does not resemble the pastoral idyll of their memories. It has become a battlefield in which every intrusion by city-dwellers is considered an affront. Managing to escape several attacks by country-dwellers, the family finally comes to a rest at a nice picnic spot. But the narrator's description of his grandparents in this moment as "happy ghosts" (38) already foreshadows the following set of events. Just when the grandparents decide to part ways with the protagonist in order to continue their lives in the countryside, Alzheimer's takes hold of the grandmother again. Knowing there won't be another chance of self-determined life, the grandfather gives himself and his wife a deadly cocktail of pills. Deprived of his family and without any other social attachments, the lonesome narrator decides to head west, towards the "endless land" (47) he hopes to find there. His desire to escape to the wild and 'untouched' West and to live a life 'on the road' echo key topoi of American culture, which has been elaborated on by Ursula Heise. She explains, "Americans have seen themselves as modern nomads, and have always felt ambivalent about their mobility, perceiving it by turns as their greatest social asset and their deepest cultural deficiency" (49). This conflict is also foregrounded in Amsterdam's novel. As the story proceeds and the narrator moves west, he increasingly finds himself caught in climate change–driven riskscapes, which impede any form of 'settlement' and thus force him to be 'on the move'. His mobility and uprootedness are then permanent, worsening the protagonist's solitude and sense of alienation. The hostility of riskscapes thus revokes the positive notion of the 'modern nomad,' who is no longer a traveller by choice.

The third chapter, entitled "Dry Land", set at a later point in the future, describes these riskscapes in greater detail, as they turn nomads into refugees, travellers into eternal passengers. This chapter paradoxically describes how the land is anything but dry, because climate change has led to increased rain patterns. The reader discovers that the protagonist narrator now works as an evacuation officer for "Land Management", looking for "the shaky light of candles burning in dark houses and evacuat[ing] whoever's still thinking the sky's about to clear" (Amsterdam 48-9). While his only companion, a 'rain horse,' has "been sensitized to travel in downpours without complaint" (48), for him it is more difficult to travel in constant rain but government medication helps him to endure these wet conditions. The narrator describes the transformation of the places he encounters on his evacuation route: the solar sheets which collect "nothing but water now" (51), and the "thousand-dollar appliances you can't use since the grid went down" (52) in a once-precious summer house which now stands abandoned and uninviting. Also, the surrounding landscape is no longer what it used to be, but the "grass or whatever was here before has been stripped by a thousand new rivers coming down from the mountain" (51), ultimately turning this piece of land into an "area for wildlife now, not people" (60). Stressing the volatility of riskscapes, this passage demonstrates how places and landscapes constantly come to be reconfigured.

While living conditions in these changeable riskscapes have become extremely difficult and dangerous, many of the people that the protagonist encounters 'dwell in crisis' instead of realistically assessing the hazards they confront. Similar to Frederic Buell's discussion of contemporary society's domestication of crisis, the characters in Amsterdam's novel try to adjust to life in riskscapes. However, as the narrator explains, the state of 'dwelling in crisis' needs to be overcome by one's acceptance of the deterritorializing processes of climate risks. This is most prominently illustrated by the narrator's comment about his job. He complains,

> It's the people part of the job that isn't so great. . . Some guys who come out on these gigs are full of compassion for the human suffering and want to help the families *come to terms, deal with their loss, adjust.* It's a noble calling, if you see it like that, but all I see is people being washed away by life and I think the respectful thing to do is treat them efficiently, not ask them *how it feels*. (49, emphasis orig.)

For the protagonist, dealing with this climatic risk situation is a matter of moving on and not one of dwelling on the life and place one has been attached to. After all, in a climatically changed world, those lives and places will sooner or later be "washed away" along with everything else. To continue dwelling in a place in the face of further risks or to develop any emotional personal attachments is futile. Instead, as it becomes evident that landscapes, places, and lives all undergo constant transformations, survival must become as mobile and independent as possible.

The hostility of riskscapes is mirrored in the personal interactions of the characters. When the narrator meets a woman and her daughter in one of the abandoned houses, their contact revolves around the question of survival at the cost of betraying each other. The protagonist quickly decides that both the alcoholic mother "whose body feels like life's gone from it" (66) and the daughter "that's got no instinct to make it" (58) are a lost cause. He considers their attachment to one another and their clinging to the past as particularly counterproductive to adaptability, which to him is crucial for survival. Eventually, it is the narrator who is deceived by mother and daughter and forced to leave them and the house behind. He starts to contemplate "what it's going to take to make them give up on each other, turn them into survivors" (69). Startled by a deer passing by, he further wonders, "what these animals were holding on for, before they finally decided to save themselves" (69). The protagonist thus muses on the value of personal as well as place-related attachments and ponders at what point risks become life-threatening enough to break these bonds. Only at a later point in the novel, however, does he give a partial answer to this question: "if you lose everything once, running becomes a part of you" (101). Accordingly, only once people have experienced complete destruction and catastrophe will they take their vulnerability to future risks seriously. They thus begin to realize that survival in riskscapes depends on detachment from place and even solitude.

Despite the fact that in the two next chapters the narrator is no longer on his own but accompanied by a woman named Margo, isolation and uprootedness remain prominent themes. When a quarantine is declared in the city (which is again nameless and not further defined), the couple moves out into the woods and builds a camp. Margo—who has been restless already in the city and disappeared sometimes for several days (often to go stealing things)—does not stop her wandering once she and the protagonist have moved to the country. Surprisingly, the narrator seems to be bothered by her absence and independence: "It hurts to think what she really wants is solitude. I liked it better when I thought she was after more material comforts" (75). His admission reveals how important personal attachment really is to him and that his isolation is a painful state that has been forced upon him as a result of trying to survive in an unpredictable riskscape. However, he soon is reminded of the advantages of a life in isolation. When their camp is invaded by a deadly, infected intruder who describes himself as a "barely surviving humanist in an inhuman world" (81), the narrator is no longer confronted solely with the fear of not finding enough food or water or with the question of when Margo will return, but faces the risk of being infected as well. He paints a vivid image of the scene:

> [The intruder is] on all fours, throwing up blood under the tree. Such a pastoral scene . . . the pale late-afternoon sky, the dried green of the trees, the little man bent over like a dog on the ground beneath it all, and the splash of red at the bottom of the canvas, seeping into the soil. (73)

The blood not only figuratively breaks the pastoral idyll of the image, but it also literally contaminates the soil and thus ultimately the place that the protagonist inhabits and which served as the basis for his survival. The risk of being infected then functions as another deterritorializing moment, forcing the protagonist to abandon the camp he and Margo have built.

Upon Margo's return from one of her wanderings to the contaminated site, she and the protagonist immediately begin to look for a new place to install themselves. Coming to what looks like an abandoned campsite, the protagonist feels the urge to "go see what's been left" and to "move in and make their world mine" (89). However, he anticipates that in doing so "I am *sure in my blood* we'll doom ourselves to always live exactly as we have lived, inhabiting whatever corner of the world isn't nailed down, never staying anywhere long enough to make anything real. We will be the ghosts that feed off the edges of life" (89, emphasis original). Interestingly, at this point the protagonist fears that their nomadic life will never come to an end and is overwhelmed by the yearning that attachment to one particular place is still possible and will enable them to "make something real." Yet, when the other residents return unexpectedly, "the decision is made for [them]" (ibid.) and settling at the campsite is no longer an option. At this point of the narration, all hopes for the possibility of re-inhabitation are thus shattered and the narrator's mantra is to always move on and to hurry "if we're going to make it" (109). Consequently, he and Margo are never staying long enough in one place to enliven it with socio-cultural practices because they are only waiting "for the next event to push [them] along" (104). Deprived of meaning, places are no longer reference points, but, following Augé's discussion, transit points or non-places. Wondering where to go without knowing where they are, Margo and the protagonist become the eternal passengers that the protagonist was afraid they would turn into.

As the story continues, it becomes apparent that it is not just the narrator and his partner who are forced to be continuously 'on the move'—everyone is. Due to increasingly extreme weather events, places have been rated according to a "Most Livable List" and the narrator now works as a distributor of cash grants for relocation from places that have to be abandoned. Dealing with extreme heat, droughts, and mosquito attacks, the situation is devastating, leaving staff members no choice but to take pills to cope. The few inhabitants who still remain at disasters sites are "laughing about their dumb luck for surviving. But they have this newborn worry in their faces," because "though the people in Grief [a government task force that tries to address people's emotions] work hard to push the line that rebuilding heals all . . . nothing really heals because. . . you're always looking back" (101). Knowing that their survival in riskscapes will be based on constant relocation, they nostalgically look back at what has been lost, longing for earlier and more stable times. The protagonist also continues to suffer from his constant displacement, but at this point in the narrative his longing for stability is mostly suppressed and only subconsciously emerges in nightmares about a young boy wanting to be led to his home, or materializes in panic attacks when he is overwhelmed by his fear of the future (95, 103). Aware that a return to a risk-free environment will not be possible, he makes fun of other evacuees who still believe in the volatility of the situation:

> Most evacuees don't learn. They try to start over someplace exciting (a target) or temperate (subject to floods, fires, or earthquakes). Or they identify the month's most thermopolitically neutral region. They assume they're not going to have to pack again. Even though it may be the third or fourth time for some of them, they're still completely tweaked with relocation fever . . . They take their first steps around their new home and get confident; make friends, buy appliances, plant tomatoes. You want to shake them: *Do you really think this time it's going to be different?* (104)

This passage demonstrates that while there still remains an urge for re-territorialization and a need to seek psychological comfort through the socio-cultural attachment to place, this strategy is ultimately pointless. Riskscapes no longer allow for re-inhabitation. Juxtaposing rootedness and mobility, the narrator clearly indicates that only the latter can serve as the 'route to survival.' Humans then literally become what environmental studies scholar Neil Evernden has called "natural aliens": a species without fixed habitat. As a result of the global climate crisis, their "world falls away and loses all significance" with the result that they are completely "unattached, at home nowhere" (120). All that remains are eternal passengers in meaningless spaces of transit, that is non-places.

The chapter "The Forest for the Trees" critically envisions this placelessness and effectively demonstrates the difficulties between the negotiation of risks, uprootedness, and eternal mobility on the one hand and security, emplacement, and stability on the other. In what seemingly are fairly stable times, the narrator works as a speechwriter for a woman named Juliet, the political leader of a fourth of the population of the country, while also leading a very intimate relationship with both her and Margo. However, pressured to conform to Juliet's wishes, he and Margo, as the narrator explains, are always pretending to be on their best behavior. Returning to Augé's discussion helps to illustrate how the passenger always performs identity ("shells") anew in non-places. Augé explains, "subjected to a gentle form of possession, to which he surrenders himself with more or less talent or conviction—he tastes for a while like anyone who is possessed—the passive joys of identity-loss, and the more active pleasure of role-playing" (103). Indeed, for a while the protagonist enjoys playing the new role that has been ascribed to him, especially because all records of his and Margo's criminal activities in the past have been erased. However, the narrator is aware that this is only a performance and he hopes that by being more thoughtful and better intentioned "[we] someday . . . will be who we really are" (Amsterdam 120), invoking again the need to "make something real." When the time comes to renew his "practical union" with Margo, the narrator also sees it as an opportunity to secure their relationship with Juliet, a person known to let "people go as easily as she has taken [them] on" (121), by adding Juliet to their practical union contract. He is tired of not knowing what the future will bring and of thus being continuously prepared to change again. This is illustrated most explicitly when he explains his plan to Margo: "Simple security. Wouldn't it be nice to know where we're going to be next year?" (123). According to the protagonist, a three-way union would not only benefit him and Margo by providing them with stability, but it would also help Juliet, who is often questioned by the public about 'settling down.' The union would credit her with a much-needed "uniter" (125) image, mirroring her own attempts to politically and territorially unite the country.

The narrator's attempts to reduce his exposure to risks by striving for more security in climatically and politically unstable surroundings, however, become absurd towards the end of the chapter, when his plan literally goes up in smoke. Forced by Juliet to participate in one of her power games, his urge for longer-term security is dismissed by his own short-term risk-taking, as she convinces him to put on a supposedly fireproof suit and puts a forest on fire. Though Juliet and Margo assure him that "everyone, everything is safe" (135), the flames of the forest surrounding him stand in stark contrast to this assertion. Upon Margo's fatalism "Light one [branch] and they all go," the protagonist realizes that ultimately his relationship with her has never been comforting but that "as long as [he] ha[s] known her, [he] ha[s] never known peace" (134). Also his plan to gain security by a three-way union with Juliet and Margo has been an illusion. His final thoughts, "I no longer want anything at all" (136), suggest his resignation as he looks at the fire quickly spreading around him and finally understands holding on to a person, an idea, or even a place is pointless because no matter where he will be, his environment will never be free from risk.

Finally, in *Things We Didn't See Coming*, not only the environment, but also the human body itself is turned into a riskscape. Even though the protagonist believed himself to be healthy, he discovers a medical report which indicates that his body has several "ticking bombs inside" (148), with symptoms in the nervous, lymphatic, and digestive system expected to manifest over the next several years. As riskscapes function as a stressor to human health conditions, the inner space (the human body) increasingly figures as the broken mirror of the non-places it inhabits—something that has already been foreshadowed by the infected intruder in the novel's campsite scene. Thus, body and environment alike pose significant threats to the characters in the novel. Apart from the physiological diagnosis, the medical report, moreover, gives insight into the protagonist's social and psychiatric condition:

> [...] strong cognition and problem-solving, weak emotive-spiritual; *tendency toward risk-taking/impatience/dishonesty when stressed*; *formative years yielded strong desire/ability to trust, make attachments—countered by apparent experience*; optimism subnormal, conflicts with strong survival instinct; isolationist, dysthymic tendencies expected to increase with age. (147, emphasis added)

This risk account then functions as a short summary of the narrator's psychological development so far and reinforces his need for attachment. This need, however, has remained unanswered by the outer riskscapes he has moved through. Ultimately, uprootedness and continuous displacement not only have had an effect on his psychological constitution, but have also led to bodily suffering. Again, being put in a situation of risk evaluation, the narrator follows his 'survival instincts', thereby confirming what the report has said about him: he betrays a community he lives with temporarily. Even though he "really wanted to call this place home" (149), he breaks the rules and leaves the group behind in order to take his body "full of problems" (147) to a medical complex. After a quick and efficient medical treatment, he vacillates between returning to the community he left and taking care of the young boy that came with him to the treatment center. Finally, he decides against both options and chooses the road instead. He explains, "it feels good, it's where I belong: I've escaped" (161).

However, this escape is only temporary, since neither the roads he travels on nor the medical treatments he receives will provide security. Instead, as the final chapter of the novel reveals, the narrator's body is no longer able to bear the riskscapes of the future, climatically changed world and finally breaks down. Working as a tour guide for groups of people with "at least two major cancers or a primary ailment" (184), who have been through many ineffective medical treatments and now just want to experience some thrill (volcano outbreaks, safaris) before they die, the protagonist realizes that he himself looks "like the rest of them" (194). He himself has become part of the terminally ill. Not only is his skin disintegrating, but in the final encounter with his father (who now lives as a healer in the countryside), the protagonist lets go of the last string of life he is still holding on to, and "without the slightest incantation, [the father] closes [his] eyes" (199). Circling back to the beginning and the moment in which the first decisions in the face of risk were taken, the novel then seems to repeat the narrator's question: Since crisis is inevitable, how can one best prepare for the volatility of riskscapes and changing environments—especially if crisis forces one to live without 'homes' or communities of belonging? And are we psychologically and physically equipped to adapt to a life as passengers in non-places?

Conclusion

Amsterdam's *Things We Didn't See Coming* figures as an innovative response to what Mike Hulme has called "the sterile idea of a disembodied and unsituated global climate with its universalizing demands on our imaginations and behaviours" (273). It zooms in on the personal experience and puts a human face on this otherwise 'disembodied idea,' while at the same time giving credit to the deterritorializing aspects of global climate change. As the novel illustrates, deterritorialization does not mean that place is completely annihilated, because, as Tomlinson points out, "we are all, as human beings, embodied and physically located" (149) and thus the need to re-territorialize continues to exercise significant power over our behavior and psychology. However, what global risks such as climate change confront us with is that as places are continuously transformed, ties to them are significantly weakened. Amsterdam's work thus challenges our understanding of place-attachment because it illustrates that in the future climatically changed world humans will move in riskscapes, in which uprootedness will become the norm.

Ignoring issues of social inequality that climate change–related deterritorialization introduces, the novel's emphasis on nameless places and mostly nameless characters seems to suggest that in riskscapes, it longer matters where we come from or who we are and thus reflects the notion that these events may happen anywhere and to anyone. Whereas other works of climate change fiction, such as T.C. Boyle's *A Friend of the Earth* or Dana Stein's *Fire in the Wind*, provide more territorially defined stories, Amsterdam's novel illustrates how place is transformed into non-place through the deterritorializing aspects of climate risks. For the characters' survival, these hostile and ever-changing environments mean constant adaptation and a life of isolation and solitude. Thus understood, deterritorialization and mobility do not enable a cosmopolitan thinking—described by Ulrich Beck as an emergence of a global moral consciousness based on shared risk experience (*World Risk Society* 14-15)—but rather create solitary passengers as the tragic unintended consequences of today's risk society.

Amsterdam's novel is significant to the growing body of climate change fiction because it engages with the representational challenge that global risks pose in novel ways. Through its fragmented story-telling, it puts characters and readers alike in a position where they cannot know what is coming, which effectively illustrates that although one cannot fully 'know' risks, one nevertheless has to make decisions in the face of them—that is, the characters have to decide whether to change location and readers whether to continue reading. The novel furthermore innovatively deals with the deterritorialized and global dimension of climate change–related risks without having to rely on digital networks or other means of disembodied, virtual communication, which Heise considers suitable for the representation of large-scale phenomena such as climate change. *Things We Didn't See Coming* provides a narrative template for the representation of global risks because it refuses to focus on one particular locality or place. Instead, it painfully relates to the reader that if she or he were to zoom in on place in a climatically changed world of the future, that place would no longer be recognizable because it would have become part of ever-shifting global riskscapes. Amsterdam's novel thereby forces us to think beyond territorial boundaries and postulates that survival depends on the letting go of place-based routines.

Works Cited

Amsterdam, Steven. *Things We Didn't See Coming*. London: Random House UK, 2011. Print.
Appadurai, Arjun. *Modernity At Large: Cultural Dimensions of Globalization*. Minneapolis: University of Minnesota Press, 1996. Print.
---. "Disjuncture and Difference in the Global Cultural Economy." *Theory, Culture, Society*. 7.2. (1990): 295-310. Print.
Augé, Marc. *Non-Places: Introduction to an Anthropology of Supermodernity*. London, New York: Verso, 1995. Print.
Beck, Ulrich. *World Risk Society*. Cambridge: Polity Press, 1999. Print.
---. "The Reinvention of Politics: Towards a Theory of Reflexive Modernization." *Reflexive Modernization*. Ed. Ulrich Beck, Scott Lash and Anthony Giddens. Cambridge: Polity Press, 1994. Print.
---. *Risk Society: Towards a New Modernity*. London: Sage Publications, 1992. Print.
Buell, Frederic. *From Apocalypse to Way of Life: Environmental Crisis in the American Century*. New York: Routledge, 2004. Print.
Buell, Lawrence. *The Environmental Imagination: Thoreau, Nature Writing, and the Formation of American Culture*. Cambridge, MA: Harvard University Press, 1996. Print.
---. "Toxic Discourse." *Critical Inquiry* 24.3 (1998): 639-665. Print.
Canclini, Nestor Garcia. *Hybrid Cultures: Strategies for Entering and Leaving Modernity*. Trans. Christopher L. Chiappari & Silvia L. Lopez. Minneapolis: University of Minnesota Press, 2005. Print.
Clark, Timothy. *The Cambridge Introduction to Literature and the Environment*. Cambridge: Cambridge University Press, 2011. Print.
Cutter, Susan and William Solecki. "Setting Environmental Justice in Space and Place: Acute and Chronic Airborne Toxic Releases in the Southeastern United States." *Urban Geography* 17.5 (1996): 380-399. Print.
Cutter, Susan. *Hazards, Vulnerability and Environmental Justice*. London: Earthscan, 2006. Print.
Deleuze, Gilles, and Felix Guattari. *A Thousand Plateaus: Capitalism and Schizophrenia*, trans. Brian Massumi. Minneapolis: University of Minneapolis Press, 1987. Print.
Edwards, Paul N. "Representing the Global Atmosphere." *Changing the Atmosphere: Expert Knowledge and Environmental Governance*. Ed. Clark Miller. Cambridge, MA: MIT Press, 2001. 31–67. Print.
Evernden, Neil. *The Natural Alien: Humankind and Environment*. Toronto: University of Toronto Press, 1993. Print.
Gabrys, Jennifer, and Kathryn Yusoff. "Arts, Sciences and Climate Change: Practices and Politics at the Threshold." *Science as Culture* 21.1 (2012): 37–41. Print.
Giddens, Anthony. *Consequences of Modernity*. Oxford: Blackwell Publishers, 1991. Print.
Heise, Ursula. *Sense of Place and Sense of Planet: The Environmental Imagination of the Global*. New York: Oxford University Press, 2008. Print.

Hulme, Mike. "Cosmopolitan Climates: Hybridity, Foresight and Meaning." *Theory, Culture Society*. 27:2-3 (2010): 267-276. Print.

Killingsworth, Jimmie and Jaqueline Palmer. "Millennial Ecology. The Apocalyptic Narrative from Silent Spring to Global Warming." *Green Culture: Environmental Rhetoric In Contemporary America*. Ed. Carl Herndl and Stuart C. Brown. Madison: University of Wisconsin Press, 1996. 21-45. Print.

Rushdie, Salman. *Imaginary Homelands: Essays and Criticism 1981-1991*. London: Vintage, 2010. Print.

Tomlinson, John. *Globalization and Culture*. 2nd ed. Chicago: University of Chicago Press, 1999. Print.

Trexler, Adam, and Adeline Johns-Putra. "Climate change in literature and literary criticism." *Wiley Interdisciplinary Reviews: Climate Change* 2 (2011): 185-200. Print.

Tuan, Yi-Fu. *Space and Place. The Perspective of Experience*. Minneapolis: University of Minnesota Press, 1977. Print.

Ziser, Michael. "Home Again: Peak Oil, Climate Change, and the Aesthetics of Transition." *Environmental Criticism for the Twenty-First Century*. Ed. Stephanie LeMenager, Teresa Shewry, & Ken Hiltner. New York: Routledge, 2011. 181–196. Print.

II

Representations of Nuclear Risk

HOLGER KERSTEN

"These Rays May Be Helpful or Harmful": The Depiction of Radium in Early 20th Century American Newspapers

On September 2, 2011, a group of local residents of Ottawa, Ill., gathered for the unveiling of a statue representing a young woman holding a paintbrush in one hand and a tulip in the other. Located near the former site of the Radium Dial company, the monument was created to commemorate the fate of the "Radium Girls," a group of workers who, in the 1920's, became victims of radium poisoning in a factory that produced luminous watch dials and other objects that needed to be visible in the dark ("Ottawa memorial"). To do their work accurately, the painters required a very fine point on their paintbrushes. Told that radium was a harmless substance, they pointed their brushes with their lips, a procedure that needed to be repeated "about six times to every watch dial" (Neuzil and Kovarik 53), and in this way ingested significant amounts of the radioactive material. As more facts emerged about the routines in radium processing factories, it was revealed that this was not an isolated occurrence. The Ottawa tragedy had its equivalents at various locations throughout the United States and left a total of 112 workers dead from what was later called an occupational disease (Mullner 5).

The story of radium as a deadly chemical agent reaches beyond the suffering of the mostly female factory workers employed in the industrial application of a highly radioactive substance. Its impact is in no way limited to a specific workplace at a specific time in history. The effect of the widespread and enthusiastic use of an element with a half-life of 1,600 years during the first decades of the 20th century is felt to this day. Many of the locations where radium was mined, processed, and used have been designated "Superfund" sites, places which the United States government endeavors to clean up with great financial effort to protect American citizens from health hazards. By September 2004, approximately $40 million dollars had been spent on remedial efforts in the Ottawa, Ill., region (EPA). 2011 estimates have set the cleanup costs for Ottawa at a total of $80 million (Farabaugh). In 1996, the *New York Times* reported that $120 million had been spent on removing radium contamination from various properties near Orange, N.J., the site of a U.S. Radium Corporation factory

(Galant). Other radium processing and production locations that have been placed on the Superfund list include communities in the states of New York, Massachusetts, and Colorado. Cleanup efforts there similarly involve funding that may well run into hundreds of millions of dollars.

Although many former radium sites have been identified and are in the process of remediation, it is not clear that the problem is now fully under control. As Mullner warned in 1998, "many factories, chemical processing plants, laboratories, physicians' offices, watch repair shops, and homes" may still be contaminated with the element and may continue to "pose serious public health problems" (Mullner 142). In this way, the early of story of radium can serve as a chilling illustration of how "unknown and unintended consequences come to be a dominant force in history and society" (Beck 22). The introduction of radium into therapeutic use and into consumer products represents the dawn of the atomic age and may thus be regarded as the earliest manifestation of what sociologist Ulrich Beck has termed the "risk society" since the experiments with the highly radioactive element and its irreversible effects antecede the construction and deployment of the atomic bomb by more than a generation. "Risks," in Beck's sense, emerge above all from radioactivity which "completely evades human perceptive abilities." Because risks "initially only exist in terms of the (scientific or anti-scientific) knowledge about them" they "are particularly *open to social definition and construction*" (23). This is why, according to Beck, the mass media, as a forum where these definitions are presented and debated and by which they are disseminated to the general public, occupy a central social and political position. As this essay will show, American newspapers did not frame their radium coverage in terms of risks. Instead, they spent most of their time and effort on trying to follow and digest the most recent scientific developments and to integrate them into speculations about how they might lead to a better future.

In view of the disastrous consequences which the commercial use of radium had with regard to human health and the environment the question arises how and why it was possible that Americans in the first quarter of the 20th century willingly engaged in such a risky enterprise. By looking at the record preserved in the newspaper coverage between 1900 and 1925, this essay suggests that the excitement and enthusiasm about a scientific novelty overshadowed the evidence of the dangers that were inherent in radium. Buoyed by the optimism that science would control nature and thus pave the way to a better life, and hampered by the lack of an adequate model for risk assessment, any awareness that the new technologies and objects involving radium might imply a large-scale and long-term risk appears to have been completely numbed. To substantiate its claim, this essay will first present a survey of the predominantly positive representation of radium research and radium applications in the American press. Focusing on an influential article published in *McClure's Magazine*, the second section will show that information about the dangers of radium and its uses was in fact available but that this knowledge triggered no warning signals. The survey ends in 1925 when the extensive press coverage of the suffering and death of the "Radium Girls" turned the dangers of radium exposure into a topic of national debate.

From Miracle Substance to Household Aid: The American Press as a Promoter of Radium

In the early years of the 20th century newspapers were the main source of information on innovations in science and technology and their potential applications for the average American citizen. This observation particularly applies to the coverage of radium research. As early as September 1903, the *New York Times* noted an "absorbing and almost exciting public interest" with regard to radium and radio-active substances. As the general public was seeking information about the newly discovered element, the *Times* highlighted the "increasing importance of the daily press in the dissemination of scientific news." These journalistic efforts, the paper proclaimed with a tone of self-confidence, led to the situation that the "average man in every civilized country knows as much about radium as do the most advanced physicists" ("Women and Radium"). A few days later, the *Times* supported its claim by referring to Oliver Lodge, an English physicist and writer, who had stated that "real educators in applied science are the daily newspapers of the countries where great facts are taken seriously" ("The Popular Interest"). For this reason, American newspapers of the time constitute an important source for an understanding of the public perception of radium in American culture.

Radium was discovered in 1898, but it took Marie Curie until 1902 to accumulate enough material to determine its atomic weight (Malley 27–32). Although the difficulties involved in obtaining sufficient radium for conducting the experiments which were needed to study the characteristics of the new element were considerable, radium quickly acquired a reputation as a miraculous substance. Even before the Nobel Prize Committee acknowledged the achievement of Pierre and Marie Curie by awarding them the Nobel Prize for Physics in 1903, the American mainstream press began to write about the uses of radium in enthusiastic terms and continued to do so until the mid-1920's when a series of incidents involving radium resulted in injuries and death that alarmed the American public.

The very first reports in American newspapers described radium as a "light giving metal." What made it particularly interesting was the fact that it seemed to be light without heat, "a long sought and much hoped for possibility" ("A Light Giving Metal"). As is illustrated by the *Boston*

Globe, journalists made an effort to convey a sense of what appeared to be the mysterious qualities of "his marvelous metal, which burns eternally without lighting and whose light is so powerful that placed in a man's stomach he would be completely lighted up for purposes of medicine and surgery" ("Wonders of Radium").

In September 1902, the *Arizona Republican* admitted that "thus far only the most preliminary steps have been made toward the discovery of the properties of radium." And yet, the "field for speculation seems boundless." Simultaneously, people began to look for commercial applications of the new substance. It was speculated that "within a few years salts of radium attain the position of a merchantable commodity, perhaps even to the extent of revolutionizing certain of the world's industries" ("New Field").

Under the headline "Radium Now the World's Wonder," the *Chicago Tribune* emphasized the enormity of the discovery by speaking of a "great revolution in science." Although relatively little was reliably known about radium, the existing knowledge sparked tremendous expectations about the future. For the *Tribune* it promised "a knowledge so gigantic that it is only limited by the capacity or the human mind to receive it" ("Radium Now"). In a lengthy article written for the Sunday edition of the *St. Louis Republic*, a journalist proposed many applications for radium in the industrial world where "a few grains might provide energy to drive our locomotives, motor cars and mechanical engines and carriages of every description." But the new element also promised to be valuable for private households whose energy needs would be covered by electric generating stations powered by radium. People's houses would be heated by "a minute quantity of the element," and "domestic cooking would be done on radium stoves" ("Some Practical Uses"). When, in May 1903, the *London Times* was still wondering what the practical use of radium might be ("Powers of Radium"), American researchers began to spread the idea that "radium may prove to be the long-sought cure for cancer" ("Ounce of Radium"). This speculation received support from Pierre Curie who, in a 1904 interview, confirmed that he was "positive" about radium's ability to kill off cancer (D'Alemcourt). From this time on, reports on experimental uses of radium as a cancer cure became a fixture in American newspapers. One of the most outspoken voices in the struggle to make radium available to the medical profession was Dr. Howard A. Kelly from Baltimore, a very prominent practitioner of radium therapy and one of the founding members of the not-for-profit National Radium Institute (Mullner 27). Because he had seen cases in which radium made possible "complete cures of cancer," Kelly was convinced that radium therapy represented a breakthrough for medical science. He passionately called for support in the struggle to make the rare and expensive substance available for cancer research and treatment at the largest possible number of hospitals. Because radium was so important but only available in very limited supply, Kelly argued that its distribution needed to be controlled by the federal government so that "it may be used properly for the benefit of all the people" ("Real Cancer 'Cure'"). Ten years earlier, Pierre Curie had also expressed his opposition to a commercial exploitation. "Radium is humanity's property," he said in an interview, "it would be profanation to use it for financial ends" (D'Alemcourt).

These idealistic positions notwithstanding, radium-laced patent medicines appeared on the market almost immediately after the first claims for radium as a potential remedy were published. In California, for example, "Rexradio, the famous London healing 'Radium King'," offered his services in the *San Francisco Call* ("Rexradio"). His "truly extraordinary radium" treatment cured "all alleged incurable diseases," including deafness, imminent blindness, sciatica, and paralysis ("Rexradio's Bulletin"). Similarly spectacular medical results were promised by the "British-American Medical Institute" of Los Angeles that used an exclusive "Electric-Ozo-Vilo Radium treatment machine" ("From the Summit"). Russell Burner, one of the men behind this scheme and a figure who had been active on the shady side of the health business for many years, also publicized himself as "The Radium King." In 1906, he founded the "Los Angeles Temple of Health" where he staged public events which combined lectures, musical entertainment, and an exhibition of radium and radium appliances. His visitors were offered refreshments, consisting of "milk, water, and other beverages, all charged with radium" ("Health Temple"). Burner also founded a chain of "Radium, Milk, and Rest Cure sanatoriums" in Southern California. He used large-sized newspaper advertisements to promote his "Radium Treatment System" and to explain the extraordinary action of radium to his potential customers. According to Burner, the effect of radium resembled "the way a ferret works when taken on a hunt for rats": Introducing radium into a patient's bloodstream unleashes a "battle" "between clean, healthy life and the deadly disease germ, and the new life never gives up until not only the disease germ is gone, but every trace of its terrible work has been wiped out and the affected parts replaced by new, strong, healthy tissue" ("From the Summit").

"Rexradio" and Burner were soon joined by many other peddlers of radium products. Throughout the early decades of the 20th century countless business notices appeared in local newspapers throughout the United States. Under slogans such as "Take baths in liquid sunshine. It sparkles and foams like champagne" they promised instant and complete relief from a long list of ailments ("Radium Sulphur Spring"). As radium "health products" became available in local drugstores, their number increased further over the next years. In 1922, the *Binghampton Press* (N.Y.) carried an advertisement for Arium Radium tablets which were supposed to restore people's energy, vitality, and strength. Modern living conditions, the text suggested, had weakened the human body. Thankfully, "Mme. Curie, that wonderful woman, who gave the world radium, unlocked the life power of the ages." At the same time, the advertiser saw a need to reassure potential customers that the product was "harmless as pure water yet as necessary to health as the food you eat" ("Radium!").

In this situation it mattered little that representatives of the medical profession, such as Dr. Francis Carter Wood, director of the Crocker Cancer Research Fund, openly stated that "most of the claims trumped up for radium were ridiculous." He feared that the public would be fooled by "medical quacks and fake cures" and blamed the newspapers for not providing reliable information. "If the newspapers would only publish the facts behind all these affairs the public would be quickly disillusioned," he said, "but cold facts are rarely of news value" ("Student of Cancer"). According to another view the press was following its own economic interests by focusing on sensational news and by doing so had so extensively exploited "the wonders of radium" that it was difficult to stop the spread of ineffective pseudo remedies and preposterous and potentially dangerous messages by which they were promoted ("Points Out Dangers").

The examples presented so far show a development that expanded the application of radium from a remedy that targeted specific diseases to a broad-spectrum tonic that supposedly restored a person's strength and waning vitality. When it made the transition from the health sector to the realm of ordinary household products, radium took full possession of the homes of average Americans. A 2008 catalog compiled for the U.S. Nuclear Regular Commission (Buchholz and Cervera) displays the wide range of consumer products that were "enhanced" with radium. The table of contents identifies more than 160 items, including building and industrial materials, luminescent devices, medical devices, toys and novelties, as well as consumer products and foods. As a record of the almost boundless inventiveness of business-minded people, the catalog illustrates the extent to which radium entered the living space of the American people.

Given that cleanliness became an important issue in 20th century America (Hoy), it comes as no surprise that radium sprays were offered as a powerful alternative to ordinary cleaning supplies. A 1909 advertisement marketed "Radium Spray" as a product that could be used on carpets, for cleaning furniture, for the protection of horses and cattle and for killing insects ("Seasonable Specials"). A Hawaiian newspaper ad described radium spray as "a liquid cleaner and polisher, a dust layer, disinfectant, deodorizer and a sure death to vermin, such as moths, bedbugs, fleas roaches, etc." To calm potential worries that customers might have about a product that prided itself on its ability to kill all vermin, the ad promised that "Radium Spray will not injure the finest fabrics," and boldface letters reassured potential buyers that the product contained "no acids" and "no poisons." The product was designed to "kill everything that has no lungs," at the same time, it was said to be so safe for humans that "you can drink it" ("Something New").

In what might have been an attempt to emphasize the harmlessness of its radium cleaner and to give it a folksy appeal, the Radium Spray Company of Richmond, Virginia, employed advertizing poetry to advance its business interests. Built to resemble the rhythmic pattern of Oliver Wendell Holmes's very popular "The Deacon's Masterpiece, or The Wonderful 'One-Hoss Shay'," the lines announced that "The greatest thing in the South today / Is the wonderful, wonderful Radium Spray." The lines recommended that the product be used on barnyard animals to rid them of insects, praised the product's efficiency as a cleaning agent, and promised relief from bothersome flies and mosquitoes. The application seemed to require no safety precautions whatsoever, not even when the product came into very close proximity with a person. One of the couplets suggested: "On the beds in the house use Radium Spray / And sleep while the bed bugs die away" ("[The Greatest Thing]").

Shortly after America entered World War I, the Radium Chemical Company promoted its "Radium Cleanser" in a large ad that combined visual material with nursery rhymes and war rhetoric. While the US military and the armed forces of all the European combatants were caught up in some of the most violent battles of the war, the manufacturer declared in dramatic terms that it had "opened war on the great pest of America, the fly which is the most deadly enemy of mankind." Without any sense of incongruity, the ad promised to deal out death "to flies and all dangerous summer pests," while at the same time cleaning, refreshing, and renewing furniture, and diffusing "sweet refreshing odor, like the breath from a pine forest." To eliminate any doubt that may have lingered about the safety of such a powerful product, the ad declared in all capital letters that "Radium Cleanser" was "perfectly harmless to human beings" ("The Fly War").

The impression that radium-enhanced products were safe to use in everyday contexts was reinforced when the presentation of these inventions for domestic use moved from the newspapers' classified sections to their news columns. In 1920, journalist and women's rights activist Doris E. Fleischman informed the readers of the Sunday edition of the *Sun and New York Herald* that radium was becoming a "household aid" that helped to eliminate danger and inconvenience for American families. In her article, she wrote about the multiple uses that radium products can have around the house: Radium tacks attached to furniture made them visible at night and thus prevented "danger to unwary shins." Keyholes, light switches, telephones and "countless other things for which the householder is always groping in the dark" could be illuminated by radium markers. Such luminous labels, the article suggested, would also prevent fatal accidents in the house because "poison bottles will glow in the dark of the medicine chest." In addition to its practical usefulness, radium was also destined to enrich the lives of children who "soon will play with its [radium's] by-products as toys. "There is more than one youngster already," Fleischman reported, "who will not go to sleep at night without having his pet bear with radium eyes beside him" (Fleischman).

Two years after Fleischman's article, the *New York Tribune* printed a similar article listing the uses for radium in the home. Here radium is called "a friendly servant in the house" because, when attached to a slipper, its glow-in-the dark effect counteracted "the universal propensity of bedroom slippers to stray under the bed." In its overall judgment, the New York paper praised radium because it afforded "comfort and convenience to busy women and their families, brightening up the corners of countless homes and shedding a soft comforting glow over the dark hours of the night." At a time when household matters were predominantly in the hands of women, radium-product manufacturers frequently targeted their ads at them. Resorting to a logic that reflects the gender concepts of the time, the *Tribune* wrote that "since a woman, Mme Curie, discovered radium it is appropriate that radium has been made to afford comfort and convenience to busy women and their families" ("Radium at Home"). Ten years earlier, an ad used a drawing of an attractive woman to proclaim that "she is beautiful because her work at home is made easy by the use of radium spray" ("She is Beautiful"). Soon, however, radium products were offered to enhance women's beauty in a more direct manner than by eliminating hard work in the home and by giving them more time to care for themselves. Its intimate association with medical applications, human health, youth and longevity made it all but inevitable that radium would become an ingredient in cosmetic products.

Between 1918 and 1920, the London-based Radior company ran a particularly intensive marketing campaign during which full-page ads appeared in the *New York Times*, the *Chicago Tribune,* and other leading papers. The ads presented a full range of beauty products, including face creams and powders, hair tonic, soap, shampoo, and under-chin and forehead pads. The manufacturer emphasized that its products contained "a definite quantity of actual Radium," the only ingredient that generated a "vitalizing energy – imparting vigor and vitality to skin tissue, muscles, scalp and glands." Keen on supporting the claims for the effectiveness of the creams and lotions, the company frequently assured its potential customers that the advertized effects were scientifically grounded. "Science knows that the wonderful Rays of Radium energize and invigorate all living tissue," the Radior company asserted, "They revivify – rejuvenate" ("Radium and Beauty").

As this survey documents, by the early 1920s the popular press had provided a forum in which advertisements and news reports established radium as a fixture in the consciousness of the American public. From the early reports describing the extraordinary qualities of the new element the news coverage tracked the path which radium took from what appeared to be a chemical curiosity that might be used to supply an inexhaustible light source to a substance that promised to be a powerful remedy in the fight against cancer and other dreaded diseases. The final step in the domestication of radium was achieved when it expanded its reign from the confines of specialized applications into the center of the everyday world: Gasoline gauges provided convenience to early motorists, radium-sighted rifles made night-hunting possible, radium-enhanced cleansers cleaned, disinfected and deodorized American homes, and cosmetic products made an appeal to all women "who value perfection of complexion [. . .] a healthy skin and beautiful hair" ("Radium and Beauty," 10 Nov 1918). In the public perception, radium enhanced the functionality of existing consumer items and became closely associated with human health and beauty.

From today's perspective, it is striking to note that for almost twenty years the discourse about the new chemical element was thoroughly optimistic, full of hopes and expectations that radium might be the key that would open the door to much improved living conditions. In surveying the articles and reports of the period, a modern reader cannot help but notice an almost complete absence of doubt or fear. Instances of apprehension or any indication that an interaction with the new substance might involve any danger are virtually non-existent. It is tempting to assume that people simply had no reason to think that the use of radium might involve risks or dangers of any kind. Since the discovery of radium introduced scientists and the lay public to something truly new, knowledge about the specific characteristics of the chemical element emerged only very slowly and so there was little understanding about how this mysterious and revolutionary element might affect human life. This is, in fact, the position taken by a federal court in 1935: A review of the literature had convinced the judges that, prior to 1925, there was no knowledge about the harmful effects brought about by close contact with radium. Although the court conceded that there were some indications that radium may be hazardous, most evidence seemed to be in favor of the view that radium was popularly regarded "as a great boon to humanity" and that "its internal uses by injection, inhalation, etc." were frequently advocated (quoted in Mullner 89).

Detached Journalism: Cleveland Moffett Reports on Radium's "Formidable Powers of Destruction"

There seems to be a consensus among scholars that the majority of newspaper articles and reports described the benefits and promises of radium (Weart 35). It is worth adding, however, that some of these positive depictions contained a brief mention that radium also had a dangerous side. By focusing on a particularly instructive example, Cleveland Moffett's article "The Wonders of Radium," published in *McClure's Magazine* in 1903, the following section attempts to fill a gap in the discussion of the early representation of radium in American life. The close reading of the text is intended to show that, even at an early stage, the American public did in fact have fairly detailed information about the extraordinary characteristics of radium and its risks and that it was likewise aware of the directions that early research on radium was taking.

In 1903, Moffett, a popular journalist, who according to the *New York Times*, enjoyed "a most enviable reputation [. . .] as a writer of magazine articles covering a wide variety of topics" ("Cleveland Moffett's Novel"), conducted an exclusive interview with Pierre Curie in Paris. Previous to his visit, Moffett had written several articles on scientific matters, including one on Roentgen rays. His 12-page article, "The Wonders of Radium," was published in the November issue of *McClure's Magazine*, one of America's most important and influential periodicals in the first decade of the 20th century that catered to an audience of several million readers. Moffett's piece opened an issue that featured articles by Lincoln Steffens and Ray Stannard Baker, who together with Ida B. Tarbell and Jacob A. Riis, had built *McClure's* reputation as a "muckraking" magazine. In October and November, several large newspaper advertisement for *McClure's Magazine* in the *New York Times*, the *Chicago Tribune* and other papers promoted the article by saying: "Cleveland Moffett tells all there is to know of the marvelous new element – most of it never before put in print – from information he got first hand from the discoverer himself."

The impact of the article was further enhanced when, a few weeks after its original appearance, it was reprinted in full in *Strand Magazine*, a popular English periodical. Additionally, Moffett's text provided much of the substance for the first chapter ("The Miracle of Radium") in Ray Stannard Baker's *Boys' Second Book of Inventions* (1903). In view of this widespread exposure, the article constitutes an important piece of evidence documenting that the American reading public had access to original and in-depth science reporting on the risks of radium

Moffett had gone to Paris to learn about the mysterious substance from Pierre Curie, the most prominent radium scientist of the time. His report of the interview covered all the areas that were of interest to contemporary readers. It provided scientific information and explanations, both in the words of Curie and his laboratory assistants and in Moffett's paraphrases. In this way, *McClure's* readers learned about the way in which radium was extracted and refined (5), about its physical characteristics, especially the fact that radium was emanating heat and light without being consumed by it (6). In the interview, Curie confirmed that there was only a minute quantity of radium available in the world, a fact which made radium the most expensive substance in existence, with a value of "three thousand times its weight in gold" (9). Curie also explained that radium emanations made other objects radioactive (12) and he suggested that there might be medical applications for radium, most notably in the treatment of lupus and cancer (15).

In view of the generally enthusiastic tone that is found in most of the news coverage of the time, it is worth noting that Moffett presented radium as a "strange substance" with "startling" properties. As a matter of fact, on the first page of his article the journalist introduced radium as an element of an ambivalent nature. "These rays may be helpful or harmful," Moffett reported to his readers, "they may destroy life or stimulate it. They are capable not only of shortening life or prolonging it, but of modifying existing forms of life, that is, of actually creating new species. Finally, by destroying bacteria, they may be used to cure disease" (3).

Despite the fact that he stood in Curie's Paris laboratory, the original center of radium research, Moffett conveyed the impression that even here the new chemical element was not fully understood. When he asked for an explanation how radium could give off energy without exhausting itself, Curie's assistant Jacques Danne, who later founded *Le Radium*, the first scientific journal devoted to radioactivity, responded: "There are various theories, but they really explain very little" (3). The fact that the French scientists were ignorant of important aspects of the chemical element led to unexpected events during experiments. Moffett mentioned an accident in which Curie lost a significant amount of radium in an explosion "which shattered the tubes and scattered their precious contents." Curie had "absolutely no explanation" and contented himself by saying that "it was one of the tricks that radium is apt to play on you" (5). Moffett noted that the French scientist's face "lighted with quite a boyish smile" when he made this comment about an incident which deprived him of a significant portion of the expensive substance and must have led to a significant amount of contamination in the lab.

In spite of this seemingly carefree attitude, Curie was fully aware of the risks that purified radium presented. During his research he had discovered that the "harmful rays [. . .] make trouble" (5) when he had, at first inadvertently and then purposefully, exposed himself to the radioactive rays. The problem with this type of radiation was, as Curie had found out to his detriment, that the injury did not appear until a few days after the exposure. Like his colleague Henri Becquerel before him, he had suffered several burns which resulted in deep and painful wounds which took an unusually long time to heal. At one time, Curie's hands "were much peeled, and very sore from too much contact with radium." The pain had been been so intense that "for several days he [Curie] had been unable to dress himself" (10). Prompted by Moffett's questions, Curie was willing to admit that radium "undoubtedly [. . .] has a power of destruction" (6). In the course of Moffett's tour through Curie's laboratory it became clear that radium's powerful rays constituted an obstacle to many of the applications that had been envisioned for the new element. Whereas some newspaper reports had hailed radium as "the light of the future," Curie explained that if people used radium as a light source they would probably be "stricken with paralysis, blindness, and various nervous disorders" (9). This was an opinion that stood in contrast to the sensational reports which had previously been spread by American newspapers. It is a curious fact that Curie, although he was well aware of the damage that radium could do, continued to interact with the substance and allowed his visitors to test the effects of the element on themselves. He instructed Moffett to press a radium tube against his closed eyelid so that he might experience the light effect that resulted from this experiment. Although Curie warned Moffett that leaving the radium in close proximity to the eye too long could result in "a serious disturbance to the eyesight, or even blindness," he had hopes that it might still be used "in certain diseases of the eye" (9).

His visit to Curie's laboratory convinced Moffett that "the most important properties of radium" were "those which influenced animal life" (12). The results of these experiments showed that radium had "formidable powers of destruction, and can by its mere presence annihilate animal life or plant life" (13). After a series of experiments which involved laboratory mice, rabbits, guinea pigs, and other animals, the researchers recorded how radium affected their test subjects. Some animals lost their furs, others became blind, and in the end all of them died. In a particularly stark passage Moffett confronted his readers with an apocalyptic image built upon the relentless repetition of the word "killed":

> Rabbits were killed, guinea pigs were killed, embryo chickens exposed to radium rays during incubation [. . .] were all killed, plants were killed, and M. Danysz is convinced that all animals, probably all forms of life, would succumb to the destructive force of radium if employed in sufficient quantities. (13)

These experiments clearly suggested that radium would have the same deadly effect on human life. Jean Danysz, a biologist at the *Institut Pasteur* and one of Curie's assistants, sketched out the scenario that would ensue if a large amount of radium were to be released in a large city and claimed that "a kilogram of radium would be sufficient to destroy the population of Paris" (14). Moffett may have been aiming at achieving a chilling effect when he reproduced the gruesome vision of mass death by radiation in the words of the French scientist:

> Men and women would be killed just as these mice were killed. They would feel nothing during their exposure to the radium nor realize that they were in any danger. And weeks would pass after their exposure before anything would happen. Then gradually the skin would begin to peel off, and their bodies would become one great sore. Then they would become blind. Then they would die from paralysis and congestion of the spinal cord. (13)

Such a lengthy passage on the dangers of radium might have invited reflections on whether or not it was safe and responsible to work with radium. However, Moffett's article turned in the opposite direction. His conversation with the scientists at the *Institut Pasteur* did not dwell upon "this rather gloomy prospect." Apparently without any sense of contradiction, Moffett expected his readers to make the transition from Danysz's apocalyptic scenario of death by radiation to an acceptance of the prediction that "radium is destined to bring substantial benefits to suffering mankind." The strategy employed to make such a move plausible was by way of an appeal to the belief that scientific progress would solve any remaining difficulties in the future. In order to "derive immense good from radium" scientists only needed to use radium "within proper bounds," bounds which were to be set "when we have gained a fuller knowledge of the subject" (13). In a move that was not going to lose anything of its effectiveness in the following decades, the solution to the existing problem was to envision a technological fix and to defer the technical details of how it might be achieved into the future. The rhetorical strategy employed in this context was that of a reverse logic in which a beneficial effect of radium was predicted on the basis of experiments which, taken at face value, resulted in rather disquieting outcomes.

At the *Institut Pasteur,* Moffett also met biologist Georges Bohn who, in experiments with tadpoles, had been able to "modify various lower forms of life as to actually produce 'monsters,' abnormal deviations from the original type of the species." In his tests with the eggs of lower animals he also obtained "monsters" which survived for a short period of time. The conclusion Bohn drew from his research was that radium could be used "*to create life* where there would have been no life." As to the ultimate purpose of his experiments, Bohn was convinced that radium could be used to "to produce new species" that showed "interesting changes [. . .] in the coloring and adornment" (14).

Although it would seem that the exceptional events that were taking place in the Paris laboratory called for a comment, the use of the terms "monster" and "abnormal deviations" were the only indication that something out of the ordinary was happening there. In the manner of a detached journalist, Moffett refrained from offering his personal views on any of the issues and never indicated that any of the things he heard or any of the activities he witnessed might pose an immediate threat. Instead, his tone conveyed a sense of excited anticipation when he implied that radium research might deliver into human hands the key to the mystery of life. The American journalist closed his report with the prediction that the acquisition of larger amounts of radium would open the door to a new era for humanity. Moffett concluded that "there is certainly reason to believe that we are entering upon a domain of new, strange knowledge and drawing near to some of nature's most hallowed secrets" (15).

If Moffett's article was the earliest and most comprehensive report on the implicit dangers of radium, it was not the only one. For the next twenty years, journalists throughout the country inserted brief information on radium's destructive powers when they covered the popular subject. In an otherwise positive account of radium's characteristics, the *St. Louis Republic* cautioned that the element also had a dangerous side. "Its effect on man internally has yet to be investigated," the article stated, "although there is little doubt [that] an extremely minute quantity even of a preparation of radium would have fatal results, and it will in all probability, prove to be one of the most dangerous and poisonous substances known to him" ("Some Practical Uses"). The *New York Sun* informed its readers that "the use of radium is very dangerous, even in hands comparatively skilled." The paper drew special attention to the delayed effect that radium exposure has on the human skin. "There is something uncanny in the experience of a man who faces radium rays for hardly much more than several minutes," the article said, "and then wakes up to the fact that he has received a terrible burn" ("Wonders and Dangers").

That continuous exposure to radium adversely affected human beings soon became a well known fact. Many of the prominent radium researchers, including Henri Becquerel and Pierre Curie, suffered from radiation burns. When reports came from Paris that Marie Curie had suffered a breakdown in 1912, William James Morton, an American physician and author of the book *The X Ray, or Photography of the Invisible*, confirmed that prolonged contact with radium would indeed have a negative impact on a person: "If a person stayed continually within the force of the radium rays cells would be killed and a general breakdown would result." "There is no known cure for this," Morton said but expressed his belief that if a patient's body was "strong enough to rebuild itself a cure will result" ("Mme. Curie's Illness"). A 1914 article entitled "False Hopes as to Radium" weakened exaggerated claims about radium's efficacy as a cancer cure and informed the public that the New York State department of Health had issued a warning against "unscrupulous impostors and fake establishments" ("False Hopes"). In 1923, George S. Willis, a physician and director of Radium Luminous Material Corporation, attempted to correct the erroneous belief that radium was a harmless substance. He predicted that, without sufficient precautionary measures, extended exposure to radium "may result in serious injury to the radium workers" (quoted in Wilson). Only two years later, American newspaper readers received ample evidence for Willis's concern. On the occasion of the death of Jean Bergonié, a prominent French radiologist, the *New York Times* stated that "[t]he perilous qualities of the X-ray and radium are well known now. They burn and sear with agonizing pain those who work with them unless the greatest precautions are taken" (Emery). The *Washington Post* estimated that since the discovery of the X-ray and radium about 140 deaths had occurred among the scientists who worked with the new technology ("Condemn Themselves"). Only a few months later, the investigations of the "radium deaths" of female workers at the East Orange, N.J., plant of the United States Radium Corporation triggered a massive press coverage during which the American public learned about the destructive impact that radium had on those who encountered it in workplace (Neuzil and Kovarik 42–48).

Conclusion: The Absence of Risk Communication in Early Reports on Radium

As Moffett's article and the selections from other news reports have shown, information on radium as a dangerous substance coexisted with the depictions that highlighted radium's benefits, even if on a smaller scale. This material provides the evidence that the most disquieting features of radium's radioactive rays were established as common knowledge. From 1903 on, readers knew that radium rays had the ability to inflict painful wounds that took a long time to heal; that they interfered with developmental processes and had the potential to create "monsters"; and that intensive exposure would result in the death of a living organism. It was also known that radium kept its radioactivity for a very long time and that it could bestow it on other substances. And yet, although it was apparent that even the leading scientists of the day were not in a position to fully explain the features of the new substance, newspapers of the time do not show that this resulted in feelings of insecurity, ambivalence or apprehension. Similarly, a modern reader misses instances of critical reflection on whether the consequences of this form of scientific progress could be sufficiently controlled or whether there might be any danger in the proliferation of radium products. In this way, a study of the radium phenomenon confirms Frank Furedi's observation that there is no "association between scientific advance and [a] parallel growth in risk awareness" (Furedi 61).

As a matter of fact, it is striking to note the absence of the notion of "risk" in the press coverage related to radium. Although the word "risk" was used in headlines about financial, economic, and political challenges, there are few instances in which it appeared in the context of science. When newspapers expressed reservations about radium they predominantly referred to the question of how effective the chemical element might be as a remedy. Articles warning that a radium treatment might do more harm than good are virtually nonexistent. There is sporadic evidence that the activities of the scientists who worked regularly and intensively with radium were seen as potentially dangerous for these individuals. This type of risk, however, was seen as inherent in the kind of work that scientists did and it appeared to be deplorable but acceptable for the "crusaders of science" to sacrifice their lives "in the cause of humanity" (Emery).

The conception of risk expressed in the scant record of risk communication about radium at this time was circumscribed by a perspective which conceived of "risk" as a personal matter. Although relevant information about the physical and chemical characteristics of radium was available as early as 1903, the newspaper coverage gives no indication that scientists and journalists understood that the discovery of radium introduced a risk factor of a new type – one that transcended the immediate place and time where it originated (see Beck 21). While it may go too far to say that radium in the first quarter of the 20th century already constituted a global danger, it did affect individuals and communities beyond the sites where radium was mined, processed, and sold. In the 1980s, when the Environmental Protection Agency designated the locations of former radium production Superfund sites, it became undeniably clear that the country's radium history had created a legacy of radioactive contamination for subsequent generations.

In the final analysis, a study of the "radium craze" as a historical phenomenon shows that the press in the early decades of the 20th century became a vast forum for the public display of radium and its applications in the health and business sectors of American culture. Articles, reports, and advertisements reflect an excitement about radium as well as a deep fascination with its supposed promises for medical and technological progress. Although factual knowledge about the harmful effects of radium was also available, it never accumulated sufficient weight to manifest itself in the form of critical reflections or warnings. An indication that the large-scale distribution of radium might involve unwanted results or even threats was nowhere to be found in American newspapers of the period. In the very few instances that presented radium in the context of a risk scenario, the dominant risk-perception paradigm limited the understanding of risk to the personal and the occupational spheres connected to the present time. Under these circumstances it was impossible to bring into focus the true risks lurking in a highly radioactive substance with a half-life of 1,600 years.

Whereas news coverage about environmental risk today is often criticized as irrational, distorted, sensationalist or even apocalyptic (see Cox 209, Allan et al. 35), risk communication about radium was virtually non-existent in the early decades of the 20th century. To account for this, one could perhaps argue that, in contrast to modern-day observers with the advantage of retrospective vision and ample evidence of the dangers of radioactivity, journalists of the early 20th century were incapable of imagining the long-term impact of the powerful radiation that science and business interests released into American life. If this is true, there would have been no compelling reason for journalists to write about anything else than what appeared to be the exciting possibilities of the new element.

Even if an apprehensive reporter had wanted to speculate about the hazardous potential of radium it could be argued, as Miller and Riechert do, that risk is an "abstraction about the possibility of damage and, by itself, does not possess any news value" (Miller and Riechert 48). Such a view appears to be particularly appropriate for the period under investigation which saw the emergence of a form of journalism that privileged "facts" over speculation, politicking, and moralizing. Journalists of the Progressive Era "wanted their reports of the world to be lively [...] but they believed they could do that without interpretation" (Schudson 85). As these principles were gaining ground, the American press developed a "reverence for the logic of science and faith in the power of detached observation" (Ettema and Glasser 65). In this way, the journalistic conventions of the time reflect a cultural climate which privileged the idea of a detached objectivity over interpretive commentaries, and which, because of its firm belief in science and progress, allowed speculation on the potential benefits of radium applications while showing no interest in exploring their negative side. Such an atmosphere was not conducive to the emergence of a risk consciousness that might have generated a sense of caution with regard to the effects of large-scale radium exposure. In the absence of such a safeguard, America's dominant cultural paradigms and cultural narratives encouraged its intensive involvement with the "miraculous substance" and thus ultimately burdened the country with a legacy of suffering and death, long-term environmental damage, and a substantial loss of financial resources in the required cleanup effort.

Works Cited

1. Primary Sources

"A Light Giving Metal." *El Paso Daily Herald* 20 Oct. 1900: 9. Web. 13 Apr. 2013.

"Cleveland Moffett's Novel." *New York Times* 8 Feb. 1908: Br 74. Web. 6 Apr. 2013.

"Condemn Themselves to Slow and Horrible Death!" *Washington Post* 8 Feb. 1925: Sm 2. Web. 21 Apr. 2013.

"False Hopes as to Radium." *Washington Post* 10 Feb. 1914: 6. Web. 21 Apr. 2013.

"From the Summit to the Sea Reaches the Four Link Chain[adv.]." *Los Angeles Herald* 18 Nov. 1908: 9. Web. 17 Apr. 2013.

"Health Temple Is Opened." *Los Angeles Times* 7 Aug. 1906: Ii, 12. Web. 14 Apr. 2013.

"Mme. Curie's Illness and Radium's Effect: Dr. W. J. Morton Thinks She May Have Broken Down under the Rays' Influence." *New York Sun* 10 mar. 1912: 8. Web. 23 Mar. 2013.

"New Field for Speculation: Wonderful Properties of New Metal but Little in Existence." *Arizona Republican* 11 Sep. 1902: 3. Web. 13 Apr. 2013.

"Ottawa Memorial Pays Tribute to Former Factory Employees." 4 Sep. 2011. Web. 28 Mar. 2013.

"Ounce of Radium Costs a Million Dollars." *Washington Times* 17 May. 1903: 3. Web.

13 Apr. 2013.
"Points out Dangers of Radium; Also, its Good." *Washington Post* 11 Jan. 1914: 4. Web. 23 Mar. 2013.
"Powers of Radium: from the London Times." *Washington Evening Star* 7 May. 1903: 12. Web. 13 Apr. 2013.
"Radium and Beauty [Adv.]." *New York Tribune* 10 Nov. 1918: V, 12. Web. 20 Apr. 2013.
"Radium and Beauty [Adv.]." *New York Times* 8 Dec. 1918: 60. Web. 19 Apr. 2013.
"Radium at Home." *New York Tribune* 18 Jun. 1922: 8. Web. 19 Apr. 2013.
"Radium Now the World's Wonder." *Chicago Daily Tribune* 21 Jun. 1903: 5. Web. 1 Apr. 2013.
"Radium Sulphur Springs." *Los Angeles Herald* 8 Aug. 1909: 11. Web. 17 Apr. 2013.
"Radium, Universal Light Bringer, Has Made the Blind to See." *The St. Louis Republic [St. Louis, Mo.]* 19 Jul. 1903, Magazine Section: 7. Web. 8 Apr. 2013.
"Radium! Amazing Earth Power That Gives You Super Man-power [Adv]." *Binghampton [N.y.] Press* 31 Oct. 1922: 8. Web. 17 Apr. 2013.
"Real Cancer 'Cure': Kelly Shows Congress Radium Is Long-sought Remedy." *Washington Post* 20 Jan. 1914: 2. Web. 21 Apr. 2013.
"Rexradio [Adv.]." *San Francisco Call* 21 Aug. 1904: 42. Web. 14 Apr. 2013.
"Rexradio's Bulletin [Adv.]." *San Francisco Call* 7 Dec. 1904: 13. Web. 14 Apr. 2013.
"Seasonable Specials: Radium Spray." *Wenatchee Daily World [Wash.]* 30 Jul. 1909: 8. Web. 19 Apr. 2013.
"She Is Beautiful [Adv.]." *El Paso Daily Herald* 3 Oct. 1912: 6. Web. 19 Apr. 2013.
"Some Practical Uses of Radium Rays: Few Grains Might Provide Energy Enough to Run a Locomotive." *St. Louis Republic* 13 Sep. 1903: Magazin Section [2]. Web. 31 Mar. 2013.
"Something New: Radium Spray [Adv.]." *the Maui News* 19 Jul. 1913: 5. Web. 19 Apr. 2013.
"Student of Cancer Sees Radium Peril." *New York Times* 30 Sep. 1915: 4. Web. 19 Apr. 2013.
"The Fly War [Adv.]." *Philadelphia Evening Ledger* 31 Jul. 1917. Web. 19 Apr. 2013.
"The Popular Interest in Radium." *New York Times* 9 Sep. 1903: 6. Web. 1 Apr. 2013.
"Women and Radium." *New York Times* 6 Sep. 1903: 6. Web. 1 Apr. 2013.
"Wonders and Danger of Radium." *New York Sun* 13 Sep. 1903. Web. 1 Apr. 2013.
"Wonders of Radium." *Boston Daily Globe* 11 Jun. 1903: 6. Web. 1 Apr. 2013.
"[The Greatest Thing] [Adv.]." *Richmond Times-dispatch* 11 Apr. 1911: 9. Web. 19 Apr. 2013.
D'Alemcourt, Heloise C. "The Discoverers of Radium: A Times Correspondent's Talk with Prof. and Mme. Curie." *Los Angeles Times* 17 Jan. 1904: E11. Web. 23 Mar. 2013.
Emery, Steuart M. "Roll of Martyrs to Science Is Increasing." *New York Times* 11 Jan. 1925: XX, 5. Web. 21 Apr. 2013.
Farabaugh, Kane. "'Radium Girls' Remembered for Role in Shaping US Labor Law." *Voice of America*, 2011. Web. 28 Mar. 2013.
Fleischman, Doris E. "Radium Becoming a Household Aid: Rarest Element Adaptable in Scores of Ways to Eliminate Danger and Inconvenience of Groping in the Dark." *The Sun and New York Herald* 30 May 1920: Section 7. Web. 19 Apr. 2013.
Galant, Debbie. "Living with a Radium Nightmare." *New York Times* 29 Sep. 1996. Web. 19 Apr. 2013.

London, E. S. "Radium"s Promise to the Blind." *Chicago Daily Tribune* 12 Jul. 1903: 17. Web. 19 Apr. 2013.

Moffett, Cleveland. "The Röntgen Rays in America." *McClure's Magazine* 6.5 (1886): 415–20. Web. 6 Apr. 2013.

---. "Illustrated Interviews: M. Curie, the Discoverer of Radium." *Strand Magazine* 27. (Jan-June 1904): 65–73. Web. 6 Apr. 2013.

---. "The Wonders of Radium." *McClure's Magazine* (November 1903): 3–15. Web. 6 Apr. 2013.

Szuda, Stephanie. "'A Long-time Coming': Radium Girls Receive Memorial." *The [Ottawa, Ill.] Times* 2 Sep. 2011. Web. 28 Mar. 2013.

2. Secondary Sources

Allan, Stuart, Barbara Adam, and Cynthia Carter, eds. *Environmental Risks and the Media*. London, New York: Routledge, 2000. Print.

Baker, Ray Stannard. "The Miracle of Radium: Story of the Marvels and Dangers of the New Element Dicovered by Professor and Madame Curie." *Boys' Second Book of Inventions*. New York: Mcclure Phillips & Co, 1903. 3–26. Print.

Balz, Viola, et al., eds. *Precarious Matters: The History of Dangerous and Endangered Substances in the 19th and 20th Centuries*. Berlin: Max-Planck-Institut für Wissenschaftsgeschichte, 2008. Print.

Beck, Ulrich. *Risk Society: Towards a New Modernity*. London: Sage Publications, 1992. Print.

Buchholz, M.A, and M. Cervera. *Radium Historial Items Catalog: Final Report. Oak Ridge Institute for Science and Education*, 2008. Web.

Clark, Claudia. *Radium Girls: Women and Industrial Health Reform 1910-1935*. Chapel Hill: University of North Carolina Press, 1997. Print.

Cox, Robert. *Environmental Communication and the Public Sphere*. 2nd ed. Thousand Oaks, Ca.: Sage Publications, 2010. Print.

Douglas, Mary, and Aaron B. Wildavsky. *Risk and Culture: An Essay on the Selection of Technical and Environmental Dangers*. Berkeley: University of California Press, 1982. Print.

EPA. *Ottawa Radiation Areas 1, 4, 9, 11 and Illinois Power*, 2011. Web. 21 Apr. 2013. <http://www.epa.gov/superfund/accomp/success/usradium.htm>.

Ettema, James S., and Theodore L. Glasser. *Custodians of Conscience: Investigative Journalism and Public Virtue*. New York: Columbia University Press, 1998. Print.

Furedi, Frank. *Culture of Fear Revisited: Risk-taking and the Morality of Low Expectation*. 4th ed. London: Continuum, 2006. Print.

Hoy, Suellen M. *Chasing Dirt: The American Pursuit of Cleanliness*. New York: Oxford University Press, 1995. Print.

Lavine, Matthew. "A Cultural History of Radiation and Radioactivity in the United States, 1895-1945." Dissertation. University of Wisconsin-Madison, 2008.

Malley, Marjorie C. *Radioactivity: a History of a Mysterious Science.* New York: Oxford University Press, 2011. Print.

Miller, M. M., and Bonnie P. Riechert. "Interest Group Strategies and Journalistic Norms: News Media Framing of Environmental Issues." *Environmental Risks and the Media*. Ed. Stuart Allan, Barbara Adam, and Cynthia Carter. London, New York: Routledge, 2000. 45–54. Print.

Morton, William J., and Edwin W. Hammer. *The X-Ray, or Photography of the Invisible and its Value in Surgery*. New York: American Technical Book Co., 1896. Print.

Mullner, Ross. *Deadly Glow: The Radium Dial Worker Tragedy*. Washington: American Public Health Asscociation, 1999. Print.

Neuzil, Mark, and Bill Kovarik. *Mass Media & Environmental Conflict: America's Green Crusades*. Thousand Oaks, Ca.: Sage Publications, 1996. Print.

Pratt, R. M. "Review of Radium Hazards and Regulation of Radium in Industry." *Environment International* 19 (1993): 475–89. Print.

Rentetzi, Maria. "The Women Radium Dial Painters as Experimental Subjects (1920-1990), or What Counts as Human Experimentation." *Ntm* (N.s.) 12 (2004): 233-48. Print.

---. *Trafficking Materials and Gendered Experimental Practices: Radium Research in Early 20th Century Vienna*. New York: Columbia University Press, 2008. Print.

---. "Trafficking Materials in Tin Boxes, Glass Bottles, and Lead Cases: Radium in Early Twentieth-Century Science, Medicine, and Commerce." *Precarious Matters: The History of Dangerous and Endangered Substances in the 19th and 20th Centuries*. Ed. Viola Balz, et al. Berlin: Max-Planck-Institut für Wissenschaftsgeschichte, 2008. 99–112. Print.

Schudson, Michael. *Discovering the News: A Social History of American Newspapers*. New York: Basic Books, 1978. Print.

Sclove, Richard E. "From Alchemy to Atomic War: Frederick Soddy's 'Technology Assessment' of Atomic Energy, 1900-1915." *Science Technology Human Values* 14.2 (1989): 163–94. Print.

Soddy, Frederick. *The Interpretation of Radium, Being the Substance of Six Free Popular Experimental Lectures Delivered at the University of Glasgow*. 3rd ed. New York: Putnam's Sons, 1912. Print.

Alexa Weik von Mossner

The Stuff of Fear: Emotion, Ethics, and the Materiality of Nuclear Risk in *Silkwood* and *The China Syndrome*

Two colors – black and yellow – and a three-cornered trefoil have come to signal potential or actual nuclear radiation. When the radiation symbol was introduced in 1946, the International Atomic Energy Agency and the International Organization for Standardization acknowledged that it had "no intuitive meaning and little recognition beyond those educated in its significance."[1] Today, the symbol is not only globally well known, but, in addition, imbued with emotional meaning because we have learned that it signals the presence of a substance whose radiation we cannot see, smell, hear, or taste, but that will nevertheless severely harm and potentially kill us owing to overexposure. When looking at the symbol, we are likely to feel some sort of uneasiness, a sensation that would probably increase dramatically if we noticed it on a barrel in our immediate surroundings. Perhaps we would begin to ponder what kinds of effects its material presence could have on our bodies, on our health, on our future. And because we could not be sure about the actual *risk* of the situation, we would, in all likelihood, experience a vague sense of fear.

Of course, other iconic images also remind us of the risks involved in even the peaceful use of nuclear power. These include the threatening sight of the destroyed reactor in Chernobyl and the plethora of images of the ruins at Fukushima that bombarded us during the first weeks of the catastrophic accident on March 11, 2011.[2] A number of commentators have expressed concern that the images of Fukushima actually *fail* to capture the dimensions of the catastrophe, precisely because we cannot sensually grasp the devastation wreaked by nuclear radiation. However, at the time of the

1 In 2007, the IAEA and ISO launched a new, more concrete symbol that adds wave lines, a skull and crossbones, and a running person to demonstrate the danger to humans. It now has a red rather than a yellow ground. See http://www.iaea.org/newscenter/news/2007/radiationsymbol.html.

2 The Fukushima nuclear disaster started with the Tōhoku earthquake and subsequent tsunami on March 11, 2011, followed by a series of equipment failures, nuclear meltdowns in several of the affected reactors at the nuclear power plant Fukushima II, and the release of catastrophic quantities of radioactive materials into the larger area surrounding the plant as well as into the ocean.

accident, audiences all over the world had already learned enough about the dangers of nuclear energy to know that damaged reactors and humans cloaked in protective gear stand for something unfathomable and horrible. This is one of the reasons why the news coverage of these events had a considerable impact on audiences in faraway places. It reminded people of the reality of nuclear risk and helped them imagine what the explosion of an atomic reactor may mean in their own countries.[3] As the German sociologist Ulrich Beck points out in *World at Risk*, "Risk is *not* synonymous with catastrophe. Risk means the *anticipation* of the catastrophe" (9). It was in part the anticipation – the imagination – of a future catastrophe *at home*, fueled by images and stories from a material catastrophe *elsewhere* that, within the shortest amount of time, radically changed public opinion on nuclear power.[4]

The events in Japan, and the psychological and political consequences of the media coverage of these events, have given new relevance to the two American films from the late 1970s and early 1980s I want to discuss in this essay: James Bridges's *The China Syndrome*, which was released in 1979, and Mike Nichols's *Silkwood*, which hit cinema screens four years later. Both films deal with nuclear risk and its possible or actual materialization, and with the *emotional effects* that the mixture of extreme physical danger and high uncertainty have on ethical decision-making processes. *The China Syndrome* tells the story of a news reporter and her cameraman who during a visit to a nuclear power plant witness and illegally film an emergency shutdown during which the plant comes close to a core meltdown. *Silkwood* focuses on the personal story of a nuclear fuel production facility employee who tries to inform the public about safety violations that have already led to the radioactive contamination of her own body.

Both films tell their tales as political thrillers, as stories in which courageous individuals struggle to uncover and publicize the truth about nuclear risk against overpowering opponents who will not stop at murder to silence them because they fear the resulting economic losses. In both cases, the fictional drama is heightened by the films' eerie relationships to real-world risks and events. *Silkwood* fictionalizes the biography of the American labor union activist and chemical technician Karen Silkwood, who died in mysterious circumstances in 1974 after testing positive for

---

[3] Outside of Japan, the events in Fukushima had perhaps the most drastic effects on media audiences in Germany, where public concern led to an almost immediate security inspection of all 17 nuclear power plants in the country and to subsequent the close-down of the seven oldest plants for security reasons.

[4] According to a poll by Win Gallup International, the percentage of nuclear energy supporters in Germany went down from 34% to 26% after the Fukushima accident, while the percentage opponents increased from 64% to 72% percent. See Gilani and Sahid, "Impact of Japan Earthquake on Views about Nuclear Energy" (2011).

plutonium contamination.[5] *The China Syndrome* is not based on a historical case, but it was released just twelve days before the real-life nuclear accident on Three Mile Island, a coincidence that not only helped the film at the box office, but also fueled anti-nuclear protests all over the United States.

In what follows, I will offer an ecocritical reading of *The China Syndrome* and *Silkwood* that focuses on the ways in which the two films represent the material and emotional dimensions of nuclear risk and on how these representations engage viewers. Both films, I will argue, not only illustrate Beck's claim that the determination of risk is a form of ethics (*Risk Society* 28); they also demonstrate that embodied emotional processes such as fear are vital components of ethical decision making in the face of unpredictable material agencies and the environmental risks they pose. Because they ask viewers to empathize with their protagonists – and thus to feel some of their feelings – these films have also had profound effects on the risk perceptions of their audiences. What chills our bones when we watch *The China Syndrome* and *Silkwood* is the realization that, as Stacy Alaimo puts it, "the human body is radically open to its surroundings" (*Bodily* 13) and that invisible but nevertheless material radioactive radiation is a lethal danger that manifests itself in form of cancer, deformation, and death. While the invisibility of radiation raises representational problems, we will see that both films make good use of their viewers' pre-existing risk perceptions to engage them in plotlines that are driven by the *anticipation* of catastrophes rather than by the catastrophes themselves. Before I turn to these films, however, I will first introduce my theoretical framework and explain why the analytical tools of cognitive film theory are particularly useful for the presented analysis.

---

5 Silkwood was a chemical technician at the Kerr-McGee plant near Crescent, Oklahoma. As a member of the Oil, Chemical & Atomic Workers Union she investigated health and safety issues, testifying in 1974 to the American Atomic Energy Commission (AEC) about serious safety violations at her plant. Richard Rashke's *The Killing of Karen Silkwood* (1981), one of the most influential accounts of Silkwood's case, reports that on November 5, 1974, a routine self-check showed that Silkwood body contained almost 400 times the legal limit for plutonium contamination. Two days later, she was found to be even more seriously contaminated. On November 13, 1974 Silkwood left a union meeting, allegedly planning to hand over proof of the safety violations to a *New York Times* reporter. Her body was later found in her car, which had run off the road. The documents she was planning to give to the reporter were never discovered. Following her death there were many speculations about the nature of Silkwood's sudden contamination and subsequent death.

Material Risks: Nonhuman Agency and the Body

In her *Material Cultures, Material Minds*, Nicole Boivin insists that "the workings of the mind cannot be understood independently of the environment" (75) because the very fact that our bodies are in constant physical exchange with our environment affects how we perceive and think. Building on the work of James Gibson and other environmental psychology scholars, Boivin reminds us that "just as thinking is a bodily activity, it is also an ecological or situated activity" (75). Neuroscientists such as Antonio Damasio have demonstrated that this complex interplay between the human organism and its environment involves not only perception and rational thought but also emotion. In *Descartes' Error: Emotion, Reason, and the Human Brain*, Damasio explains that "The organism interacts with the environment as an ensemble: the interaction is neither of the body alone nor of the brain alone" (xxvii). Emotions play an important role in this complex interaction because they deliver "cognitive information, directly and via feelings" (xix). "Were it not for the possibility of sensing body states that are inherently ordained to be painful or pleasurable," writes Damasio, "there would be no suffering or bliss, no longing or mercy, no tragedy or glory in the human condition" (xxv). This is because "suffering, whether it starts in the skin or in a mental image" in the end "happens in the flesh" (xxvii).

These neuropsychological deliberations about the complex interactions between minds, bodies, and environments cast an interesting light on the claims of material feminists such as quantum physicist Karen Barad and ecocritic Stacy Alaimo who insist on the living materialities of bodies and on the agency of nonhuman entities. In *Meeting the Universe Halfway*, Barad constructs a theory of "agential realism" in which agency is no longer exclusively "aligned with human intentionality or subjectivity" but rather understood "as a matter of intra-acting; it is an enactment, not something that someone or something has" (235). Causal relations, she explains, "do not preexist but rather are intra-actively produced" (236) in the complex interplay between space, time, and matter.

Alaimo draws on Barad's work on agential realism in the development of her own conception of "trans-corporeality," which "stresses the flow of substances and forces linking bodies and environments" ("Material Engagements" 69). In her *Bodily Natures*, Alaimo analyzes "particular moments of confusion and contestation that occur when individuals and collectives must contend not only with the materiality of their very selves but with the often invisibly hazardous landscape of risk society, which require scientific mediation" (17). Out of the confusing, threatening, and intriguing connections between bodies, science, and the material agency of toxic substances, she sees a "nearly unrecognizable sort of ethics" emerging that "demands that we inquire about all of the substances that surround us, those for which we may be somewhat responsible, those that may harm us, those that may harm others, and those that we suspect we do not know enough about" (18). Beck similarly suggests that in what he has called the risk society, "Determinations of risks are the form in which ethics … is resurrected inside the centers of modernization" because "[r]isk determinations are an unrecognized, still undeveloped symbiosis of the natural and the human sciences, of everyday and expert rationality, of interest and fact" (*Risk Society* 28). Alaimo partially agrees with this but reminds us that "True awareness [of the exact nature of such risks] eludes most, if not all, members of risk society" (*Bodily* 19).

Given Damasio's important work on the role of emotions in the interactions between minds, bodies, and their environments, it is regrettable that affective engagements are not a factor in Alaimo's (or Barad's) deliberations. Beck, for his part, acknowledges that fear and other negative emotions play important roles in the complex dynamic of the risk society, but he also pays insufficient attention to the ways in which emotional engagements are an integral part of human cognition and ethical decision making.[6] More interesting in this regard is the work of decision research scientist Paul Slovic, who draws on the work of Damasio and other clinical neuroscientists in his analyses of human risk perception. In *The Perception of Risk*, Slovic explains that over time he has "come to recognize just how highly dependent [risk perception] is upon intuitive and experimental thinking, guided by emotional and affective processes" (xxxi). In an article entitled "Risk as Analysis and Risk as Feelings," Slovic and his co-authors go even further, stating that "analytic reasoning cannot be effective unless it is guided by emotion and affect" (311) and that "we cannot assume that an intelligent person can understand the meaning of and properly act upon even the simplest of numbers such as amounts of money or numbers of lives at risk … unless these numbers are infused with affect" (321). This builds directly on Damasio's claim that "Emotion and feeling, along with the covert physiological machinery underlying them, assist us with the daunting task of predicting an uncertain future and planning our actions accordingly" (xxiii). What is more, philosophers such as Robert Solomon and Martha Nussbaum and psychologists such as Keith Oatley, Dacher Keltner, and Martin Hoffman have all demonstrated that affective responses play a central role in moral reasoning and ethics.[7]

---

[6] In *World at Risk*, Beck explains that "Fear determines the attitude towards life" (8). His own attitude towards fear, however, is decidedly negative. He predicts that in what he calls the "world risk society" fear can easily lead to totalitarian modes of governance with the "fear business" profiting "from a general loss of nerve" (9).

[7] See Roland de Sousa, *The Rationality of Emotions* (1987); Martha Nussbaum, *Upheavals of Thought* (2002), Robert Solomon, *True to Our Feelings* (2007). For psychological approaches see Oatley and Keltner *Understanding Emotions* (2006) and Martin Hoffman, *Empathy and Moral Development* (2002).

As we will see, *The China Syndrome* and *Silkwood* both explore the highly complex relationships between the material and potentially toxic substances within a given environment, the risks they pose for individual human bodies and those of whole communities, and the role that affect and emotion play in both the perception of these risks and in the ethical decision making in the face of it. Because they are fiction films, they also do something else: they engage viewers emotionally as well as cognitively in their fictional risk scenarios. This is why I want to introduce yet another group of theoretical approaches, one that is concerned with the ways in which cultural texts, including film, work on their audiences. These cognitivist approaches in fact draw on the same neuropsychological research previously introduced and they similarly emphasize the close interactions between our brains, our bodies, and the imagined environment of a film in the viewing experience.

Imagined Risks: The Conditional Realism of Fiction Film

As Lisa Zunshine explains in *Introduction to Cognitive Cultural Studies*, the work of scholars in this emerging field combines "literary and cultural analysis with insights from neuroscience, discursive psychology, cognitive evolutionary psychology and anthropology, cognitive linguistics, and philosophy of the mind" (1). In film studies, the emergence of cognitive approaches in the mid-1990s marked a conscious departure from what tends to be called screen theory.[8] Cognitive film scholars with an interest in the emotional appeal of film – among them Noël Carroll, Carl Plantinga, Ed Tan, Torben Grodal, Murray Smith, and Greg Smith – draw on the work of clinical neuroscientists and cognitive psychology rather than on psychoanalytic research. With reference to this alternative psychological framework, these scholars argue that the spectator's faculties of cognition and judgment are of central importance in the process of eliciting an emotional response to film and that such emotional responses in turn influence the spectator's cognition and judgment. Narrative film is understood as an "emotion machine" that "generates … like a moving belt … a continuous emotional situational meaning … that results in an ongoing, genuine emotional response" (Tan 251). Plantinga calls this phenomenon the "conditional realism" in spectator response: spectators experience emotions that are very similar to what they would feel in a "real" situation, with the difference that they are at the same time aware of

[8] David Bordwell and Noël Carroll's edited volume *Post-Theory: Reconstructing Film Studies* (1996) is very helpful for a better understanding of how cognitive approaches challenge the long-standing dominance of poststructuralist and psychoanalytical approaches.

the fact that what they watch is fiction and that this fiction is mediated ("Trauma" 239). Furthermore, the viewer will usually have an understanding of genre conventions and thus bring previous knowledge to the film that might amplify his or her emotions or interfere and conflict with them.

The key element in our understanding of narrative is the human capacity for empathy, defined by Martin Hoffman as "an affective response more appropriate to another's situation than one's own" (48). Recent neuroscience research suggests that the *mirror neuron* system plays a key role in our ability to empathize and socialize with others and that it is also the basis of what literary and film scholars call "character identification." "We have empathy for the fictional character," explains the Italian neurologist Marco Iacoboni, "because we literally feel the same feelings ourselves" (4). Keith Oatley emphasizes the cognitive component of such processes, arguing that we respond emotionally to what we see on a cinema screen because we mentally simulate the experiences of a character (see x). The nature of this mental simulation, however, is at least partially guided by the cues or "invitations" provided by the film. As Carroll points out, "the filmmakers have already done much of the work of emotionally organizing scenes and sequences for us through the ways in which [they] have foregrounded what features of the events in the film are salient" (28). Films guide our emotions while we watch them; as Greg Smith puts it, they continually "offer [us] invitations to feel" in certain ways (12). We can accept those invitations and "experience some of the range of feelings proffered by the text," or we can reject them (12). If we choose to accept them, the film becomes a full body experience because emotions, as Carroll explains, involve both cognition and "feelings," the latter being "sensations of bodily changes, like muscle contractions," or the welling of tears (24).

What Plantinga calls "conditional realism" – the fact that the viewer experiences emotions as well as bodily feelings during the viewing process while at the same time understanding that what they see is not "real" – has the interesting consequence that viewers may experience negative emotions such as anxiety, fear, and disgust as ultimately pleasurable. Plantinga has written extremely lucidly about the intricacies of this phenomenon, which is the basis for the success of whole film genres, among them horror, psycho-thriller, and melodrama.[9] Only very few people would want to see a psycho-thriller such as Jonathan Demme's *The Silence of the Lambs* (1991) if it were not for the fact that they can live through (real) sensations of fear and disgust while at the same time know that Hannibal Lecter is actually the actor Anthony Hopkins and that he won't pose any danger to anyone beyond the screen (or, in fact, to the other actors involved in the movie).

9 See Plantinga, "Trauma, Pleasure, and Emotion" (2009). See also Julian Hanich, *Cinematic Emotion in Horror Films and Thrillers* (2012).

This phenomenon is what makes enjoyable viewing experiences possible in cases where the viewer is confronted with the depiction of situations that pose a serious risk to the protagonist and/or people the protagonist cares for. On the one hand, the viewer is likely to feel empathetic fear on behalf of the protagonist (who may or may not show fear himself); on the other hand, there is the suspense and excitement that results from the reassuring knowledge that no one in the film will really get harmed and that there is also no danger to the viewer's own health. However, this pleasurable sense of personal safety and control may be threatened when the depicted events have what Suzanne Keen has called a "chance relevance to particular historical, economic, cultural, or social circumstances" (70). In such moments the fictional events on the screen may feel all too real to the empathizing viewer. With this in mind, I now turn to *The China Syndrome*.

Risk Perception and Ethical Decision Making in *The China Syndrome*

In American parlance, the "China syndrome" stands for the worst-case result of a nuclear meltdown. Coined in 1973 by the nuclear physicist Ralph Lapp, the term describes a scenario where reactor components melt through their containment structures into the underlying ground and through the crust of the earth "all the way to China."[10] While it is clear that this is neither physically nor geographically possible, the term still conjures strong mental images and emotions. The China syndrome is not only a strong metaphor for the uncontrollable power of a physical process; it also evokes fears of large-scale nuclear contamination, which is invisible but nevertheless distressingly material. Already through its title, then, Bridges's film communicates a notion of risk and plays on viewers' desires to engage in a pleasurable way with real-world fears and anxieties. The film offers a thought-provoking look at, firstly, the ways in which risk perceptions, and the emotions associated with them, shape ethical decision making, and, secondly, the central role of the media in the "staging" (Beck, *World at Risk* 17) and amplification of risk.

The China Syndrome opens on a black screen with several male voices speaking the kind of jargon that makes viewers realize they are inside a television newsroom. The first image we see is a test pattern followed by a somewhat peculiar close-up of one of the film's three protagonists: a round hand mirror hides most of the pretty face of Jane Fonda, who plays up-and-coming television news reporter Kimberly Wells. Seen through the lens of a television camera, Kimberly seems strangely exposed and objectified. Moreover, the peculiarly positioned mirror gives the impression of an "empty" face, suggesting that Kimberly, at this point at least, mostly

[10] Lapp was a collaborator in the Manhattan Project.

reflects other people's images and ideas. Indeed, one of the – for us invisible – men in the control room remarks dryly that "she will do what we tell her." The remark refers to the color and length of Kimberly's hair, but it also comments ironically on her future development as a character, since before long the young woman will become a fully fledged investigative reporter who is driven by her ethical principles (and her journalistic instinct) rather than by what the men at her station "tell her."

Eager to climb the journalistic career ladder, Kimberly jumps at the opportunity to film a special for her station's "Energy in California" series on the (fictional) Ventana Nuclear Power Plant, which is located just outside Los Angeles. Her first report from the plant captures the official stance on nuclear power in the mid-1970s, as she refers to it as "that almost magical transformation of matter into energy that the experts tell us may be our best shot at energy self-[sufficiency]." The public relations representative of the plant then offers some dumbed-down technical details of this "magical" and "absolutely safe" transformation of matter into energy, giving viewers the information they need to understand the drama that is about to unfold. Kimberly's maverick cameraman Richard (Michael Douglas) provides the much less comforting version of the story. "Wait until you get into that other room," he says mockingly to Kimberly, "and get that radiation all over that cute little body." While no one takes him seriously at this point, Richard names the specter that will haunt the rest of the film: the uncanny nature of radiation and the horrific things it can do to what Alaimo has called our "radically open" bodies (*Bodily* 13).

Only thirteen minutes into the film, the narrative changes its tone and pace as Kimberly and Richard happen to be present when the Ventana plant goes into an emergency shutdown. This is the moment in which the filmmakers are confronted with the dilemma of how to make a material threat that is *invisible* visually compelling and emotionally engaging. Given sufficient funds, the depiction of a nuclear blast is no problem for filmmakers; a good example being the famous final sequence of Stanley Kubrick's *Dr. Strangelove* (1962) which seduces viewers with the sublime aesthetic beauty of the mushroom cloud that is at odds with the bomb's lethal material impact. The devastating *result* of nuclear warfare is also visually compelling, if in very different ways. Nicholas Meyer's *The Day After* (1983) and John Hillcoat's *The Road* (2009) are pertinent examples.[11] These films fall into the post-apocalyptic movie genre, and they derive part of their cinematic power from the visual spectacle they present.

The China Syndrome, however, chooses a different path. Instead of showing the disaster itself or its aftermath, the film relies on what Beck

---

[11] While it is not certain whether the devastation in Hillcoat's *The Road* is the result of a nuclear war, some commentators have suggested that the cold, ash-covered environment is reminiscent of a nuclear winter.

calls the "anticipation of catastrophe" and thus on the perception of risk and the ethical consequences of that perception. The material hazard that causes the emergency shutdown of the Ventana plant is visualized through a slight tremor, accompanied by flashing annunciators, unnerving alarm bells, and the eerie sound of a needle printer sounding a lot like a Geiger counter. This is quite effective, but it does not make viewers jump back in their seats. In order to make the invisible and indeterminate danger of radiation *visceral*, the filmmakers must psychologize the idea of contamination. In the absence of spectacular or fear-inducing imagery, it is viewers' empathetic engagement with the protagonists of the film and *their* perceptions of risk that gives them a sense of danger and impending disaster.

The most important character for viewers' empathy in *The China Syndrome* is Shift Supervisor Jack Godell (Jack Lemmon). While Kimberly and Richard offer viewers an outsider perspective on the events – mirroring in most cases that of the viewer herself – Jack provides the insider (expert) perspective. He is an "old hand" who, unlike his collaborators in the Ventana control center, initially reacts with supreme equanimity to the emergency shutdown. "What have we got … turbine trip?" he asks calmly, coffee mug in hand. He seems further reassured when the technical surveillance system of the plant confirms that the problem is indeed a turbine trip. But when he puts his coffee down on the table next to the needle printer, he notices another slight tremor, and although he does not say anything, the expression on his face suggests that he finds it unsettling. Barely a second later, a red flashing annunciator signals "radiation in containment 8." Jack still keeps his composure, asking his colleagues to relax, giving instructions and voicing the thoughts of viewers when he demands that "someone turn off that goddamn alarm." The discontinuation of the unnerving sound is a relief for viewers, and for a few moments they are led to believe that the men are indeed getting the reactor under control. However, the moment of relief does not last long. At precisely the moment when Jack tells the plant's nervous PR man that everything is fine, the alarm starts again, announcing an unusually high water level in the reactor. Jack seems alarmed now and – against the rules of "the book" – decides to open two relief valves to "get rid" of the water. Only moments after his decision he learns that another indicator says that the water level is in fact dangerously low, and for a few long seconds he is puzzled by this contradictory information. He now seems tense and stressed, thinking feverishly. He knocks against the display signaling the high water level, and then in horror observes the needle moving down swiftly. It had been stuck. Panic in his face, Jack calls his superior and tells him in a low voice that they "may uncover the core."

In this crucial scene, the filmmakers offer viewers close-ups of all of the main characters, allowing them to empathize with their perspectives and emotions. "A central way the *visual* aspect of film is significant," explains Plantinga, "is in the use of the human face in the *scene of empathy*" ("The Scene" 239). Of central importance to the scene of empathy is emotional contagion, defined by psychologists Elaine Hatfield, John Cacioppo, and Richard Rapson as "the tendency to automatically mimic and synchronize facial expressions, vocalizations, postures, and movements with those of another person and consequently, to converge emotionally" (81). Crucial for social interaction in real life, emotional contagion is also central to our understanding of fictional characters. As Plantinga points out, "even given a lone closeup of a character's face the spectator can often comprehend the relevant emotion because we recognize that particular facial expressions signify identifiable emotional experiences" ("The Scene" 242). Lemmon plays Jack with great psychological intensity, and as his character – who says of himself that he "loves" the Ventana power plant – becomes increasingly alarmed about the situation, so does the empathizing viewer.

As the story develops into a political thriller in which Jack, Kimberly, and Richard try to prove and publicize scandalous safety cover-ups at the plant that threaten the lives of millions of people in the Los Angeles area, viewers are invited to arrive at the same ethical conclusions regarding the dangerous implication of safety violations and nuclear risk. Jack uncovers evidence that in order to save money, X-rays of welds in the nuclear reactor have been falsified. When he wants to make that evidence public, he is chased by employees of the power company who try to cover up the scandal. The film ends with a dramatic scene in which Jack is shot by a SWAT team in the control room of the plant while he is giving Kimberly a television interview in order to communicate to the public the extreme danger posed to their lives by the safety problems in the reactor. Jack thus dies for his ethical decision in the face of nuclear risk, and it is suggested that because of its immense profitability for the operators and the State of California, the plant will go back on the grid after some superficial safety checks and repairs, a disaster waiting to happen. As Kimberly puts it ambiguously in one of her reportages: "Power is what it's all about."

As mentioned earlier, *The China Syndrome* tremendously affected public opinion on nuclear power in the United States. In this context, it is important to remember that viewers' empathy and cognitive responses to situations depicted in fiction are contingent upon exterior conditions. The empathy American viewers felt with the fictional characters of *The China Syndrome* and their emotional responses to the depicted events on the Ventana Nuclear Power Plant were in all likelihood mediated by pre-existing anxieties about the hazards of nuclear power. These anxieties were whipped up into an acute state of fear when only twelve days after the release of the film, a real-life partial core meltdown happened at the Three Mile Island nuclear generating station in Pennsylvania, resulting in the release of approximately 2.5 million curies of radioactive gases and approximately 15 curies of iodine-131 (Rogovin 153). The population's concern about the unknown risks of the accident drove many to watch the film, not least because it offered them an imagined "inside view" of what might be happening on Three Mile Island. It certainly did not help them relax when one of the characters says that the accident portrayed in the film would render "an area the size of Pennsylvania permanently uninhabitable." Such fictional statements were bound to interact with viewers' real-life perceptions of risk, and the film is generally credited with having contributed to the (temporary) turn of public opinion against nuclear energy in the United States in the early 1980s.

However, despite its concern about the dangers of nuclear radiation for human bodies (we see groups of protestors at the security hearings showing pictures of their endangered children), *The China Syndrome* always remains at the level of anticipation. The closest it gets to visualizing the *material* side of nuclear radiation is when, at the beginning of the film, Richard puts into his mouth one of the pellets of simulated uranium the plant uses for demonstration. The pellet turns out to be not quite colorfast, leaving a dark hue on Richard's tongue. "I think you are contaminated," Kimberly comments dryly, but the actual contamination of human bodies never happens in the film. Mike Nichols's *Silkwood* is very different in this regard, obsessed as it is with the material contamination of the human body.

Material Bodies and Fear of Contamination in *Silkwood*

Silkwood shares a number of plot elements with *The China Syndrome*, which is remarkable given that it is based on the life story of a real person. Like Jack Godell in *The China Syndrome*, the protagonist of *Silkwood* tries to inform the public about safety violations at her plant, and like Jack, the evidence she uncovers becomes a serious – and in the end lethal – danger to her own life. Karen Silkwood (Meryl Streep) is a worker at the Kerr-McGee Cimarron Fuel Fabrication Site, which, unlike the Ventana plant, is not fictional, a fact that will not be lost on most viewers. Karen, her boyfriend Drew (Kurt Russell), and her lesbian friend and roommate Dolly (Cher) make plutonium fuel rods at Kerr-McGee, which are then delivered to nuclear reactors. The film gives viewers insights into the workers' tedious work routines and how they deal with the constant threat of exposure to radiation. The explanation given to visitor groups who ask about the possible effects of handling plutonium is that the effect of radiation on the human body is "exactly like" sunburn: "it can't hurt you unless you're careless with it." However, the company is generally rather lax when it comes to security measures. When, in Karen's absence, a contamination is detected in her section, the plant is closed down for two days, but after that employees are expected to continue their work, wearing additional protective gear. Absurdly, Karen is suspected by her superiors of having deliberately contaminated her section because she wanted the weekend off. As one of her co-worker explains to her, "the company has to blame somebody" because "otherwise it's their fault."

When soon after one of Karen's co-workers gets "cooked" – meaning contaminated – viewers get their first inkling of what that means for the person affected. The woman is stripped naked by employees in protective gear and then scrubbed down violently under a hot shower. The company tells her after the scrubbing that the exposure she has had is "under the acceptable body burden" but the woman is inconsolable and convinced that she will "get cancer and die." Karen tells her co-worker to make her superiors give her a nasal smear to check for internal contamination because that is what they are "supposed to do." The next day, sirens go off as Karen monitors her hands on the Geiger tube before leaving her section, and she has to undergo the scrubbing procedure herself. Viewers are confronted with close-ups of her horrified face when the water jet is put into her mouth and ears, her skin red and sore from the violent scrubbing. The invasiveness and humiliation of the procedure communicates easily as viewers cannot help but put themselves into Karen's position, imagining what it must feel like to be treated in this way.

Later, Karen is told to bring in urine samples to check for interior contamination. She is now becoming increasingly concerned about the effects of plutonium on the human body and, for the first time, reads the information she had been given by the union years ago. Like most of her co-workers, she has so far ignored the dangerous effects of plutonium and the fact that, as sociologist Andrew Pickering puts it, the material world is "continually doing things, things that bear upon us … as forces upon material beings" (6). Only after she has experienced the scrubbing and read about cancer and genetic defects does Karen begin to understand what the invisible material agency of plutonium can do to her and other peoples' bodies. As a result, she joins the union and begins to pay attention to the safety problems at her workplace. She discovers that the negatives of X-rays of faulty fuel rods produced for a breeder reactor are being retouched to disguise their inferior quality, a procedure, she is told by a union official, which could easily be responsible for the deaths "of two million people." Karen accepts the moral imperative involved in her discoveries and begins to fight against her powerful employer.

Like *The China Syndrome*, *Silkwood* uses the narrative conventions of the melodrama in a story that is "all about power." As melodramatic narratives, both films feature suffering protagonists who fight against overpowering antagonists for the greater good of society, and in both films the hero of the story is on the losing end.[12] What is different is that in *Silkwood* nuclear risk does not remain at the level of anticipation. What was only a threat in *The China Syndrome* – the risk of physical contamination – has become painful reality in *Silkwood*, and once again viewers are invited to empathize with the heroine's shock and horror at learning that she is, in fact, internally contaminated and that from now on the plutonium will begin to manifest itself inside of her body in the form of cancer and, eventually, death. They are also invited to empathize with Dolly's disbelieving fear when a Geiger counter tells her that her own living environment, which seemed perfectly normal, is in fact dangerously contaminated, and to imagine what it would be like to have that same experience in their own homes. As Alaimo argues, ethical considerations from the viewpoint of transcorporeality must emerge from the perplexing and often painful place "where the 'human' is always already part of an active, often unpredictable, material world" (*Bodily* 17). Karen moves within a material world that is highly unpredictable and risky, not only because handling plutonium can at any time lead to severe contamination but also because her ethical considerations have led her to a point where her employer is actively fighting her. She does not really know how the plutonium got inside her body, although she has reason to suspect that there are people who find her dangerous enough to want her dead.

The film ends with the fatal car accident that ended the real Karen Silkwood's life, bright lights in the darkness behind Karen's car suggesting that it was not an accident after all, but a deliberate killing. In his review for the *New York Times*, Vincent Canby called the film "a precisely visualized, highly emotional melodrama that's going to raise a lot of hackles," although he had problems with the filmmakers' attempt "to impose a shape on a real-life story that, even as they present it, has no easily verifiable shape" (Canby). However, this is of course where the film takes a political stance and where it makes use of the power of fiction. What Canby considers an inconsistency – the fact that in the final moment of the film a text insert explains that "the precise circumstances of Karen's death are unknown" – can also be interpreted as the deliberate creation of tension, with the text giving the official position and the images confirming what many commentators have suggested: that Karen Silkwood was deliberately killed in order to keep her from providing evidence of the massive safety violations at her plant. In my reading, the cognitive tension between these two final moments, the last shot of the car accident and the

[12] The fact that both films rely on melodramatic storytelling conventions is not unusual for Hollywood productions. As Linda Williams has shown, melodrama is not so much the specific *genre* of the tear-jerking "women's film" as it is the dominant form of American popular film in general, and it is the dynamic relationship of strong emotional appeals and various types of action that keeps the spectator engaged in a melodramatic narrative (see 49).

text insert, is exactly what invites viewers to ponder a little longer whether Silkwood's fears were perhaps justified.

Conclusion

Emotional responses are therefore important for viewers' cognitive engagement with the fictional stories and real-world contexts of both *Silkwood* and *The China Syndrome*. In both cases, they are also shown to be central for the protagonists' rational decision making in the face of nuclear risk. Jack Godell and Karen Silkwood are characters whose ethical considerations and actions are fuelled by emotional engagement. When Jack Lemmon's character realizes in *The China Syndrome* that he may be personally responsible for a nuclear core meltdown and when Streep's character in *Silkwood* is forced to accept the fact that her urine contains plutonium, they experience strong emotions that hit home the fact that "our scientific understanding of unpredictable material agencies will never be sufficient to protect us from unforeseen harms" (Alaimo, *Bodily* 22). Both films invite viewers to share these insights and to make them part of their own ethical decisions and actions; and there is evidence that some viewers have accepted those invitations, resulting in a changed attitude towards nuclear power in their lives outside the movie theater.

"In the age of ecological crisis," Serenella Iovino has argued, "literature can choose to be 'ethically charged', and to communicate an idea of responsibility" (31). The same, I would suggest, is true for film, and the two films I have considered here exemplify well how this can be done. Although they do not offer images of large-scale nuclear disaster and devastation, and although they cannot show the long-term physical consequences of nuclear contamination, they remind viewers of the complex interrelations and potentially fatal entanglements between (intentional) human agency and the (unintentional) material agency of uranium, plutonium, and other radioactive substances. The events in Fukushima have demonstrated once again that technical progress tends to produce unintended side effects, which are often uncontrollable despite our best efforts. The uncanny conjunction between the human agency that was behind the building of nuclear power plants in an earthquake-prone area in Japan, the unintentional material agency of a sea quake and the resulting tsunami, and the resulting agency of uncontrollable nuclear chain reactions painfully reminds us that humans are indeed not the only actors on planet earth, regardless of the fact that they sometimes tragically believe that they are.

Works Cited:

Alaimo, Stacy. *Bodily Natures: Science, Environment, and the Material Self.* Bloomington: Indiana University Press, 2010. Print.

---. "Material Engagements: Science Studies and the Environmental Humanities." *Ecozon@: European Journal of Literature, Culture, and Environment* 1.1 (2010): 69-74.

Barad, Karen. *Meeting the Universe Halfway: Quantum Physics and the Entanglement of Matter and Meaning*. Durham, NC: Duke University Press, 2007. Print.

Beck, Ulrich. *Risk Society.* Cambridge: Polity Press, 1986. Print.

---. *World at Risk*. Cambridge: Polity Press, 2007. Print.

Boivin, Nicole. *Material Cultures, Material Minds: The Impact of Things on Human Thought, Society, and Evolution*. Cambridge: Cambridge University Press, 2008. Print.

Bordwell, David and Noel Carroll, eds. *Post-Theory: Reconstructing Film Studies*. Wisconsin Studies in Film. Madison: University of Wisconsin Press, 1996. Print.

Canby, Vincent. Review of *Silkwood. New York Times*. December 14,1983. Web. 10 January 2012 http://movies.nytimes.com/movie/review?res=9C07EFD61638 F937A25751C1A965948260>.

Carroll, Noël. "Film, Emotion, and Genre." *Passionate Views: Film, Cognition, and Emotion.* Ed. Carl Plantinga and Greg M. Smith. Baltimore: Johns Hopkins University Press, 1999. 21-46. Print.

The China Syndrome. Dir. James Bridges. Perf. Jane Fonda, Michael Douglas, Jack Lemmon. Columbia Pictures, 1979.

Damasio, Antonio. *Descartes' Error: Emotion, Reason, and the Human Brain.* 1994. London: Vintage, 2006. Print.

The Day After. Dir. Nicholas Meyer. ABC, 1983.

de Sousa, Ronald. *The Rationality of Emotion*, Cambridge, MA: MIT Press. 1987. Print.

Dr. Strangelove or: How I Learned to Love the Bomb.. Dir. Stanley Kubrick. Perf. Peter Sellers and George C. Scott. Columbia, 1964.

Gilani, Ijaz Shafi and Rushna Shahid. "Impact of Japan Earthquake on Views about Nuclear Energy. Findings from a Global Snap Poll in 47 countries by WIN-Gallup International." *Win Gallup International*. April 19, 2011. 1-15. Print.

Hanich, Julian. *Cinematic Emotion in Horror Films and Thrillers: The Aesthetic Paradox of Pleasurable Fear*. London and New York: Routledge, 2012. Print.

Hatfield, Elaine, John T. Cacioppo and Richard Rapson. *Emotional Contagion.* Cambridge: Cambridge University Press, 1994. Print.

Hoffman, Martin. *Empathy and Moral Development: Implications for Caring and Justice.* Cambridge: Cambridge University Press, 2000. Print.

Iacoboni, Marco. *Mirroring People: The Science of Empathy and How We Connect to Others.* New York: Picador, 2009. Print.

Iovino, Serenella. "Ecocriticism and a Non-Anthropocentric Humanism: Reflections on Local Natures and Global Responsibilities." *Local Natures, Global Responsibilities.* Ed. Laurenz Volkmann, Nancy Grimm, Ines Detmers, and Katrin Thomson. Amsterdam: Rodopi, 2010. 29-53. Print.

Keen, Suzanne. "Narrative Empathy." *Toward a Cognitive Theory of Narrative Acts*. Ed. Frederick Luis Aldama: Austin: University of Texas Press, 2010. 61-92. Print.

LeDoux, Joseph. *The Emotional Brain.* New York: Simon and Schuster, 1996. Print.

Oatley, Keith. *Such Stuff as Dreams: The Psychology of Fiction*. Malden and Oxford: Wiley, 2011. Print.

Oatley, Keith and Dacher Keltner *Understanding Emotions*. Malden, MA: Blackwell, 2006. Print.

Pickering, Andrew. *The Mangle of Practice: Time, Agency, and Science*. Chicago: University of Chicago Press, 1995. Print.

Plantinga, Carl. "The Scene of Empathy and the Human Face on Film." *Passionate Views: Film, Cognition, and Emotion*. Ed. Carl Plantinga and Greg M. Smith. Baltimore: Johns Hopkins University Press, 1999. 239-255. Print.

---. "Trauma, Pleasure, and Emotion in the Viewing of *Titanic*: A Cognitive Approach." *Film Theory and Contemporary Hollywood Movies*. Ed. Warren Buckland. AFI Film Readers. London: Routledge, 2009. 237-56. Print.

Rashke, Richard. *The Killing of Karen Silkwood: The Story Behind the Kerr-McGee Plutonium Case*. 1983. Second Edition. Ithaca: Cornell University Press, 2000. Print.

The Road. Dir. John Hillcoat. Perf. Viggo Mortenson, Kodi Smit-McPhee, Robert Duvall, Charlize Theron, and Guy Pearce. 2929 Productions, 2009.

Rogovin, Mitchell. *Three Mile Island: A Report to the Commissioners and to the Public*. Volume I. Nuclear Regulatory Commission, Special Inquiry Group, 1980. Print.

The Silence of the Lambs. Dir. Jonathan Demme. Perf. Anthony Hopkins and Jody Foster. Orion Pictures, 1991.

Silkwood. Dir. Mike Nichols. Perf. Meryl Streep, Kurt Russell, Cher. 20th Century Fox. 1982.

Smith, Greg M. *Film Structure and the Emotion System*. Cambridge, Mass: Cambridge University Press, 2003. Print.

Slovic, Paul. *The Perception of Risk*. London: Earthscan, 2000. Print.

Slovic, Paul, Melissa L. Finucane, Ellen Peters, and Donald G. MacGregor. "Risk as Analysis and Risk as Feelings: Some Thoughts about Affect, Reason, Risk, and Rationality." *Risk Analysis* 24.2 (April 2004): 311-322. Print.

Solomon, Robert C. *True to Our Feelings: What Our Emotions Are Really Telling Us*. Oxford and New York: Oxford University Press, 2007. Print.

Tan, Ed S. *Emotion and the Structure of Narrative Film: Film as an Emotion Machine*. London and New York: Routledge, 1995. Print.

Williams, Linda. "Melodrama Revisited." *Refiguring American Film Genres: History and Theory*. Ed. Nick Browne. Berkeley: University of California Press, 1998. 42-88. Print.

Zunshine, Lisa, ed. *Introduction to Cognitive Cultural Studies*. Baltimore: Johns Hopkins University Press, 2010. Print.

Anna Thiemann

Nuclear Risk, Domestic Responsibility, and the Uses of Comedy: Elizabeth Stuckey-French's *The Revenge of the Radioactive Lady*

Eileen Welsome's prize-winning *Plutonium Files* (1999) about secret human radiation experiments during the American Cold War era draws on various sources to illuminate a dark chapter in U.S. history. One of the many voices the author includes is that of Martha Stephens, an English professor and novelist who happened to be on the first committee to review such a government-sponsored research project. Stephens explains what it was like for her to read the records of Eugene Saenger's total-body irradiation study, which harmed unsuspecting patients at the University of Cincinnati in the 1960s and 70s: "I was used to reading in plays and novels about tragic deaths full of pity and sorrow. But I was not used to *this* pity, *this* sorrow of powerless and sick people asking for help and then being brutally abused. Many of these deaths seemed to me executions. And they still do today" (qt. in Welsome 405; emphasis in the original). By comparing Saenger's experiments to tragedy and "executions," Stephens makes a strong judgment about cause and blame. It is clear to her that the patients in Cincinnati died from radiation and that Saenger is directly responsible for their death, an idea that has been refuted by the medical establishment to this day.

Predictably, Saenger was unwilling to accept responsibility for his actions. In her book-length investigation, *The Treatment* (2002), "the story of one tragedy of medical research" (xi), Stephens recounts that he dispelled her accusation with the following argument: "Well, if I'm responsible for those [subjects] who died early, why am I not also responsible for those who lived long?" (qt. in Stephens 160). Saenger's defense takes advantage of the uncertain effects of radiation on the human organism, which characterize many manufactured risks of the twentieth and twenty-first centuries. Manufactured risks such as radioactivity are by-products of scientific and technological development. According to Anthony Giddens, they create new risk environments "for which history provides us with very little previous experience. We often don't really know what the risks are, let alone how to calculate them accurately in terms of probability tables" ("Risk and Responsibility" 4). As a result, these risks have triggered a crisis of accountability, the emergence of what Ulrich Beck calls "organized irresponsibility" (*Ecological Politics* 2).

Welsome's and Stephen's historical studies were published at the turn of the millennium—only five years after the U.S. government launched a groundbreaking investigation into human radiation experiments (Clinton)[1]—yet, it would take more than another decade for the material to be adapted into other genres and forms. Facing the dilemma of moral uncertainty in the late modern age, the author of the first fictional work on U.S. radiation studies, Elizabeth Stuckey-French, significantly abandoned the tragic mode of her journalist and historical scientist predecessors, drawing on various comic traditions instead, to explore the complex implications of contemporary risk society. Her 2011 novel, *The Revenge of the Radioactive Lady*, was inspired by a study at Vanderbilt University, where hundreds of pregnant women from low-income families were given free "little cocktail[s]" (Welsome 220) with radioactive iron. "Touted as a nutrition study," the experiments were meant to determine the "long-term effects of radiation on children" (LeBaron 98). A follow-up study revealed that the women were afflicted with various health problems and that four children had died of cancer at an unusually early age (Welsome 220-28). Like Welsome's *Plutonium Files* and Stephens's *The Treatment*, *The Revenge of the Radioactive Lady* seeks to undermine the principle of organized irresponsibility by giving a voice to the victims of human radiation studies and by reconstructing doubts and moral scruples within the scientific community.[2] Yet, the multifaceted comic mode of Stuckey-French's novel enables her to convey and negotiate the epistemological and ethical challenges of contemporary "riskscapes"[3] in a way that tragedy cannot. Rather than proving the Aristotelian notion that comedy is "almost 'subpolitical'" (Downey 122), *The Revenge of the Radioactive Lady* illustrates the genre's critical and transformative potential in the late modern age.

Philosophers of humor have pointed out that comic amusement is often triggered by the self-ignorance and irresponsibility of others or the unexpected juxtaposition of events, objects and ideas, thereby achieving its

---

1 See also Jonathan D. Moreno's *Undue Risk: Secret State Experiments on Humans*, which was published in 2001. As a bioethicist, Moreno served on Clinton's Advisory Committee on Human Radiation Experiments, which released its final report on October 3, 1995.

2 In an interview, Stuckey-French explains that her novel tries to imagine how the doctors justified their behavior to themselves: "They weren't all 'bad' people. Arrogant and monomaniacal perhaps, but not necessarily evil. Certainly the Cold War offered them rationalizations, but there was more to it than that. I wanted to explore what might have gone on in their heads, and how they lived with themselves afterwards" ("An Interview").

3 The term "riskscape" was prominently defined by Susan Cutter who uses it to refer to the "interplay of social, political, and economic factors—interacting separately, in combination with one another, and with the physical environment—[which] creates a mosaic of risks and hazards that affect people and the places they inhabit" (87).

main purpose: the release of nervous energy (Morreall 4-26). *The Revenge of the Radioactive Lady* displays all these features, but I am particularly interested in the correlation between (ir)responsibility, risk, and comedy, which has attracted the attention of risk theorists and literary critics alike. After providing a more detailed discussion of risk and responsibility, I will take a closer look at the role of comedy in the age of uncertainty. In this context, I will draw mainly on the sociological work of Ulrich Beck, who compares late modern risk society to the Kafkaesque "comedy of the absurd" (*Ecological Politics* 62), and the work of literary critics who scrutinize the transformation of comedy in the late modern age. Scholars from both disciplines, sociology and literary criticism, develop surprisingly similar arguments about comedy and the irresponsible self in Western fiction, which I am going to compare to the use and function of comedy in *The Revenge of the Radioactive Lady*. In doing so, I will address a deficit or blind spot in the emerging field of literary risk criticism, which has been oblivious to the pivotal role of comedy in social science and literary historical explorations of late modern risk society. Moreover, I will join critics who take the existing debate over comedy, risk and responsibility in the age of uncertainty one step further by moving beyond the American black humor tradition of the 1960s.[4]

Risk, Responsibility and the Comic Imagination

The concept of risk has not always implied human agency and responsibility. When the term emerged in the context of maritime navigation in the late Middle Ages, it was linked to fateful events like sea storms, which were attributed to a force majeure or divine intervention, thus excluding the idea of human fault. The scientific and disciplinary regimes of the industrial era turned risk into a calculable and thus insurable entity to be subjected to political regulation. As a result, risk came to be associated with decision, control and intervention, the idea that something can be done to prevent damage and disaster (Lupton 5-7). Yet, this newly established relationship between risk and responsibility changed dramatically with the proliferation of manufactured risks during the late modern era, which paradoxically triggered a crisis of accountability. According to Beck, man-made risks such as genetic engineering, chemical pollution and atomic radiation have created global, unprecedented, and incalculable risk environments, which force modern institutions to embrace the logic of "organized irresponsibility":

[4] Paul Lewis's *Cracking Up: American Humor in a Time of Conflict* (2006) is the only study to date that focuses on humor and global risks in the late twentieth and early twenty-first century. Yet, drawing on Anthony Giddens and Joanna Macy, Lewis tends to highlight the alleviating function of humor and comedy rather than its subversive potential.

> The concept of 'organized irresponsibility' helps to explain how and why the institutions of modern society must unavoidably acknowledge the reality of catastrophe while simultaneously denying its existence, hiding its origins and precluding compensation or control. To put it in another way, risk societies are characterized by the paradox of more and more environmental degradation—perceived and possible—coupled with an expansion of environmental law and regulation. Yet at the same time, no individual or institution seems to be held specifically accountable for anything. (*World Risk Society* 149)

The omnipresence and proliferation of historically new hazards give rise to an ever-expanding and highly organized legal apparatus, which nonetheless fails to identify the causes and culprits of environmental degradation.

The reason for this failure is not only the rapid development of unprecedented risks, which escape the meshes of the law, but also the fact that legal regulations undercut their own competence by relying on scientific experts, the main producers of risks, who are neither impartial nor able to anticipate the unintended effects of their research. Apart from these issues, Beck identifies an even more fundamental problem: the fact that all participants in this system of organized irresponsibility uphold "the old industrial patterns of rationality and control" (*World Risk Society* 56). These patterns include the principle of individual causation and accountability, which no longer fit the multi-causal risk environment of late modernity. Predictably, Beck maintains that we need to resist our nostalgic impulses and find new ways of imagining and dealing with the ethical implications of contemporary risk scenarios (*Risk Society* 235).

Since the new millennium, cultural critics have become increasingly interested in the imaginative rendering of risk environments in narrative texts. Ursula Heise maintains that contemporary risk fiction "foreground[s] the increasingly urgent search for an aesthetic of uncertainty" ("Cultures of Risk" 41). Discussing literature and film, she points out that fictional riskscapes come in various genres and modes including epic, science fiction, *bildungsroman*, satire, pastoral, apocalypse, gothic, comedy, and tragedy.[5] Yet, lacking in aesthetic complexity, so Heise, these works fail to capture the workings of late modern risk society. She concludes that contemporary risk environments require "more experimental forms of storytelling, and perhaps even the resources of new narrative media such as the multiple links of hypertext" ("Toxins" 773). Due to her focus on the literary representation of late modern risk society, Heise has been accused of "a kind of mimetic fallacy" (119) by literary scholar Susan Mizruchi, who focuses on ethical rather than epistemological concerns. Highlighting the problem of class, she analyzes texts like Don DeLillo's *White Noise* (1984), which satirize upper-class eccentricity and ironic detachment in the face of risk, as well as

[5] These genres are mentioned in different contexts of Heise's work on environmental risk and literature ("Cultures of Risk" 18, 37; "Toxins" 763; *Sense of Place* 3).

realist works about individual suffering and redemption like Richard Powers's *Gain* (1994), which are meant to evoke empathy across class lines. According to Mizruchi, contemporary risk narratives encourage us to stop insisting on the rational distinction between victims and perpetrators. Yet, at the same time, they privilege "a social order founded on more rational, more benevolent principles" (129). Mizruchi provides valuable insights into the ethical implications of risk narratives, but in the end it is not quite clear how the tension between the incalculability of risk and the desire for rationality and justice is to be resolved.

What both Heise and Mizruchi fail to fully analyze is the nexus between epistemology, ethics and aesthetics in late modern risk society, the development of unknowable risks and organized irresponsibility on the one hand and its translation into narrative form on the other. These issues have significantly been addressed by risk theorists themselves, who routinely draw on novels and films to illustrate their arguments—a fact that has been largely ignored by literary and cultural critics.[6] When discussing "adaptive reactions to the risk profile of modernity" (*The Consequences of Modernity* 134), Giddens refers to cynical parodies like *Dr. Strangelove* (1964) and other black comedies which dampen the emotional impact of risk-related anxieties (136). While Giddens uses fictional texts only as occasional examples,[7] Beck goes as far as to postulate a co-evolution of modern risks and aesthetic forms. In *World at Risk*, Beck proposes that the history of the European novel can be described "in terms of the historical metamorphosis of risk" (5-6), which is closely linked to the transition from religious to secular societies. "As a gulf opened between God and risk," so Beck, "the European novel entered into an association with risk," revealing its logic and existential dimensions (4).

Beck distinguishes three stages in the literary exploration of risk: Cervantes's emphasis on the ambiguity of risk and fateful decision-making, Balzac's focus on the administration of risk by modern social institutions, and Kafka's transformation of risk-associated freedom into "self-obstruction, self-accusation and self-subjection" (6). Ignoring later developments of the novel, Beck chooses to compare late modern risk society to Kafka's "comedy of the absurd":

> Life and praxis in the risk society have become Kafkaesque in the strict sense of the word—if this concept designates the absurd situations available in real life to the individual in a totalitarian, labyrinthine world that is opaque to himself. [...] The further one goes down the branching corridors, rooms and subterranean

[6] Mizruchi briefly mentions that the trauma theorist Kai Erikson draws on literary texts, but she does not give any examples or insights into their specific function in the sociologist's argument (118).

[7] *The Consequences of Modernity* contains further references to Carolyn See's *Golden Days* (1986) and Saul Bellow's *Herzog* (1964) (132, 146).

> tunnels of hazard manufacture and administration, […] the more apparent it becomes that there is a great bureaucracy, extending into and out of the factories themselves; it consists of general recklessness and uncertainty, growing ignorance or half-baked knowledge, falsification, cover-ups, etc., under the truly inspired organizational principle of unaccountable non-liability. (*Ecological Politics* 61-62)

Focusing on Kafka's *The Trial* (1925), Beck argues that the uncertainty of risk and the concomitant principle of organized irresponsibility result in the protection of individuals and institutions that are guilty of causing risk. Protest and accusations by risk victims are silenced by an impenetrable "maze of information" (*Ecological Politics* 61), and the ultimate "inability-to-know [Nicht-Wissen-Können]" (*World at Risk* 5) forces them into a cycle of self-blaming. Beck praises the comedy of the absurd for its exposure of organized irresponsibility, but he maintains that effective protest "must speak in the language of […] science" (*Ecological Politics* 62), which is unlikely to happen as scientific experts are implicated in the production of risks.

Beck's history of the novel traces a linear development of mutually exclusive forms, which is quite surprising in view of the fact that he charges late modern risk society with a nostalgic longing for 'outdated' values and principles. His literary historical excursions seem to fall short of explaining the complex relationship between late modern risk society and the postmodern literary imagination, which draws on various genres and modes from the past. I am going to prove this assumption with my exemplary analysis of *The Revenge of the Radioactive Lady* in the next section of this essay. However, before I do so, I will explore the similarities and differences between sociological and literary critical perspectives on comedy in the age of uncertainty.

What unites Giddens and Beck is their focus on twentieth-century comedy of the absurd, which is apparently a suitable genre for negotiating the epistemological and ethical implications of late modern risk society. They are joined by literary critics who have focused on the transformation of comedy in the age of uncertainty. These scholars are not directly connected to the emerging field of risk criticism, but their findings imply that the history of comedy is in fact closely linked to the evolving concepts of risk and organized irresponsibility. Comedy has always been interested in the irresponsible self as an object of comic amusement, yet its moral status has changed according to cultural notions of knowledge and progress, which correspond to shifting perceptions of risks. In the introduction to his essay collection *The Irresponsible Self: On Laughter and the Novel* (2004), James Wood argues that the pre-modern "comedy of correction" follows the principles of transparency and moral reasoning by putting a window into the characters' hearts and holding them accountable for their actions and decisions (4). Moving from opinion to knowledge, so Northrop Frye tells us (*Anatomy* 158), traditional or new comedy[8] aims at the punishment and reintegration of the irresponsible self into society and is thus geared towards a happy ending and "the crystallization of a new society" ("A Natural Perspective" 184), which is often symbolized by an unlikely marriage or other social rituals like "a feast, or a dance" at the end of the narrative (Abrams and Harpham 39).

In modern and late modern risk society, on the other hand, comedy is informed by decidedly different epistemological and ethical frameworks. Wood links the rise of modern fiction in the late nineteenth and early twentieth centuries to modern uncertainty and irresponsibility, pointing out that the "modern novel replaces the knowable with the unknowable, transparency with unreliability" (8). Marking the end of rationality and moral certainty, this epistemological shift turns the irresponsible self into a showcase example of the human condition. Responsible decision-making is based on the anticipation of the consequences of one's actions, but such an analysis becomes impossible in the complex risk environment of the twentieth century. In other words, irresponsibility is unavoidable, a universal problem rather than an individual character flaw. As a consequence, modern comedy promotes, not remorse and punishment, but stoicism and forgiveness. It still focuses on inclusion and endeavors to create "an alternative community" (Wood 4); yet, this community is no longer based on clear-headed judgment and correction but on shared acknowledgement of uncertainty and irresponsibility.

Serving as an introduction to a heterogeneous essay collection that covers a wide range of authors from Shakespeare and Dostoevsky to Jonathan Franzen and Bohumil Hrabal, Wood's theory about comedy and responsibility in the age of uncertainty is necessarily vague and abstract. Critics who have focused on late twentieth-century American comedy have come up with a more differentiated conceptual and historical outline, tracing the main differences between new comedy, existential fiction and the American black humor tradition of the 1960s, which is often presented as a reaction to World War II atrocities and science-related risks like the threat of nuclear annihilation (Pratt xix).[9] In contrast to new comedy, existential fiction and black humor literature assume that the world is irrational and absurd, lacking logical order and ultimate justification. Yet, while existential fiction is deadly serious and celebrates the desperate humanist efforts to ease

[8] "Traditional comedy" and "new comedy" are closely linked to the concept and history of pre-modern comedy. I use the term "traditional comedy" to highlight the notion that pre-modern comedy has not died out in the modern age; "new comedy," on the other hand, designates a well-known subgenre that plays a central role in Frye's argument.

[9] Even though black humor is not limited to the American literary scene, U.S. writers "on the whole appear to be more articulate about it, and American audiences more susceptible to the form" (Numasawa 41).

the pain (Janoff 32-33), black humor chooses to laugh at modern absurdities. Black humor not only refuses to avoid taboo topics such as rape and murder and "to treat […] tragic materials tragically" (O'Neill 65); it also refrains from offering "explicit [or] implicit proposals for improving, reforming, or changing the painful realities on which it focuses" (Pratt xix). The most widely debated novel of the American black humor tradition is Joseph Heller's World War II satire *Catch-22* (1961),[10] which chronicles the absurd and horrifying experiences of a U.S. Air Corps bombardier who refuses to risk his life in mindless missions. Heller's novel illustrates not only the epistemological and ethical aspects of black humor—its focus on modern uncertainty and organized irresponsibility—, but also its political dimension which offers a critical revisionist perspective on U.S. history. What many debates about Heller and black comedy tend to ignore is that *Catch-22* is a highly complex text which negotiates different ideological positions. Even though the novel is often introduced as a showcase example of black humor fiction, some critics have pointed out that it actually presents "a curious mixture of philosophical attitudes" (Janoff 34) ranging from hedonistic nihilism to altruistic existentialism, which arguably dominates the protagonist's mindset at the end of the novel (Janoff 33-34).

Social scientists and literary critics thus develop similar arguments about the role of comedy in the age of uncertainty. Most strikingly, they draw on the same examples, including Stanley Kubrick's *Dr. Strangelove*[11] and Kafka's comedy of the absurd, which is often seen as a precursor or early representative of the black humor tradition (O'Neill 77). Beck and Giddens use these texts mainly as an illustration of organized irresponsibility and charge science with the task of solving the problems of the late modern age.[12] Literary critics, on the other hand, claim a much more active role for black humor fiction and other cultural forms by underlining their critical and subversive potential.

What has been lacking in the contemporary debate about risk, responsibility and the comic imagination is an integration of social science and literary studies perspectives as well as a profound discussion of more recent literary developments that have redefined the black humor tradition of the 1960s. After this brief overview of existing arguments about comedy in late modern risk society, I will now take the debate further by analyzing a twenty-first century risk narrative which adapts and transforms the comic traditions of previous centuries.

---

[10] The index of the edited volume *Black Humor: Critical Essays* (1993) contains no less than twenty-five references to Heller's novel (370-71).

[11] The index of the edited volume *Black Humor: Critical Essays* (1993) contains six references to Kubrick's film (369).

[12] Giddens tends to be more optimistic in this regard (Alario and Freudenburg 196-97).

Elizabeth Stuckey-French's *The Revenge of the Radioactive Lady*

The title of Elizabeth Stuckey-French's 2011 novel holds the promise of a new perspective on risk and responsibility. Its reference to revenge summons the pre-modern principles of agency, moral accountability and correction. At the same time, it "is playfully retro" (Willett), thus hinting at the novel's comic and self-reflexive tone. In good postmodern fashion, *The Revenge of the Radioactive Lady* turns out to be a mixture of traditional and modern comedy, including elements of correction, punitive violence, self-blaming and forgiveness, which are thoroughly scrutinized and negotiated. To be more precise, Stuckey-French's novel manages to deal with late modern uncertainty and the phenomenon of self-incrimination without forsaking morality and responsibility.

The Revenge of the Radioactive Lady revolves around Marylou Ahearn, a seventy-seven-year-old victim of a secret government study, which was conducted at Memphis University in the early 1950s. When being pregnant with her first child, she was given a "deadly radioactive cocktail" (4) that left her with lingering health problems and ostensibly killed her daughter Helen, who died of cancer in 1963. Although Marylou received financial compensation in a government settlement, she seeks personal revenge on Dr. Wilson Spriggs, the physician who poisoned her. Upon learning that he lives with his daughter's family in Tallahassee, Marylou moves from Ohio to Florida and makes preparations to confront—and kill—her enemy. Yet, news that Wilson has Alzheimer's forces her to change her plans. Instead of murdering the disoriented physician, she decides to punish him by ruining his family, which consists of Vic and Caroline Witherspoon and their three children, Ava, Otis and Suzi. However, to Marylou's dismay, Wilson's family turns out to be short of self-destruction, thus thwarting her backup plan. Stuckey-French's novel may have the basic ingredients of revenge tragedy, but its character constellation and unexpected plot development turn it into a full-fledged comedy, which is peopled with irresponsible selves: Caroline spends her entire energy on Ava, who has Asperger's syndrome, while her husband Vic is obsessed with hurricanes and short of sliding into an extramarital affair. Suzi misses Olympic soccer camp because of a risky move in a lost game and falls in love with a minister who turns out to be a child molester. Ava loses her virginity to a practical stranger, and Otis, the second child with Asperger's, spends most of his time in his shed to build a nuclear breeder reactor.

With human experiment, murder and child abuse, Stuckey-French's comedy takes on typical topics of black humor fiction, and reviewers as well as the author herself have routinely placed her text in this genre.[13] In fact,

[13] See the anonymous review in *Kirkus Reviews* and the *Lit Show* interview with the author ("Stuckey-French"; Stuckey-French, "Elizabeth Stuckey-French").

however, *The Revenge of the Radioactive Lady* draws on various comic traditions to negotiate the question of responsibility in late modern risk society. In terms of style, Stuckey-French's novel uses the comic tools of traditional humor. The text abounds with classic comic elements such as irony, surprise, and exaggeration, starting with the title page illustration which conveys the idea of a cheery 1950s housewife turned serial killer. The comic discrepancy between Marylou's character and her brutish scheme of revenge is further emphasized when the novel reveals that the "nice old lady" (34) is already seventy-seven years old and keeps struggling against her impulse to befriend her victims. Her enemy, Wilson Spriggs, is an equally comic figure, a "nice, polite, rather handsome gentleman" (125), who drives Marylou crazy because he is apparently too old to remember and repent his sins. *The Revenge of the Radioactive Lady* is also full of contrived ironic reversals like the ones mentioned above, and the novel caricatures late modern risk society by presenting not only an entire cast of irresponsible selves but also a wild potpourri of risks from natural disaster and nuclear energy to dementia and pedophilia.

Its traditional comic style alone is no indication that Stuckey-French's novel subscribes to the epistemological and ethical perspective of pre-modern comedy. After all, critics have pointed out that the history of comedy is characterized by very little experimentation and that even the "formal strategies of black humorists are generally conservative" (Pratt xxii). Yet, *The Revenge of the Radioactive Lady* goes beyond evoking traditional comedy on the level of form. A self-referential passage in the first chapter, the author's focalization strategies and the overall plot development indicate that the comedy of correction is a lurking presence in the novel. In the opening pages, we learn that Marylou is a retired English teacher who is more than grateful for not having to "spoon-feed Chaucer to tenth graders again" (2). Ironically, her mission has brought her to Canterbury Heights, a neighborhood "where the streets were named after Chaucer's characters. *The Canterbury Tales* had returned to mark this next big passage in her life" (2). Marylou and her enemy, Wilson Spriggs, live on Reeve's Court and Friar's Way respectively, which happen to refer to "tales where the narrative structure and expectations are those of comedy as a specific genre" (Pearsall 160). To be more precise, Chaucer's "Friar's Tale" and "Reeve's Tale" are prototypical examples of the comedy of correction, in which a wicked fool is punished for his hubris and selfishness. Variable focalization also evokes the moral clarity characteristic of the premodern comedy of correction. In all twenty-three chapters, the narrator takes turns entering the minds of the main characters, thus promising to lay bare their 'true' character and the motives for their irresponsible behavior. Significantly, only one chapter, chapter twenty-two to be precise, reveals the thoughts of Wilson Spriggs. With Wilson being the first irresponsible self and final focalizer of the novel, the plot moves towards his punishment and reintegration into society. In the end, he gets to drive a car again, breaks his silence about the experiments, and falls in love with Marylou, who actually agrees to marry him. With the traditional comedy of correction, Stuckey-French evokes the pre-modern principles of rationality and moral certainty, which are anachronistic, yet still relevant, in late modern risk society, revealing 'our' unwillingness to deal with the absurdity of modern existence. Yet, rather than indulging in the nostalgic impulse of late modernity, the novel ridicules its rational vision by transcending pre-modern comic traditions.

The most striking difference between *The Revenge of the Radioactive Lady* and the classic comedy of correction concerns the way in which Stuckey-French handles the question of responsibility. In her novel, moral clarity and the attribution of blame are complicated by the inherent uncertainty of risk, its positive and negative effects, which results in chaos and irresponsibility. Each action is embedded in a complex network of interdependent forces that renders reasonable and responsible decision-making extremely difficult—if not impossible. This fatal principle affects each and every character of the novel and leads to self-blaming—beginning with the "Radioactive Lady" herself. Borrowing from the modern comedy of the absurd, the novel dramatizes the victim's self-accusation. Marylou blames herself not only for accepting and swallowing the radioactive cocktail without asking any further questions but also for taking other risks while she was pregnant like going to a party and drinking alcohol: "Nowadays pregnant women knew better. What kind of damage had she done to Helen that night? Maybe all those mimosas had contributed to Helen's cancer as well" (140). Similarly, Wilson's daughter Caroline assumes that she caused the autism of her first child:

> Caroline hadn't been able to step away, at all, ever, because part of her, deep down, was sure that she was somehow responsible for Ava's autism—that it was caused by something Caroline ate or drank or did while she was pregnant, or that her genes were bad, or the fact that her labor had gone on for a week and Ava had been yanked out by forceps with the umbilical cord wrapped around her neck. And those fucking mercury-laced shots. (312)

Unable to deal with the uncertainty of late modern risk society, both women devise destructive strategies to calm their guilt, which throw them into a cycle of (self-)condemnation. Caroline sacrifices her husband and other two children to focus her entire attention on Ava's wellbeing, and Marylou reinvents herself as the Radioactive Lady who channels her energy into punishing the 'evil' Dr. Spriggs.

In keeping with the principles of the late modern risk society, the novel refrains from offering comic revenge as a viable alternative to self-accusation. Marylou's vision of "some unfolding drama starring the Radioactive Lady and the American Nazi" (221) is compromised by the unpredictable outcomes of her own risky scheme. Instead of achieving her aims, the Radioactive Lady triggers several unintended catastrophes. Her plan to steer Ava "away from her studies and toward the trashy world of modeling" (134) gets the eighteen-year-old involved in a nude photo shoot, which ignites the lust of the photographer's friend Reverend Coffey, and her attempt to turn Suzi into a "religious freak" (276) drives the thirteen-year-old into the arms of the same pedophile minister. Moreover, Marylou realizes that she has quite unexpectedly come to like her victims, which renders the fatal outcome of her mission all the more regrettable.

Similar to the scientist's research, Marylou's risky experiment has also some positive effects: She encourages Vic to be a responsible husband and father, and she makes sure that the USEPA, the United States Environmental Protection Agency, takes care of Otis's radioactive shed. But rather than weighing the good against the bad, Marylou focuses on the harm she has done. Like Wilson several decades earlier, the Radioactive Lady finds herself at the top end of an unpredictable chain reaction, which forces her to review her own accountability: "This whole thing was her fault. She had taken Suzi to that church for her own devious purposes and delivered her into the clutches of that creep. [...] The Radioactive Lady, it seemed, was just as destructive as the nasty shit she'd swallowed" (228). Marylou's self-characterization and self-accusation highlight the central dilemma of late modern risk society, its belief in logic and justice, which clashes with the irrationality and irresponsibility of modern existence: On the one hand, she blames herself for the negative outcome of her plans and decisions. On the other hand, she likens herself and her actions to the unpredictable effects of radioactive materials, which cannot be controlled and handled responsibly.

It is remarkable that, within this fictional universe of maximum uncertainty, Marylou does not follow the example of other characters in the black humor tradition who tend to adopt a nihilistic outlook on life and existence (Janoff 32). The fact that she is not able to control the future does not destroy her sense of responsibility; nor does it stop her from trying to learn from the past. In the long run, she realizes that revenge is risky and immoral as it entails unintended consequences and "*just hurts more people*" (281; emphasis in the original).

Marylou's insight echoes the episode in which Wilson mentions his harmful radiation study for the first time and admonishes Otis not to repeat his grandfather's mistakes: "I was involved in a research study, a long time ago […]. We thought we were doing the right thing but we weren't. We hurt innocent people. Caused deaths. I don't want you to ever take those chances." (266-67) Wilson repeats his confession in front of his victim and the scientific community when Marylou takes him to Memphis University. At his former workplace, Wilson opens up about the experiments, supporting

Marylou's assumption that false optimism and the Cold War research environment lured him into a misjudgment:

> He admitted that his was the wrong side, but he said there had been a Cold War going on and he was scrambling to get research money. He was an ambitious young scientist trying to get data, a doctor trying to help determine how much radiation was safe. Back then, these sorts of studies were conducted all over the country. They knew virtually nothing about radiation, but they'd all thought that small amounts had to be safe. (325)

Wilson knows that he cannot change the past but he sincerely regrets Helen's death and is willing to change and to embrace responsibility in an uncertain and rapidly changing world by admitting to his past mistakes. Accordingly, he rejects his colleagues' praise for his pioneering work in radioisotope therapy and calls the young researchers at Memphis University "a couple of blisters who've shown up after the real work's been done" (322).

Despite their disillusioning experience in a highly irrational world, both protagonists preserve a strong sense of responsibility, which prevents them from sliding into nihilistic apathy. The existential twist of Stuckey-French's black comedy, its altruistic vision and ultimate rejection of fatalistic thinking, invites a comparison to the most prominent 'showcase example' of black humor fiction, Heller's *Catch-22*. Both novels highlight the absurdity of modern life and expose instances of organized irresponsibility in modern systems and institutions. In *The Revenge of the Radioactive Lady*, however, the critique of those in power is considerably softened. The young scientist Wilson Spriggs is presented as ambitious and naïve, but he ends up expressing his respect for human life and his willingness to learn from past mistakes. Stuckey-French's renegotiation of Heller's perspective is rendered explicit by an intertextual echo at the end of the novel. In chapter twenty-two (!), Wilson mentions his favorite memory concerning his time in the Army Air Corps during World War II, which he spent in "England and then Italy and occupied France" (317). In contrast to Heller's protagonist, Wilson highlights only the positive sides of his war experience, boasting about his pivotal role in the defeat of German air power. Marylou responds to Wilson's story with an ambivalent "little smile" (317), which expresses her amusement and admiration. Even though she ridicules Wilson's idealization of his bombing missions, she still acknowledges that they constitute a noble episode in his life. The scientist's 'heroization,' however, does not imply that *The Revenge of the Radioactive Lady* abandons the historical revisionist impulse of black humor fiction.

To remove any doubts about the critical perspective of her work, Stuckey-French has two members of the third generation, Ava and her friend Travis, make plans to study archeology and history because they want "to recreate the past" (257). Another example of how the author deals with the

U.S. perspective on world history is the opening passage of chapter eighteen, where the injured and posttraumatic Suzi comforts herself by reading Anne Frank's diary:

> Anne Frank was her go-to girl. Suzi stayed in her room as much as they'd let her, rereading Anne Frank's diary for the millionth time so that she would not feel sorry for herself. After all, all that had happened to Suzi was that 1. She hurt her knee playing soccer and had missed Olympic soccer camp; and 2. She'd given a grown man a blow job. Big deal. It wasn't like he'd raped her or she'd been forced to hide in an attic for years. (268)

Anne Frank's 'optimistic' diary and its various U.S. adaptations have been said to symbolize the American tendency "to downplay or deny the dark and brutal sides of life and to place a preponderant emphasis on the saving power of individual moral conduct and collective deeds of redemption" (Rosenfeld 37). Similarly, Suzi trivializes her trauma and reinvents herself as her sister's keeper, who acted as a shield against the minister's desire for Ava: "I only did it [...] so he'd leave Ava alone. I did it so she would not have to" (245). Yet, entering Suzi's mind, the novel soon reveals that "[t]hat idea had occurred to her only after the fact" (268) and that she actually feels responsible for her personal tragedy. By linking Suzi to Anne Frank's diary, Stuckey-French's novel satirizes America's overoptimistic interpretation of world history, which tends to ignore unpleasant realities and to nurture the idea of U.S. moral superiority.

The Revenge of the Radioactive Lady proposes, not to abandon, but to adapt 'our' self-image and optimism to the realities of the past and the puzzling conditions of the late modern age. Wilson's confession and regret about the human radiation experiments reveal his sincere intention to 'come clean' and to do what he can to prevent human suffering in an irrational universe. Stuckey-French's novel presents his paradoxical optimism as the only viable response to a world that lacks logic and moral certainty. This moral solution to the dilemma of late modernity is also evoked in the final chapter of the novel, which deals with the uncertain outcomes of Otis's nuclear experiments and Marylou's redefined relationship to Wilson and his family. No matter what political and scientific authorities such as the federal government or the USEPA will say, the Witherspoons will never "*really* know" (330; emphasis in the original) if their home is safe. Moreover, the parents and grandparents can only speculate if their autistic son and grandson is able to grasp the implications of his experiment: "Was he thinking about what he'd done, regretting it, or was he planning how to make his next nuclear device? Who knew?" (334). Marylou's adopted family is far from perfect and perhaps short of another catastrophe. Nevertheless, she "like[s] feeling responsible for them" (334).

Stressing Marylou's desperate hopefulness in the face of uncertainty, the novel turns out to subscribe to the "marginally optimistic system" of existentialism, "which is characterized by human involvement and the ideal of service" (Janoff 32). But rather than adopting the serious tone of existential fiction, Stuckey-French conveys her relatively positive ending by appropriating and transforming the happy ending of the classic comedy of correction: "There was a certain lightness in the air, the way it feels when a storm has finally passed over. A relief, a renewed purpose. [...] Marylou expected someone to get up and dance, would've done it herself if she wasn't nearly eighty" (363). This ironic evocation of optimism and renewal ridicules the rational vision of the pre-modern comic imagination, which no longer fits the realities of late modernity. The protagonists of Stuckey-French's novel illustrate this lesson: Wilson and Marylou present an odd old couple that is bounded by a painful past rather than a glowing future. In the end, they emerge as equally irresponsible characters who have taken great risks in their fights for justice and the common good. They are both heroes and fools as their deeds triggered unpredictable chain reactions with both good and harmful consequences. Yet, what counts according to Stuckey-French's comedy is the willingness to learn from the past and to take responsibility for an uncertain future, which is lacking in late modern risk society.

Conclusion

With my theoretical contextualization and exemplary analysis, I hope to have shown that the role of comedy for the rendering of late modern riskscapes is worth further exploration. Even though social scientists and literary scholars have dealt with comic risk narratives from different disciplinary perspectives, their common interest has gone unnoticed in the emerging field of literary risk criticism. A more thorough investigation of this largely neglected interdisciplinary dialogue over risk and the comic imagination promises to shed new light on the epistemological and ethical perspectives of contemporary risk fiction and its relationship to risk theory. With *The Revenge of the Radioactive Lady*, I have analyzed a work that consciously plays with elements of pre-modern comedy, existential fiction and black humor, thus refuting Beck's notion of a parallel linear development of risk society and Western literature. Stuckey-French's novel satirizes the overoptimistic vision of the traditional comedy of correction and the nihilist attitude of black humor fiction, highlighting their obsolescence and moral inadequacy. After exploring the epistemological and ethical implications of these comic forms, Stuckey-French ends up opting for the altruistic vision of existential fiction, which presses for honesty and humanist commitment in an irrational and uncertain age. In doing so, she offers a new perspective on responsibility and uncertainty that distances itself from Beck's preoccupation with the comedy of the absurd and his "fatalistic view of the human condition" (Jarvis 44). The comic imagination of *The Revenge of the Radioactive Lady* illustrates that risk fiction can do more than compete with science in the race for 'high-tech' representations of contemporary riskscapes. It can envision new ways of dealing with the moral challenges of late modernity, which have beset science and political systems and institutions.

Works Cited

Abrams, M. H., and Geoffrey Galt Harpham. *A Glossary of Literary Terms*. 5th ed. Boston: Thomson, 2005. 38-41. Print.

Advisory Committee on Human Radiation Experiments. *The Human Radiation Experiments: Final Report of the President's Advisory Committee*. Ed. Ruth Faden. New York: Oxford University Press, 1996. Print.

Alario, Margaritta, and William Freudenburg. "The Paradoxes of Modernity: Scientific Advances, Environmental Problems, and Risks to the Social Fabric?" *Sociological Forum* 18.2 (2003): 193-214. Print.

Beck, Ulrich. *Ecological Politics in an Age of Risk*. 1988. Trans. Amos Weisz. Cambridge: Polity Press, 2002. Print.

---. *Risk Society: Towards a New Modernity*. 1986. Trans. Mark Ritter. London: Sage, 2005. Print.

---. *World at Risk*. 2007. Trans. Ciaran Cronin. Cambridge: Polity Press, 2009. Print.

---. *World Risk Society*. 1999. Cambridge: Polity Press, 2001. Print.

Clinton, William. "Executive Order 12891 of January 15, 1994: Advisory Committee on Human Radiation Experiments." *Federal Register* 59.13 (1994): n. pag. National Archives and Records Administration, 1994. Web. 20 Aug. 2013.

Cutter, Susan L. *Hazards, Vulnerability and Environmental Justice*. London: Earthscan, 2006. Print.

Downey, Patrick. *Serious Comedy: The Philosophical and Theological Significance of Tragic and Comic Writing in the Western Tradition*. Lanham: Lexington, 2001. Print.

Frye, Northrop. *The Anatomy of Criticism: Four Essays*. Ed. Robert D. Denham. Toronto: University of Toronto Press, 2007. Print.

---. "A Natural Perspective: The Development of Shakespearean Comedy and Romance." *Northrop Frye's Writings on Shakespeare and the Renaissance*. Ed. Toni Grande and Garry Sherbert. Toronto: University of Toronto Press, 2010. 127-225. Print.

Giddens, Anthony. *The Consequences of Modernity*. Cambridge: Polity Press, 1990. Print.

---. "Risk and Responsibility." *Modern Law Review* 62.1 (1999): 1-10. Print.

Heise, Ursula K. "Cultures of Risk and the Aesthetic of Uncertainty." *Scientific Cultures—Technological Challenges: A Transatlantic Perspective*. Ed. Klaus Benesch and Meike Zwingenberger. Heidelberg: Winter, 2009. 17-44. Print.

---. *Sense of Place and Sense of Planet: The Environmental Imagination of the Global*. Oxford: Oxford University Press, 2008. Print.

---. "Toxins, Drugs, and Global Systems: Risk and Narrative in the Contemporary Novel." *American Literature* 74.4 (2002): 747-78. Print.

Janoff, Bruce. "Black Humor, Existentialism, and Absurdity: A Generic Confusion." *Black Humor: Critical Essays*. Ed. Alan R. Pratt. New York: Garland, 1993. 27-39. Print.

Jarvis, Darryl S. L. "Risk, Globalisation and the State: A Critical Appraisal of Ulrich Beck and the World Risk Society Thesis." *Global Society* 21.1 (2007): 23-46. Print.

LeBaron, Wayne. *America's Nuclear Legacy*. New York: Nova Science Publishers, 1998. Print.

Lewis, Paul. *Cracking Up: American Humor in a Time of Conflict.* Chicago: University of Chicago Press, 2006. Print.

Lupton, Deborah. *Risk*. 2nd ed. London: Routledge, 2013. Print.

Macy, Joanna. *Despair and Personal Power in the Nuclear Age.* Philadelphia: New Society Publishers, 1983. Print.

Mizruchi, Susan. "Risk Theory and the Contemporary American Novel." *American Literary History* 22.1 (2009): 109-35. Print.

Moreno, Jonathan D. *Undue Risk: Secret State Experiments on Humans*. New York: Routledge, 2001. Print.

Morreall, John. *Comic Relief: A Comprehensive Philosophy of Humor*. Malden: Blackwell, 2009. Print.

Numasawa, Kōji. "Black Humor: An American Aspect." *Black Humor: Critical Essays*. Ed. Alan R. Pratt. New York: Garland, 1993. 41-60. Print.

O'Neill, Patrick. "The Comedy of Entropy: The Contexts of Black Humor." *Black Humor: Critical Essays*. Ed. Alan R. Pratt. New York: Garland, 1993. 61-88. Print.

Pearsall, Derek. "The Canterbury Tales II: Comedy." *The Cambridge Companion to Chaucer*. Ed. Piero Boitani and Jill Mann. 2nd ed. Cambridge: Cambridge University Press, 2003. 160-77. Print.

Pratt, Alan R. "Introduction: The Nature of Black Humor." *Black Humor: Critical Essays*. Ed. Alan R. Pratt. New York: Garland, 1993. xvii-xxv. Print.

Rosenfeld, Alvin H. "The Americanization of the Holocaust." *Commentary* 99.6 (1995): 35-40. Print.

Stephens, Martha. *The Treatment: The Story of Those Who Died in the Cincinnati Radiation Tests*. Durham: Duke University Press, 2002. Print.

Stuckey-French, Elizabeth. "Elizabeth Stuckey-French (4-12-2011)." Interview. *The Lit Show*. Web. 10 July 2013.

---. Interview with Forrest Anderson. *SalisburyPostables*. Web. 15 Feb. 2012.

---. *The Revenge of the Radioactive Lady*. New York: Doubleday, 2011. Print.

"Stuckey-French, Elizabeth: THE REVENGE OF THE RADIOACTIVE LADY." *Kirkus Reviews* 15 Dec. 2010. Academic OneFile. Web. 13 July 2013.

Welsome, Eileen. *The Plutonium Files: America's Secret Medical Experiments in the Cold War*. New York: The Dial Press, 1999. Print.

Willett, Jincy. "Nuclear Reaction." Rev. of The Revenge of the Radioactive Lady. By Elizabeth Stuckey-French. *New York Times* 11 Feb. 2011. Web. 15 Jan. 2012.

Wood, James. *The Irresponsible Self: On Laughter and the Novel*. 2004. London: Pimlico, 2005. Print.

III

Environmental Risks Across Media

CHRISTINE GERHARDT

Beyond Climate Refugees: Nature, Risk and Migration in American Poetry

In current debates about environmental risks, migration does not play as prominent a role as one might expect given the complex ways in which human-nature relationships intersect with the dynamics of movement in place. In particular, sociological and anthropological studies that have shaped the discussions about modern society as risk society, including Mary Douglas's controversial *Risk and Culture* (1982), Anthony Giddens's *Runaway World* (2002) as well as Ulrich Beck's *Ecological Politics in an Age of Risk* (1995) and *World at Risk* (2007), all address climate change, loss of biodiversity and other environmental risks without talking about human migration in greater detail.[1] Yet as we live at a cultural moment that is equally characterized by global environmental change and by people's increasing mobility within and across national borders, our understanding of human-nature interactions and the risks they involve might well profit from a more in-depth exploration of migration as a cultural practice that interacts with the natural environment in particular ways. Moreover, studies about environmental risk often engage a language of mobility—Beck, for instance defines risk as "the perceptual and cognitive schema in accordance with which a society *mobilizes* itself when it is confronted with the openness, uncertainties and obstructions of a self-created future" (*World at Risk* 4), and stresses that "the anticipation of climate change sets a fundamental transformation *in motion* in the here and now" ("Climate for Change" 258; both emphases mine). Therefore, a more explicit discussion of the role migration plays in the context of environmental risks also promises fresh insights regarding the essentially mobile dimensions of our human ways of being in the world, of the natural environment itself, and of the peculiar threats that emerge from such a highly dynamic constellation.

---

1 Conversely, Beck's *Cosmopolitan Vision* (2006), which centrally deals with issues of (im)migration, does not say much about climate change. Only more recently has Beck begun to link both topics: in "Remapping Social Inequalities in an Age of Climate Change" (2010) he discusses ways in which those who are in power shift environmental risks to those who cannot escape certain places, and in "Climate for Change, or How to Create a Green Modernity" (2010), he calls for a transnational response to climate change that would not limit people's mobility.

An important starting point is provided here by a growing interest in human migrations caused by negative environmental change. This interest manifests itself not only in such documentary films as Al Gore's *An Inconvenient Truth* (2006) and in particular Michael Nash's *Climate Refugees* (2010), but also in geographical and other place-oriented analyses that explore when and how historically specific cases of drought, sea level rise, and other forms of extreme weather have lead certain social groups to migrate.[2] These studies address a remarkably broad spectrum of risks, from the risks of negative environmental developments (such as floods or storms) via the risks people are willing to take before they consider migration (such as the loss of houses and livestock) to the risks of the migration process itself (such as security or public health threats); moreover, they consider people's responses both to anticipated catastrophes and to problems already tangible in the here and now (which, after all, can be difficult to distinguish in the case of gradual environmental changes such as droughts). Yet on another level the very focus of these studies on environmental refugees also narrows their perspective, because it suggests a surprisingly linear if not one-dimensional relationship between environmental change and migration. While research on climate refugees clearly draws attention to important and politically pressing developments, negative environmental change and migration, with their various causes and unforeseen consequences, are intertwined in ways that also point beyond the notion of one being primarily the cause and the other the effect. Environmental change alone, depending on the geographical and historical parameters taken into account, has to do with phenomena as diverse as desertification, forest dieback, and sea level rise, with species extinction, ozone depletion, and the exhaustion of natural resources; and migration, most commonly understood as the movement "from one country, place, or locality to another" (Webster), can refer to national and international (im)migration, individual and collective movements, chain, seasonal and return migration. With these dynamics being linked in multi-dimensional ways, and notions of risk playing into them on a number of levels, what interests me here is how poetry as a particularly complex and open mode of expression that invites us to see the world with different eyes participates in this ongoing cultural conversation about human-nature interaction and migratory processes. More specifically, I explore how North American poetry imagines the links between environmental change, risk, and migration as a dynamic triangular relationship that is rich in metaphorical dimensions and sidesteps simple cause-and-effect patterns, emphasizing instead the limits of human understanding vis-à-vis the complexities of the natural world and our place in it.

---

2 For a critical survey of the field see, for instance, Sabine L. Perch-Nielsen, Michèle B. Bättig and Dieter Imboden's essay "Exploring the Link between Climate Change and Migration" (2008).

The first challenge at this point involves identifying and defining a body of texts relevant to such a discussion. Over the past few decades, a vibrant body of poetry has emerged that, I believe, deserves attention for the complex and suggestive ways in which it brings environmental considerations, shifting notions of risk and migratory movements to bear upon each other. For example, Amy Clampitt's well-received *The Kingfisher* (1983) intertwines the migratory movements of birds and plants and the risks they involve with those of explorers and settlers, and her later collection *Westward* (1990) combines expressions of environmental loss with meditations on the crises brought by historical and present westward movements. Coming from a different direction, W.S. Merwin's *Travels* (1993) includes poems on the explorations of early naturalists, while his most recent book of collected and new poems, called *Migration* (2005), highlights how much the threat of ecological disaster and various kinds of geographical movement lie at the heart of his work. In Canada, as early as 1970 at the onset of modern environmental concern, Margaret Atwood's *The Journals of Susanna Moodie* explored the encounters of a nineteenth-century English immigrant author with North America's "wilderness" from the perspective of the contemporary environmental crisis, while more recently, Don McKay's collections of verse *Camber* (2004) and *Field Marks* (2006) have linked ideas about bird and other migrations to thoughts on human displacement and fate. The African American poet Ed Roberson, in *To See the Earth Before the End of the World* (2010) reflects on the blindness that accompanies the excessive mobility of the twenty-first century, and Craig Santos Perez's *from Unincorporated Territory [Hacha]* (2008) talks about the threats Guam's environment is facing as an incorporated American territory. In Native American poetry, Michael Kabotie's *Migration Tears: Poems about Transitions* (1987) describes his people's shifts between rural and urban places, intertwining the history of environmental degradation with that of white settlement, while Joy Harjo's *How We Became Human* (2001) testifies to her overlapping concerns with environmental memory and (forced) migrations. Finally, a number of transnational or multicultural collections, for instance Gloria Anzaldúa's *Borderlands/La Frontera: The New Mestiza* (1987) and Lorna Dee Cervantes's *Drive* (2005), Carolina Hospital's *The Child of Exile* (2004) and Virgil Suárez *90 Miles* (2005), as well as anthologies such as *American Diaspora: Poetry of Displacement* (2001) and *Inclined to Speak. An Anthology of Contemporary Arab American Poetry* (2008) also include individual poems that engage environmental perspectives, and the potential risks of human-nature relationships, in conjunction with the dynamics of (im)migration. This diverse body of texts significantly broadens and also destabilizes the ways in which studies on climate refugees have begun to link environmental concerns, risk and migration. As poems, they do so not only thematically—that is, by emphasizing different histories and geographies, ethnic traditions and political concerns—but also conceptually, by bringing the imagination, and in particular, a focus on subjectivity and language, suggestiveness and paradox, to the intersection between environmental crisis, risk, and migration.

So far, American poems that address the specter of negative environmental change in conjunction with the dynamics of migratory unrest have not received any sustained critical attention. To my knowledge, the only book-length study that combines an interest in ecological and migratory issues in American poetry is Robert Boschman's *In the Way of Nature: Ecology and Westward Expansion in the Poetry of Anne Bradstreet, Elizabeth Bishop and Amy Clampitt* (2009). A few years earlier, Bonnie Costello's *Shifting Ground: Reinventing Landscape in Modern American Poetry* (2003) already included a chapter on the nomadic aesthetic of Clampitt's nature poetry, but neither Boschman nor Costello explicitly deal with notions of risk.[3] That there are no more publications in this vein can only in part be explained by the marginal status poetry continues to assume in ecocritical and transnational studies. This reluctance may also have to do with the prevailing notion that environmental and overtly social concerns somehow belong to different realms. The idea that literature that focuses on the natural world has little to say about social differences and vice versa has already been unsettled by studies in such newly emerging areas as African American ecocriticism, post-colonial ecocriticism and, more recently, Marxist ecocriticism; in each of these fields, critics have come to identify unexpectedly diverse bodies of literary texts that address environmental issues in relation to social and political conflicts, and have kept refining their analytical tools in order to address the questions that emerge from such texts. I believe that American poetry that is concerned with the relationship between environmental change and migration invites precisely such a multiply-oriented critical perspective, the notion of risk providing a productive reference here both as thematic point of intersection and as conceptual common ground between concern for the environment and migration. The following analysis is an attempt to systematize how such poems talk about environmental change, risk, and migration as interrelated themes, which formal and stylistic choices are particularly suggestive in these constellations, and how the concepts of mobility and environmental risk come into play here, informing each other while also being redefined in the process.

---

3 Also worth mentioning here is Denise Low's essay "Two Aspects of Western Landscape: Migration Trail and Landmarks" (2008), which pulls together a considerable body of texts, both prose and poetry, that link the topic of migration to fresh perspectives on the natural environment.

I. Human Migration, Nature's Destruction, and the Risk of Nature's Revenge

A first group of American poems that combine the concern for the environment and migration in ways that push beyond the critical interest in climate refugees does so by turning towards migrations that were not caused by, but did themselves cause negative environmental change and the anticipation of future catastrophe. In particular, such poems imaginatively revisit the colonization and progressive European settlement of the American continent, linking these migratory movements to the destruction of America's primeval flora and fauna and to a growing sense of foreboding. As such, they are part of a longer tradition of environmental poems that criticize the destruction of nature caused by first settlers and later generations of (im)migrants, a tradition that includes texts as diverse as the 1904 ballad "The Revenge of the Forest Primeval" by the German-American Konrad Nies, and W.S. Merwin's 1967 "The Last One." Yet where these poems spell out how the destruction of America's forests by presumptuous immigrants caused a veritable environmental catastrophe in which a vengeful nature is already striking back, the poems I am interested in here bracket this actual catastrophe, focusing on its anticipation—in other words, on risk. Rather than simply reverse the cause-and-effect pattern that underlies the concept of environmental refugees, these poems engage the fear of nature's revenge as multidimensional trope to rethink the conflicts that emerge from our historically mobile interrelationship with the natural world.

A particularly revealing poem that activates such an environmental risk scenario is "The People of the Boat," published in Morton Marcus' collection of prose poems *When People Could Fly* (1997). Marcus was a Californian descendant of Russian immigrants and author of eleven volumes of poetry, including *The Santa Cruz Mountain Poems* (1972) about nature as seen from the perspective of a hiker, and *Pages from a Scrapbook of Immigrants* (1988), which explores his ancestors' commitment to mobility as well as to place. In "The People of the Boat," the first person (collective) speaker surveys the entire history of America's European settlement, calling attention to the natural destruction that followed each wave of migration, and registering the immigrants' intensifying sense of "foreboding."

This combined concern for the environment, risk and migration characterizes the poem from the very beginning: in the opening lines, the first settlers watch "the shaggy shoreline," perceive the land with its "rocks and trees," and experience "a moment of questioning as well as foreboding"; in the next paragraphs, new groups of settlers swing "axes and sledgehammers," fell "birch tree and pine," and eradicate "animals and the painted people" from the land, whose "ghosts," however, grow along with the sense of foreboding; and in the end, recent immigrants realize that the long-anticipated negative consequences of such destruction are now about to materialize in the form of nature striking back:

> Storms gather behind the buildings, cloudbanks that rumble like old forebodings. "It is weather, only weather," the people say. "It will vanish in a deluge of rain." But by this even the newcomers mean a new kind of rain, one that bites at the buildings and streets like teeth in the jaws of avenging ghosts. (*When People Could Fly* 43)

This fear of acid rain, imagined as unpredictable "avenging ghosts" that threaten to devour America's cities, marks the culmination here of a historical process in which nature's exploitation has been accompanied, but was never actually averted by a growing sense of risk.

Marcus' metaphor of avenging ghosts crystallizes the perspectives this poem unfolds in terms of the role migratory movements have long played in the context of environmental change and risk. First of all, the trope of vengeful ghosts highlights how much the fear of an environmental catastrophe that has been caused in part by global migrations is linked to a perceived shift in agency from humans to nature: where the beginning of Marcus' poem is dominated by the mobile colonists' vigorous logging, lashing and tarring, up and against an overall passive and static nature, the end reduces recent immigrants to a "wild-eyed and mumbling" mass, "shipwrecked sailors, lost and penniless" who are stuck locally and mentally, while faced with aggressive and dynamic "storms" that "gather" and "cloudbanks" that "rumble"; a series of questions and passive constructions, and the constant repetition of the term "foreboding," further undermine the sense of human agency and control. Moreover, the trope also foregrounds the central role the very idea of mobility plays in conceptualizing environmental risk in conjunction with migration. The metaphor of avenging ghosts not only casts nature as active and uncontainably, unpredictably mobile, but the risk of environmental catastrophe, too, is understood in geographically mobile terms. Finally, the image of the most recent migrants fearing nature's revenge in the form of bad weather that rumbles "like *old* forebodings" yet will turn out to be a "*new* kind of rain" (emphasis added) also foregrounds an often neglected historical continuity between the old biblical fear of God's revenge and the new global sense of environmental risk, without disregarding the qualitative difference between the two.

A second poem that imagines historical migrations as originating moment of environmental destruction and risk, in terms that rethink the fear of God's revenge as fear of nature's revenge, is Nicole Cooley's "John Winthrop, 'Reasons to be Considered for … the Intended Plantation in New England,' 1629." Cooley is a New Orleans-born author whose most recent book of poetry *Breach* (2010) focuses on hurricane Katrina, anticipating the destructive force of this violently mobile event, and surveying its effects on the landscape and social structures, including people who resist migration. The poem "John Winthrop" that concerns me here is from her earlier volume *The Afflicted Girls* (2004) about the Salem witchcraft trials and shows how the Puritans' movement to the "new world," their subjugation of nature, and a sense of impending disaster were intertwined with the demonization of women.

Because the poem pulls together Winthrop's arguments for migration months before the Arbella's actual journey, it is all anticipation, an anticipation that, from a late twentieth-century perspective, also has to do with fearing environmental disaster. After the poem's title calls attention to the Puritan great migration, and an epigraph quotes Genesis 1:28, "Increase and multiply, replenish the earth and subdue it," which seems to advocate people's exploitation of nature to their own advantage, the poem's opening question "Who is the author of Disaster?" immediately links the migrants' relationship to nature to a profound sense of danger. This sense of danger points beyond the religious fear that the new continent might turn out to have more in common with hell than with a new Garden of Eden. And the surprising suggestion that "for an answer," one should "read / The Book of Nature or / a woman's face" indicates that the cause for a future catastrophe might lie less in God's punishment than in nature' active resistance to being "subdued," and in the resistance of women symbolically linked to the natural realm. After stanzas two and three briefly outline the Puritan idea of repeating the migration from "Egypt" to "New Jerusalem" as well as their notion of the New World as "wife,/her body City on the Hill," the poem culminates in a fourth stanza plus a concluding couplet that highlight once more how much the subjugation of nature was at the heart of the Puritans' overarching sense of fear:

> Split the trees at the root,
> slash the salt grass to clear
> a long road to the future.
> Lock your wife in the house.
> Keep yourself safe.
> Remember that the Invisible World is full of women.
> (*The Afflicted Girls* 2)

If it is difficult to say in these lines whether the Puritans lashed out against nature and women or against nature as woman, and whether the sense of fear was the reason or the cause of this destruction, this seems to be precisely the point. Assuming the voice of Winthrop himself, the poem offers a forceful account of how these migrants' fear of a feminized nature and of actual women, and their relentless subjugation of both, continually perpetuated each other.

As this poem reimagines the destructive dynamics of historical migrations from the perspective of the current environmental crisis, it again employs the notion of nature's revenge. Here too the trope crystallizes how the dynamics of people's migratory activities segue into evocations of nature's potential agency, shifting the attention from the destruction of a passive nature that sustains human survival towards the uncontrollable energies of an equally destructive nature: in the beginning, human activities linked to the "Intended Plantation in New England," especially the biblically sanctioned subjugation of nature, lead to a fear of disaster that is cast as nature's active "answer"; in the end, a vivid projection of the settlers splitting trees and slashing grass, the admonitions to "keep yourself safe" and "[r]emember that the Invisible World is full of women" imply that the maltreated nature will turn into a threat to the settlers, conflating nature and women in ways that increase a sense of nature's avenging agency. The form of the poem contributes to the impression as its stanzas create a pattern of downward stairs on the page, a movement that can neither be stopped by three inserted Winthrop lines in italics, nor by the final couplet whose call for safety remains without consequence. Moreover, the notion of nature' revenge again blurs the line between the seventeenth-century biblical fear of disaster and the late twentieth-century anticipation of an incalculable global environmental catastrophe: in the poem, the presumption of Puritan axioms is forever destabilized by an anticipatory fear of nature's (and women's) revenge, a fear that already has a presence in England before the great migration, will inflect Puritan action in the New World, and is there to stay.

Overall, these two poems, in reconsidering past settler movements as originating moments for the late twentieth-century sense of impending environmental catastrophe, bring more to the current debate than a stronger consideration of migration as a principal cause of negative environmental developments. By picturing the threat of an environmental crisis as intensifying fear of nature's revenge they also pair the perceived loss of human control with a respectful recognition of nature's agency, a humbling shift in perspective that tends to remain subliminal in most discussions about environmental risk that are primarily concerned with diagnosing and ultimately overcoming the loss of human control. Moreover, by alluding to nature's revenge as a force that is not bound to a specific place, these poems contribute to a growing recognition of environmental risk as part of a mobile world and as in itself mobile, and can indirectly be linked to what Beck called the necessary process of "overcoming the nation-state narrowness" of perspectives and politics that stand in the way of effectively dealing with the global environmental crisis ("Climate for Change" 258). Finally, by expressing a fear of nature's revenge that transcends both space and time, these poems take a long view of historical development. As such, they can be said to link current ideas and sensibilities to the early modern period when colonization and global trade first introduced the idea of "risk" that would come to shape what Beck diagnoses as the "world risk society" ("World Risk Society as Cosmopolitan Society?").

II. Human Migration, Nature's Migration, and the Risk of Collective Death

A second group of poems relevant here suggest that migration is an integral part of human existence, not only an exceptional and problematic phenomenon that occurs in response to negative environmental change and has itself contributed to such change. In these poems, movement in space belongs to being human with all the risks it involves—just as the migratory movements of certain animals and plants, with all the threats they face, are part of their existence. As they talk about nature's migratory patterns in ways that subtly resonate as metaphors for human migrations, they are related to a broad tradition of poems that symbolically link experiences of displacement, exile or alienation with the experiences certain migrating birds, fish or mammals, as for instance Lorna Dee Cervantes's "Emplumada," Virgil Suarez's "Indigo Bunting's Last Molt," and Don McKay's "Load," as well as Elena Georgiou's "Dream Diary of a Migrant Bird" and Lucy Dougall's "Migrations." The poems I am concerned with here, however, shift the attention from the existential risks individual migrating animals and, by extension, people have always faced toward a new level of risks they encounter because of environmental destruction. In particular, they engage the trope of migrating animals facing collective death due to loss of habitat and other negative developments in ways that communicate a keen awareness of a global environment risk that includes all human beings, and all living creatures, also and especially in our common mobility.

A comparatively early poem that addresses these concerns is "In a Clearing" from W.S. Merwin's collection *The Lice* (1967). Merwin moved back and forth between the American East Coast and England, Spain and France before finally settling in Hawaii, and is known for his life-long interest in nature and movement, most clearly expressed in his 1993 collection *Travels* and in his extensive 2005 volume of collected and new poems *Migration*. The plaintive poem "In a Clearing" envisions a eerie, dream-like mass migration of various kinds of animals away from the earth and off into the darkness, in ways that resonate as impending mass extinction that has not only been caused by humans, but also metaphorically includes humans in this last journey towards death.

The poem begins with herds of hooved animals "flowing" through what seems to be a purely imaginative landscape of the mind:

> The unnumbered herds flow like lichens
> Along the darkness each carpet at its height

In silence
without end
Without death
Nothing is before them nothing after
Among the hooves the hooves' brothers the shells
In a sea (*Migration* 138)

This dream sequence of animals calmly moving towards death without ever arriving does more than loosely link a specific animal migration to human movements in place, and more than rephrase the notion that all life always has been and always will be a journey towards death. This halting elegy also expresses a sense of what would soon be called global environmental risk, mainly by way of the alarming vision of a mass migration that points towards mass death. For one, the migration consists of apparently endless numbers of different species, from shells to mammals, gentle "herds" that are increasingly enveloped by death, both as a word, "death / With its many tongues that no god could speak / That can describe / Nothing that cannot die," and in images of light "go[ing] out" and of "vanish[ing]." Moreover, the actual catastrophe is ultimately withheld—culminating in the paradoxical image of a rising, yet dying sun, and aptly expressed by Merwin's characteristic lingering lines without any punctuation—which turns this deceptively peaceful animal migration into an haunting image of risk. Finally, the imaginary mass migration is caused by the devastation of natural places that these "unnumbered herds" would depend on—the speaker sees the animals "Passing through senses / As through bright clearings surrounded with pain," which evokes not simply innocent open spaces in a forest, but land whose vegetation has been brutally destroyed; when the poem ends with these ceaseless herds that are about to leave "A small place / Where a dying sun rises," it anticipates a mass migration that responds to what seems to be a global environmental devastation.

On a more abstract level, this disturbing death song conjoins notions of negative environmental change, risk and migration in multiple and paradoxical ways. The trope of a massive animal migration towards death shows that in the contemporary context of nature's large-scale destruction, migration has lost much of its environmental innocence as a basic, "natural" mode of being in the world that animals share with humans, or as metaphor for life as a journey that must ultimately lead to death. Nature's migrations, and the human migrations they evoke, now also refer to a precarious form of existence that we all share, because all life hinges on a certain degree of dependable places to sustain it; since such places are increasingly damaged and destroyed, all of us are no longer faced only with the individual risks of living mobile lives, but also with an accelerated, untimely mass extinction. At the same time, the trope highlights the differences between animal and human migrations. Even though, or precisely because, it suggests a shared vulnerability on the basis of a shared geographical mobility, it also emphasizes that this shared vulnerability was caused by human actions, including those related to the dynamics of settlement and colonization, which undermines any easy symbolic association between animal migrations and human migrations.

A second poem in which human migrations are seen in relation to nature's migrations in a context of environmental change and risk is Amy Clampitt's "Urn Burial and the Butterfly Migration," from her 1985 volume *What the Light was Like*. Clampitt, who is a descendant of nineteenth-century pioneers, grew up in Iowa, and spent her adult life in New York City, has referred to herself both as a "poet of place" (*Predecessors, Et Cetera* 163) and as a "poet of displacement" (Salter xiii). Her work is increasingly celebrated for the intricate ways in which it shows our relationship to the natural world as being constantly in flux; Bonnie Costello, for instance, has argued that her poetry relinquishes the idea(l) of a rooted identity and "imitat[es] the restlessness of nature" (117), and Robert Boschman has stressed her double-preoccupation with uprootedness and with loss of cultural memory (88). In the elegy "Urn Burial and the Butterfly Migration," the burial of the speaker's younger brother as "old settler / now among old settlers" is the occasion for an extended meditation on misleading ideas of stillness in life and death, against which the speaker sets her own notion of movement as key element of nature and human existence, which involves risks that are subtly linked to environmental concerns.

At first, the speaker seems to fully embrace the conventions of pastoral elegies, because she not only retells the old story of all life as journey towards death, but appears to express the hope that death can be overcome through nature's regenerative dynamics. A graveyard scene that revolves around the idea of "Rest for the body's residue" provokes her to exclaim "O friable repose of the organic!" and to offer various associations that show nature, human existence, and death to be mobile, and intertwined in that very mobility. She mentions "ladybirds' enameled herds," milkweed that spills their "prodigal,/ packed silks," and "the air-travelling" monarch butterflies, all of which are suggestive of human "settler" movements as well, and explicitly compares her own "scattered" family to migratory plants:

Like the dandelion,
that quintessential successful
immigrant, its offspring gone
to fluff, dug-in hard-scrabble
nurtured a generation of
the mobile, nomads enamored
of cloverleafs, of hangars, of
that unrest whose home-*our*
home-is motion. (*Selected Poems* 91)

The threat of death informs all of these migrations; the ladybirds that "gather for the winter" are "red pearls of an unsaid rosary to waking," crickets try to secure their "individual survival," mulleins "hunker," thistleheads are "frayed," milkweed "gondolas" have "wrecked stalks," and the butterfly chrysalises contain a "foreboding," while her siblings, in their "mere haste toward something else" are compared to a dandelion's "offspring gone to fluff." This connection between nature's and human migratory movements in life, in death and beyond culminates in the poem's turn to butterflies as established symbol for traveling human souls, when "caravans" of monarch butterflies in their "marathon" across America are linked to the rising ashes of the speaker's brother. In other words, nature's migrations and human migrations, and the ways in which death is implicated in these movements, are associated with each other in multiple ways, "naturalizing" our mobile existence as common journey towards death.

But the flight of the butterflies, this traditional emblem of overcoming death through resurrection, is itself threatened by death, so that in this poem, too, an animal migration faced by massive death expresses a sense of environmental risk. If modern elegies have become increasingly skeptical regarding nature's ability to console us at times of human loss, as Jahan Ramazani suggests, offering "fractured speech and memorable puzzlings" instead (ix), Clampitt subtly links this skepticism to nature's vulnerability in times of environmental crisis.[4] In the poem, the monarchs are surrounded by wind that sounds like keening and by "a treacherous long sob of apprehension," which links the mourning for the dead brother to an intense foreboding that points beyond the "normal" losses the butterflies regularly face when millions of them migrate more than 2000 miles across large parts of the US. Similarly, when the speaker refers to their passage as "a miracle that will not live to taste the scarce nectar, the / ample horror of another summer," this notion foreshadows more than the deaths of those who will not return because of their short life span, which ranges from 2 weeks to 8 months. Towards the end of the poem, the fragile butterflies, who are known to depend on exactly the same trees in Southern California and Mexico for their survival and are increasingly threatened by logging and urban development, emerge "in flickering clots, in dozens / above the parked cars of the / shopping malls of Kansas" and "along / the Dallas-Fort Worth airport's / utopian thoroughfares," and when the speaker describes them as "landless caravans" who leave an "elegiac signature of nations who have no language," an entire species seems to be signing off, turned landless because

4 While Ramazani discusses the changing role of nature in modern elegies, especially in terms of new, often ironic versions of the pathetic fallacy (217), he does not discuss how the environmental crisis plays into these re-conceptualizations of elegiac nature. Similarly, Jeffrey Thomson's essay on elegiac poems that "recognize in sorrow part of the pattern of the natural world" (160) does not look at poems that might link such sorrow to the critical state of nature itself.

the natural places they depend on have been "developed" to accommodate human mobility. The poem's halting tone, intensified by numerous enjambments, further reinforces the sense of the butterflies' impending geographical displacement, as well as the overall atmosphere of risk this poem conveys. Clampitt's elegy for her deceased brother, then, may be much less directly concerned with environmental change than Merwin's, but she, too, engages the metaphor of a large scale, potentially deadly animal migration in ways that give voice to a sense of impending environmental disaster.

Overall, such poems address the relationships between environmental crisis, risk and migration in ways that foreground how critically our human movements are implicated in nature's movements. In particular, the trope of migrating animals facing the threat of collective death due to loss of habitat and other environmental changes condenses several contradictory aspects of this relationship. On the one hand, the trope reaches back to conventionalized ways of imagining life as a journey that ultimately leads to death, casting migration not so much as an exceptional state that we can or should avoid, but as one we share with nature. But at the same time, the trope serves as an indicator of how much at risk we currently are, not only in our "naturally" mobile existence and the vulnerability such existence always entails, but also because of the environmental destruction for which we alone, in our very mobility, are responsible. Apart from these critical reconsiderations of the human position as simultaneously part of nature and separate from it, these poems, in the way they deploy and revise the conventions of pastoral elegies, also make room for mourning as an aspect of anticipating possible collective doom, for expressing an affect that remains almost wholly muted in current conversations about environmental risk. Finally, they activate the dilemma of our mobile existence, in the face of which the sense of narrative closure and simple morality fail alike. Yet while they offer no solution, they manage to invest the paradoxical implications of the forceful imagery of mass migration into death with an ethical urgency in ways that are, perhaps, only possible in poetry.

III. Human Migration, Destabilized Knowledge, and the Problem of Power

In a third group of poems, several of the previously discussed links between nature, risk, and migration come together in ways that foreground the destabilization of earlier frames of reference that the migration to unknown places tends to involve. Such poems suggest that people's geographical movement and the basic, existential risks it entails can morph into a fundamental epistemological uncertainty in terms of how to relate to the natural world. This uncertainty in turn can be transformed into new, less exploitative modes of interacting with the environment that are as much in flux as the people who migrate and the places in which they live. However, migration, as a quintessential experience in which old frameworks no longer fit the new context, does not simply become the starting point for new environmentally resonant relationships with the land here. Rather, these poems present two conflicting responses to such migratory uncertainty—one that sees the non-human world with fresh eyes and develops less domineering and destructive modes of interacting with it, and one that insists on approaching the environment along old lines of control and exploitation. The new kind of environmental risk, the anticipation of a future catastrophe caused by the unintended consequences of our own actions, emerges from the difficulty of making those risk-sensitive and potentially more environmentally oriented migratory voices heard.

An example for this dynamic can be found in the poem "The Planters," which is part of *The Journals of Susanna Moodie* (1970) by Canada's most prolific contemporary author Margaret Atwood. Atwood is mainly known as an environmentally oriented prose writer, but her collections of poetry, including *Double Persephone* (1961), *The Circle Game* (1966), and *The Animals in That Country* (1968), also receive increasing critical attention, mainly for their interest in how gender, cultural and historical differences inflect people's relationships with the natural world. In "The Planters," the nineteenth-century immigrant Susanna Moodie is supremely aware of the existential risks she and her husband are facing in their new surroundings, and also of a more profound ignorance vis-à-vis nature, and translates this multilayered uncertainty into environmental sensitivity. The particular sense of environmental risk in this poem comes from a constellation in which her recognition of human action as destructive remains of little consequence because she is in a disempowered position herself.

Throughout the poem, the first-person speaker juxtaposes two opposing epistemological relations between the migrants and the non-human environment, represented by her husband and herself:

> If they let go
> of that illusion solid to them as a shovel,
>
> open their eyes even for a moment
> to these trees, to this particular sun
> they would be surrounded, stormed, broken
>
> in upon by branches, roots, tendrils, the dark
> side of light
> as I am. (*Journals* 17)

As she watches her husband and other men farm a tiny field, she realizes that they respond to the concrete threats they are faced with and to the more profound uncertainty of their position in the Canadian "bush" with a mixture of denial and violence. "They deny the ground they stand on / pretending this dirt is the future," and engage the newly cleared Canadian wilderness by way of classical paradigms of domination. Unsettled by doubt and uncertainty, they resort to willful myopia, refusing to be changed by the unfamiliar environment. The female speaker, by contrast, realizes that the men who cultivate vegetables between a "jagged" forest line and "jagged river" are in danger, as if between two saws or the jaws of a beast. Her awareness of their precarious position in an unknown forest translates into the perception both of nature's potentially overwhelming agency, and of the destructiveness of the settlers' farming practices who turn densely alive ecosystems into a "stumpy patch of cleared land" that looks like a fresh wound. So while the men are unable or unwilling to engage the land more on its own terms, the speaker transforms the movement to and within an unfamiliar territory, and the dangers all of them are facing, in to a proto-ecological awareness of the land and their attempts to clear it.

The unresolved conflict between male migrants who rely on mechanisms of nature's control and refuse to see how their actions will imperil themselves, and a female speaker who perceives this threat as part of an increased environmental sensibility but does not and perhaps cannot act is at the heart of this poem's careful consideration of the interplay between nature, risk and migration. By way of this structure, the poem expresses more than a concern for colonial migrations as originating moment of environmental risk perception and of an increasing fear of nature's revenge, which also informs its play of tropes. The juxtaposition of these two positions also foregrounds that the links between human-nature relationships, risk, and migration are further inflected by social structures: it shows how migration can cement or subvert established hierarchies (or both at the same time), and how such processes can influence and be influenced by the migrants' different degrees of risk perception and their abilities to turn such awareness into environmentally oriented positions. On a different level, this poetic structure, this unresolved tension, addresses a new kind of environmental risk that emerges from migratory constellations precisely because the two kinds of human-nature interaction and risk perception are linked to social hierarchies. The risk is that the increasing environmental sensibilities that migration can yield do not translate into changed action because they reside with the powerless. After all, the woman may be the speaker of the poem, but she speaks it as a private journal entry and thus as relatively inconsequential text. And yet the private nature of the poem is itself a trope and the cultural context of the poem is late modernity, in which the unheard voice of the powerless is vindicated by its foresight. In this respect, the tension between two migratory perspectives on the land that remains unresolved in the world of the poem but appears in a different light in the context of twentieth and early twenty-first debates about the global environmental crisis also draws attention to environmental risks we may currently be facing due to similar exclusionary mechanisms.

A second poem in this vein is "Crossing 'a piece of earth'" by the Mexican-American writer Teresa Palomo Acosta; it was published in her 1999 book *Nile & Other Poems* and is also part of the 2005 anthology *Crossing into America: The New Literature of Immigration*. Here, a Mexican speaker is about to cross the US/Mexican border, and the awareness of the immediate risks involved in the process of simply "crossing a piece of earth" changes the migrant's perception of the land in environmentally oriented ways, while the American guards are unable to let the context of migration alter their controlling position. Since the watchmen are not migrants themselves but guardians of a boundary that serves to prevent migration, the poem offers an interesting variation on a new kind of risk that develops out of the difficulty to communicate across lines of social and political power, in a migratory context that potentially enables a more environmentally attuned outlook.

This migration poem, too, revolves around the tension between two perspectives on the land in a migratory context. "At the border the gatekeepers sit with loaded guns," men who seem subtly aware of the fact that the desert around them is honeycombed by underground waterways, that Mexican migrants identify with these mobile elements of the place, and that this dynamic threatens their own, only seemingly secure position: "the gatekeepers want so to stop /the flow of history slipping from them / as it undulates underground." In response to the peculiar risks they are facing due to their position in a place full of mobility, the representatives of US imperial power resort to traditional mechanisms of control, enforcing the "latest migra laws" to prevent people's transborder movement. For the Mexican migrant, by contrast, the imminent danger of crossing this "simple piece of land" leads to an alternative approach. Confronted with the double-risk she faces from the armed patrols and an inhospitable desert, the speaker realizes that an "official map […] cannot measure precisely the lay of the land":

> At the border
> Where the gatekeepers eye me
> I dream up a way to set my own eyes
> On other markings in the desert nearby
> - The sagüaros -
> As a means to know the land
> And our history as a fluid movement in time
> Underground […]
> It leaps through aqueducts and under the bridges
> And into paradise.

It makes its own lay of the land
And tells me that I know the time has come
To stop waiting for a ruling
Promoting the just use of land/rights
On either side of the border I cross. (*Crossing into America* 74)

The old map still in hand, the speaker "begin[s] to reconsider the rules" and imagines an alternative movement through the land—replacing the American guards with large cactuses, considering the Mexican people's collective history as part of the land and its "underground" dynamics, and arriving at a political ideal of "just" uses of the land, a vision of environmental justice that implies justice towards the land itself. This dreamt-up, fluid migration does not lead to a naïve identification with the place but remains fully aware of the risks it involves, since the land is understood as dynamic und uncontainable:

Still, I know that at the border
The places for me to discard my map and wade into the water
And assuredly swim across
Stretch farther
Than either
We
Or laws
Have eyes to see. (*Crossing into America* 75)

These lines suggest that even a migration attuned to the land and its histories is risky because it means entering a territory that has potentially unfathomable dimensions. In other words, the existential risks of migration do not lead to renewed gestures of control here, but to an alternative outlook that combines political activism with environmental sensitivity.

Again, it is significant for this poem's interplay of people's relationships to nature, risk, and migration that the conflict remains unresolved. In the end, "the men who keep the rules / Reorder the time and space and lay of the land" force the "illegal" migrants into vans and back to Mexico, where they plan the next crossing, a "cycle […] permanently fixed." Here, too, the poem remains in a state of limbo, and a new sense of risk emerges from the tension between these two positions, and especially from the power differential the speaker enacts vis-à-vis the guards; as in Atwood's poem, the environmentally more sensitive position is expressed from the perspective of the politically disempowered voice and "risks" remaining unheard. And again, the act of writing and publishing poetry can, at least in part, revoke this mechanism—an idea that goes hand in hand with the speaker's explicit embrace of imagining, or "dreaming up" an alternative approach to the land that is both mobile and environmentally inflected yet must itself remain risky, also because of the land's ultimate unknowability.

Such poems, then, turn to the ways in which human movement in place undermines old frames of reference, including those used to justify nature's domination and control, and show that such uncertainty, being part of risk consciousness, also constitutes an opportunity since it invites a new perspective on the natural world. However, rather than suggesting that the flexibility and readjustment that migration requires, and the various risks it involves, invariably lead to a heightened sensibility for the places that provide the grounds of migration in these poems, they emphasize that such destabilization can just as well cement exploitative positions vis-à-vis the land. By condensing this tension in the figure of an unresolved personalized conflict—between nineteenth century male and female colonizers, or between twenty-first century Mexican migrants and American border patrols—these poems communicate how environmental risk perception and its effects on environmental positions in the context of migration are inflected by socio-political hierarchies in complex and contradictory ways. They allow those migrants whose existential sense of risk entails environmentally sensitive perspectives to assume the role of poetic speaker, yet show them as voiceless within the social hierarchies that bind them. The point here is not that socially and politically disempowered migrants are particularly prone to develop green positions. Rather, by letting the voiceless speak, they cast environmental risk perception and the revisions in human-nature interaction it can engender as imaginative dynamic whose transformative potential pushes against but is also held back by social and politically hierarchies. By avoiding narrative closure, they remain suspended in the moment of risk, with the social and economic catastrophe perpetually looming in the uncertain future.

Taken together, all of the poems discussed here offer challenging new perspectives on the ways in which the natural environment, risk and migration intersect in America's cultural imagination. Most generally speaking, they reveal that migration is a significant parameter in contemporary literary conceptualizations of environmental risk, one that deserves critical attention in the fields of literary and cultural studies. One of the specific achievements here certainly lies in their thematic diversity and complexity, especially in their readiness to think about migration and environmental risk in ways that consistently point beyond the phenomenon of climate refugees. With their interests in America's settlement as a cause of negative environmental change, in the similarities and differences between human and nature's migrations, and in the unsettling experience of migration as a source of conflicting views of the land, these poems call attention to the intricate and often contradictory ways in which migrations can inflect human-nature interactions, and cast environmental risk perception itself as a mobile phenomenon that is shaped by but also transcends historical and geographical boundaries.

At the same time, their highly symbolic meditations bring a number of affective responses to the environmental, social and political issues involved here that rethink some of the basic parameters of human-nature interaction. When the recurrent trope of fearing nature's revenge implies a humbling sense of nature's autonomy, when the haunting image of an anticipated mass death of migrating animals enables expressions of environmental mourning, and when links between environmental risk perception and social hierarchies are discussed in terms of irresolvable interpersonal conflicts, such poems productively complicate the relationships between negative environmental change and human migrations, between environmental risks perceived by humans and the threats faced by nature, and between the human desire to control nature and our limited ability to understand it.

As such, these poems' passionate commitment to the imagination might well be their most significant contribution to the emerging cultural dialog about the environment, risk and migration. Even the most narrative of the poems discussed here engage language in ways that destabilize notions of linear progression in space and time, and of direct, one-dimensional links between cause and effect. Instead, they present environmental change, risk, and migration in complex interrelation with one another—just as they envision the human subject in relation to the natural environment, forever shifting between striving for control over nature's potentially threatening forces and gestures of subjecting oneself to them. Thus, negotiating the de-centered human subject position in the tension between migratory movement, environmental change, and the risks both involve, is at the heart of these poems. If it is true, as Ulrich Beck suggests, that the "current seductive naïve catastrophic realism" ("Climate for Change" 258) considerably limits present risk communication, poetry, as a particularly multilayered and evocative mode of expression that strains against notions of representation, linearity, and rationality, may be particularly well suited to face this multilayered moment of crisis.

Works Cited

Acosta, Teresa Palomo. "Crossing 'a piece of earth.'" *Crossing into America: The New Literature of Immigration.* Ed. Louis Mendoza and S. Shankar. New York: New Press, 2005. 73-75. Print.

Atwood, Margaret. *The Journals of Susanna Moodie*. Oxford: Oxford University Press, 1970. Print.

Beck, Ulrich. "Climate for Change, or How to Create a Green Modernity." *Theory, Culture & Society* 27.2-3 (2010): 254-66. Print.

---. *Cosmopolitan Vision*. Malden, M.A.: Blackwell, 2006. Print.

---. *Ecological Politics in an Age of Risk*. Cambridge: Polity Press, 1995. Print.

---. “Remapping Social Inequalities in an Age of Climate Change: For a Cosmopolitan Renewal of Sociology.” *Global Networks. A Journal of Transnational Affairs* 10.2 (2010): 165-81. Print.

---. “World Risk Society as Cosmopolitan Society?: Ecological Questions in a Framework of Manufactured Uncertainties.” *Theory Culture Society* 13.1 (1996): 1-31. Print.

---. *World at Risk*. Malden, M.A.: Polity Press, 2007. Print.

Boschman, Robert. *In the Way of Nature: Ecology and Westward Expansion in the Poetry of Anne Bradstreet, Elizabeth Bishop and Amy Clampitt*. Jefferson, NC: McFarland, 2009. Print.

Cervantes, Lorna Dee. *Drive: The First Quartet*. San Antonio, TX: Wings Press, 2005. Print.

Charara, Hayan, Ed. *Inclined to Speak. An Anthology of Contemporary Arab American Poetry*. Fayetteville: University of Arkansas Press, 2008. Print.

Clampitt, Amy. *The Kingfisher*. New York: Knopf, 1983. Print.

---. *Predecessors, Et Cetera: Essays*. Ann Arbor: University of Michigan Press, 1991. Print.

---. *Selected Poems*. Ed. Mary Jo Salter. New York: Borzoi-Knopf, 2012. Print.

---. *Westward*. New York: Knopf, 1990. Print.

Cooley, Nicole. *The Afflicted Girls*. Baton Rouge: Louisiana State University Press, 2004. Print.

Costello, Bonnie. *Shifting Ground: Reinventing Landscape in Modern American Poetry*. Harvard University Press, 2003. Print.

Cruz, Victor Hernández. *The Mountain in the Sea*. Minneapolis: Coffee House Press, 2006. Print.

Dungy, Camille T., ed. *Black Nature: Four Centuries of African American Nature Poetry*. Athens, GA: University of Georgia Press, 2009. Print.

Douglas, Mary, and Aaron Wildavsky. *Risk and Culture: An Essay on the Selection of Technological and Environmental Dangers*. Berkeley: University of California Press, 1982. Print.

Giddens, Anthony. *Runaway World: How Globalization Is Reshaping Our Lives*. London: Profile, 2002. Print.

Hospital, Carolina. *The Child of Exile*. Houston, TX: Arte Público Press, 2004. Print.

Low, Denise. “Two Aspects of Western Landscape: Migration Trail and Landmarks.” *Midwest Quarterly* 49.2 (Winter 2008): 200-21. Print.

McKay, Don. *Camber. Selected Poems*. Toronto: McClelland & Stewart, 2004. Print.

McKay, Don. *Field Marks: The Poetry of Don McKay*. Waterloo, CA: Wilfrid Laurier University Press, 2006. Print.

Marcus, Morton. “The People of the Boat.” *When People Could Fly*. New York: Hanging Loose, 1997. 43-44. Print.

---. *When People Could Fly*. New York: Hanging Loose, 1997. Print.

Mcleman, Robert and Barry Smit. “Migration as an Adaptation to Climate Change.” *Climatic Change* 76 (2006): 31-53. Print.

Mendoza, Louis and S. Shankar, ed. *Crossing into America: The New Literature of Immigration*. New York: New Press, 2005. Print.

Merwin, W.S. “In a Clearing.” *Migration. New and Selected Poems*. Port Townsend: Copper Canyon, 2005. 138-39. Print.

---. *Migration. New and Selected Poems*. Port Townsend: Copper Canyon, 2005. Print.

Perch-Nielsen, Sabine L., Michèle B. Bättig, and Dieter Imboden. "Exploring the Link between Climate Change and Migration." *Climatic Change* 91 (2008): 375–93. Print.

Ramazani, Jahan. *The Poetry of Mourning: The Modern Elegy from Hardy to Heany*. Chicago: University of Chicago Press, 1994. Print.

Salter, Mary Jo. Introduction. *Selected Poems*. By Amy Clampitt. Ed. Salter, Mary Jo. New York: Borzoi-Knopf, 2012. xi-xix. Print.

Suárez, Vigil, and Ryan G. Cleave, eds. *American Diaspora: Poetry of Displacement*. Iowa City: University of Iowa Press, 2001. Print.

Suárez, Virgil. *90 Miles*. Pittsburgh: University of Pittsburgh Press, 2005. Print.

Thomson, Jeffrey. "'Everything Blooming Bows Down in the Rain': Nature and the Work of Mourning in the Contemporary Elegy." *Ecopoetry: A Critical Introduction*. Ed. J. Scott Bryson. Salt Lake City: University of Utah Press, 2002. 153-61. Print.

KARIN HÖPKER

A Sense of an Ending – Risk, Catastrophe and Precarious Humanity in Margaret Atwood's *Oryx and Crake*

In his 1993 talk "The Coming Technological Singularity: How to Survive in the Posthuman Era" Vernor Vinge discusses the arrival of a technologically induced event that will radically change the world as we know it. "The Singularity," as he calls it, will bring about an age of posthumanity:

> From the human point of view this change will be a throwing away of all the previous rules, perhaps in the blink of an eye, an exponential runaway beyond any hope of control. [...] It is a point where our old models must be discarded and a new reality rules. As we move closer to this point, it will loom vaster and vaster over human affairs till the notion becomes a commonplace. Yet when it finally happens it may still be a great surprise and a greater unknown. [1]

Based on notions of accelerating technological development, be it in the field of computer science, nanotechnology, or the life sciences, the concept of the Singularity illustrates one of the grand narratives which inform contemporary Western societies' imaginations of the future. It anticipates a technological evolution which will bring about a change so fundamental that we are no longer able to conceive of its outcome or imagine a time beyond. In "What if the Singularity does NOT happen" (2007), in which he revisits his earlier proposal for change, Vinge defines the moment when technological creations will surpass the grasp of human intelligence as the beginning of a posthuman age that will be "as unimaginable to us as opera is to a flatworm."[2]

While the evolving technological complexity seems to pose a barrier to the prognostication and anticipation of such a future, the science-fictional

---

1 See Vinge's San Diego State website http://www-rohan.sdsu.edu/faculty/vinge/misc/singularity.html. The original paper was presented at the VISION-21 Symposium of NASA Lewis Research Center and the Ohio Aerospace Institute, March 30-31, 1993. First articulated in Vinge's article "First World" (*Omni*, January 10, 1983), the concept was famously relaunched by Ray Kurzweil in his 2005 *The Singularity is Near* (New York, Viking). For a critical discussion of the concept, its adaptations and its contemporary cultural functions, see Colin Milburn's *Nanovision: Engineering the Future* (Duke 2008).

2 http://www-rohan.sdsu.edu/faculty/vinge/longnow/index.htm.

imagination rises to the challenge and, in the form of posthuman fiction, envisions the other side of the temporal rabbit hole, past which, in a world altered beyond recognition, our present-day knowledge no longer holds much currency. As a literary field defined by its topic, posthuman fiction varies greatly in its treatment of the subject. It envisions slow, almost imperceptible change as well as scenarios of catastrophic abruptness, and it ranges from utopian hopes for new forms of existence to dystopian fears of cataclysm ravaging the planet after centuries of human abuse and exploitation. And yet, all variations share a common characteristic: They enact a "sense of an ending."[3]

Posthuman fiction confronts the reader with the paradoxical spectacle of an intradiegetic ending which announces the unthinkable, radical finiteness of humanity and yet remains suspended, because the posthuman theme also always proposes a story beyond this end. Instead of establishing closure, these narratives draw a divisive line right across the chronology of their diegetic world which radically puts humanity at disposition. I will discuss Margaret Atwood's *Oryx and Crake* (2003) as a recent example of posthuman fiction which characteristically employs the trope of an ending and its aftermath as a highly effective tool to critically engage with a problematic present.

The novel's engagement works on two levels. Primarily, the text establishes the temporal trajectory of posterity to cast an unflinching gaze back at humanity. Via the peculiar vantage point of a protagonist whom we encounter as literally the last human being, the novel extrapolates a world in which late-capitalist consumerism and an exploitative speciesism inform intra-societal and inter-species relations. The humanist narrative is exposed as an ideology of exceptionalism which has become all too closely interwoven with a dominant discourse of profit and risk management and has reached a point where the new probabilistic logic overrules all concerns of ethics and human sustainability.

On a second level, *Oryx and Crake* shifts its focus from society to the individual subject and explores the theme of an interspecies encounter between humanity and its posthuman other. After a catastrophic event of near-global extinction, the human protagonist Snowman finds himself ill-adapted to a damaged eco-system and struggling for bare survival. He has become the relic of an evolution which has surpassed him and has left him a mere freakish specter to the new posthuman inhabitants, reminding them of a history that is not theirs. And yet, marginalized and drastically dislocated

---

3 Frank Kermode has of course famously coined this term in his 1967 study of the same title (Oxford University Press). Yet as Frank Kelleter points out in his introduction on popular seriality, the cultural work of literary narrative rests on a characteristic uncertainty balancing between the telos of ending and closure on the one hand and its equally necessary deferral promising the non-finality of always a next installment. Cf. *Populäre Serialität: Narration – Evolution – Distinktion* (Bielefeld 2012), 11-46.

from the anthropocentric paradigm of human exceptionalism, he is able to reclaim his humanity, once he realizes that his otherness has always already been an integral part of his own humanity.

Central to my analysis will be two narrative and thematic tropes: Luhmann's temporal construct of a "Katastrophenschwelle" [a "disaster threshold"] which the novel employs for its agenda of social criticism, and Agamben's notion of an intimate caesura which illustrates how the novel problematizes humanist subjectivity. Reading the novel through these two tropes, I will show how *Oryx and Crake* employs the posthuman narrative form to generate a utopian momentum from a dystopian scenario. The text radically proposes a new mode of thinking which ventures to sidestep the actuarial logic of risk and its quantifying grasp on decision-making and which recognizes the fundamental precariousness of humanity as a new basis for an interspecies encounter. Further, the novel's narrative structure demonstrates the specific aesthetic potential of posthuman fiction to render visible the problematic cultural techniques at the heart of an escalated risk society.

I. A Voice from Beyond: Posthumanity and Posthumanism

To briefly outline some of the literary and theoretical presuppositions central to posthuman fiction, one can first of all argue that the concepts of posthumanism and posthumanity are not directly dependent on each other in so far as posthumanism does not necessarily require the existence of a posthumanity.[4] Humanism and humanity, on the other hand, correlate closely in the sense that our current, Western definition of "Man" or "humanity" requires the taxonomic apparatus of humanism, which since the early modern era has upheld the fundamental semiotic differentiation that categorically separates the human from its non-human other and thus generates a genealogy of human exceptionalism. Neil Badmington argues that

[4] Needless to say that the field is a vast one and has quickly evolved since Donna Haraway's 1985 "A Manifesto for Cyborgs" announced the arrival of a posthuman age (without ever using the term). As Vinge's thoughts on the Singularity illustrate, earlier works throughout the 1980s and '90s such as Chris Hables Gray's anthology *The Cyborg Handbook* (1995) or N. Katherine Hayle's *How We Became Posthuman* (1999) tended to focus on the new possibilities of computer science, artificial intelligence, virtual reality, and man-machine interfaces. More recently, in response to the rise of life sciences and biotechnology, scholars like Cary Wolfe (esp.in *Animal Rites* and *Zoontologies*, both 2003) or Haraway (*The Companion Species Manifesto*, 2003, and *When Species Meet*, 2008) develop a criticism of the humanist paradigm from the perspective of speciesism and the subjection of the non-human other.

> [p]osthumanism marks a careful, ongoing, overdue rethinking of the dominant humanist (or anthropocentric) account of who "we" are as human beings. In the light of posthumanist theory and culture, "we" are not who "we" once believed ourselves to be. And neither are "our" others. (374)

In that sense, posthumanist narrative provides an extension and fictional counterpoint to what history and political philosophy have in many variations discussed as the "End of History." Where Alexandre Kojève or Francis Fukuyama envision an endpoint to humanity's historical evolution as a Hegelian fulfillment of history and the struggle for recognition, posthuman literature imagines a much more literal end.[5]

In fiction, of course, the "end of man" may come in many different ways, but posthumanist narratives are united in their effort to imagine the "other side" of the singularity, be it a postapocalyptic aftermath or a bio- or technoscientifically prompted, evolutionary leap. Some of these accounts may be celebratory and utopian, others of a more ambivalent tone, but many tend to be outright dystopian and imagine the scenario of change as fundamentally menacing. They prominently employ a rhetoric of risk and endangerment, in which the imagined singularity marks an alarming temporal caesura, at which the arrival of the posthuman threatens to render humanity obsolete. As Fukuyama writes, "the most significant threat posed by contemporary biotechnology is the possibility that it will alter human nature and thereby move us into a 'posthuman' stage of history" (2002: 7, my emphasis).

Margaret Atwood's *Oryx and Crake* is both posthuman in subject—as its diegesis imagines the end of humanity succeeded by a new species— and posthumanist in its ethics—as it criticizes the detrimental repercussions of a human speciesism unfettered by considerations of sustainability or responsibility. It conjures up a future, which violently displaces humanity from the center of its humanist paradigm, reflecting Badmingtons claim that

> [p]osthumanism [...] emerges from the recognition that "Man" is not the privileged and protected center, because humans are no longer – and perhaps never were – utterly distinct from animals, machines, and other forms of the "inhuman"; are the products of historical and cultural differences that invalidate any appeal to

[5] I will not trace the multifarious cultural productions on the topos, but it is noteworthy how a more biological and species-centered discourse on the future, the end, and the possible succession of humankind has made its way from genre fiction to the mainstream. While in the 1980s and '90s science fiction writers like Rudy Rucker, Bruce Sterling, Octavia Butler, and Greg Bear explored the imaginable fringes of late- and post-human futures, the topic of biotechnologically induced posthuman speciation now echoes in novels such as *Oryx and Crake* (2003), Michel Houellebecq's *Possibilité d'une île* (2005), or Kazuo Ishiguro's *Never Let Me Go* (2005). For a discussion of Ishiguro and Atwood in the light of her 1979 *Life Before Man*, see Rosario Arias' essay "Life After Man?"

> a transhistorical human essence; are constituted as subjects by a linguistic system that pre-exists and transcends them; and are unable to direct the course of world history towards a uniquely human goal. (374)

Alternating between two plot strands of Snowman's present and that of his younger, pre-apocalyptic self Jimmy, Atwood's novel lets us witness the dawn of such a recognition. The protagonist realizes his marginality and with it the fact that notions of a "transhistorical human essence" or an anthropocentric teleology of history are a mere figment of human imagination (cf. Badmington 374).

Similar to many dystopian novels *Oryx and Crake* uses a postapocalyptic vantage point, from which the bulk of human history can be viewed as an occurrence of the past, in order to critically illuminate an anthropocentric paradigm into which a highly problematic logic of risk is inextricably embedded. The perspective of posteriority renders irrefutable what contemporaneity may only suspect, namely that processes of decision-making were faulted by overconfidence in the probabilistic calculability of risks and by fantasies of systemic control. With a narrative voice distinctive to posthuman fiction, the novel accompanies its focalizing character in the lonely role of guide and destitute raconteur. Retrospection and reminiscences are our sole source of information about pre-apocalyptic society and the events that led to its downfall. Only late in the novel do readers find out that an ecoterrorist group, led by Jimmy's former classmate Crake, had unleashed a biotechnologically devised virus on humanity to rid an overexploited ecosystem of the deadly parasite of mankind. A Robinsoniad of possibly the last man on earth, the narrative creates an obsolete chronicle without hope for a human audience or a readership capable of comprehending the strange tale of humanity's end.

Based on the foundational fiction of a "post," *Oryx and Crake* aligns narrative voice and perspective along the central divide of "before" and "after," of human and other: Its peculiar structure creates a vantage point for a radical inquiry which questions assumptions and silent operations of contemporary "risk society" (Giddens 1991/ Beck 1992). A biopolitical economy and corporate stakeholders have effectively replaced traditional government and created an environment of fear, in which semantics of risk and prevention justify an apparatus of control in the name of security and a greater common good. The novel unhinges this forceful dynamic by staging the arrival of a worst case scenario far beyond the range of all actuarial imagination. But, instead of making an end-of-humanity scenario the vehicle to an alarmist rhetoric (which might only incite a stronger desire for control and security in its readers), the text outlines the limitations of actuarial thought and opens up an alternative concern with humanity's ontological and ethical peril.

The novel's point of attack is post-apocalyptic. Only gradually do we piece together the dystopian picture of a near-future, where the exploitation of environmental resources reigns, and where society has harnessed its technoscientific achievements for maximizing corporate revenue, personal pleasure, and profit in a class-divided system. Questions of ethics and sustainability are left to resistance groups and religious sects operating in a non-corporate underground. Humanity is succeeded in evolution by a bioengineered posthuman species called "The Children of Crake."[6] Told in heterodiegetic third person, two alternating narrative strands—marked by a change in tense and by a change in the protagonist's name—converge in a catastrophic point zero that structurally iterates the temporal caesura of humanity's end. While the earlier events narrated in past tense relate to "Jimmy," the postapocalyptic segments are narrated in present tense and mark a metamorphosis of "Jimmy" into "Snowman", whose struggle for survival has little in common with his earlier life in a privileged world of advanced biotechnology and accelerated consumerism. And yet, instead of drawing on the thrill of a fatalistic course of humanity's doom, the novel builds on a more constructive critical agenda that engages inter-species relations, environmental concerns, and the use of resources as part of a trajectory of consequentiality and a problematic societal apparatus of decision-making.

To do so *Oryx and Crake* employs two central operations which hark back to and innovatively inform previous narratives of dystopian scenarios. In one movement, the novel radicalizes the extrapolation of dystopian aspects to a critical limen which Niklas Luhmann, in his 1991 *Soziologie des Risikos*, has called "Katastrophenschwelle", a "disaster threshold" (11).[7] In Atwood's novel, the radicality of the imagined catastrophic unhinges established mechanisms of risk-assessment and risk-taking and renders moot all weighing of prospects of profit and damage that serve to evaluate decision-making. In a second, parallel movement, the novel uses the spectacle of an ending that cuts across its diegesis to draw attention to the precariousness of human subjectivity and call to the fore what Giorgio Agamben termed an "intimate caesura." In his 2002 *The Open: Man and Animal*, Agamben proposes that the foundational operation of iterated differentiation which lies at the heart of the genealogy of Western "humanism" and which generates "the human" as a category apart from all non-human other has left a deep rift at the core of human subjectivity. In an ethical course remarkably close to Atwood's agenda, *The Open* argues that it is only by recognizing the

---

6 Named after their human maker, the "Crakers" are hybrid creatures, designed to lead a harmonious tribal life and adapt to an ecosystem uninhabitable to humans. The end of humanity thus also evokes the beginning as earlier mythical threshold of creation, now reiterated in the emergence of a new hominid species.

7 In the following I will cite from the translated edition *Risk: A Sociological Theory* (Transaction, 2002).

undetractable residue of the non-human other still present within our core identity and intimately binding us to the animal that mankind can become fully human.

Through these two operations, which draw a divide through the novel on the levels of chronology, narrative structure, and human subject, *Oryx and Crake* exposes the human as radically and doubly precarious, threatened by species extinction and questioned in its humanity. And yet the peril and endeavor of facing such precariousness may, Atwood's text seems to suggest, be the very prerequisite for creating an opening to transgress the categorical boundaries that bind the human subject within a socially, economically, and ecologically problematic current order.

II. *Katastrophenschwelle*: Posthuman Fiction, Risk, and Literary Form

Much has been written about Atwood's depiction of science and her stance in the two cultures debate,[8] and *Oryx and Crake* has been criticized by some for the populist "swing" it allegedly takes at genetics.[9] Yet, I would argue that in the novel both the sciences and the arts are pressed into the service of economic profit and consumption. The novel does not target the sciences per se, but a systemic shift that has rendered scientific knowledge production supplementary to its applications and instrumental to economic marketability.

In a near, fictitious future we witness the consequences of severe changes in governmentality and in the criteria for decision-making on collective and individual levels, induced by an economically driven logic of risk, within which the assessment of profit weighed against potential loss overrules criteria of common good. Phantasies of closure and security manifest spatially in the gated enclaves of corporate housing (26, 73, 225), the Wattson-Crick-Institute (196f), or its experimental biosphere (304), which all seem to promise reduced complexity and controlled environments. Corporate actors like CorpSeCorps or individuals like Crake suffer a symptomatic forgetfulness of the fundamental systemic openness and inaccessibility of future events. They rank the manageability of risk and its prevention with overconfidence but obfuscate the very basis of their systemic assessments, namely that assumptions about the future are hypothetical and become calculable only as operationally closed fictional constructs. As Luhmann puts it, recursively operating systems use their own current state as a point of orientation and base their assumptions about the future on the information gained from observing their own immediate past. Yet the generated trajectory of events obscures the fact that its continuity is a mere

8 Cf. Squier, Bouson 2004 et al.

9 See for example Griffiths' op-ed review "Genetics according to *Oryx and Crake*."

projection and that the future remains indeed inaccessible (cf. Luhmann 33-50, specifically 35)

Thus, as *Oryx and Crake* demonstrates, a logic of risk, in which an actuarial rhetoric has replaced previous notions of scientific causality, is not problematic because its calculations fail but because its criteria become an ultima ratio. Where all things are hypothetically calculable and quantifiable, all things can be put at disposition if one is willing to set a wager. It creates an economic temporality in which external dangers are translated into parameters of expectability and accidental events can be systematically related and described in terms of the evaluation of a cost and benefit calculation. Such a logic of risk generates certainty from uncertainty by introducing a quantifiable relation of exchange between endangered present and contingent future. While it functions well pragmatically and supports basic processes of decision-making, it is still based on an essentially fictional hypothesis of a closed system with limited possibilities of outcome. *Oryx and Crake* envisions what happens when the probabilistic fantasy of fully calculable and manageable risk, forgetful of its own fictional and hypothetical nature, becomes all-pervasive.

Ultimately, the novel's catastrophe is triggered by an essentially contingent series of complex systemic causes and individual actions. By realizing the catastrophe as a thing of the past, the novel strips it of all aspects of improbability: The previously feared event, then classified and discarded as improbable—the catastrophe—transforms into the actual and a sequence of events that was by no means monocausal. The pandemic that wiped out *homo sapiens sapiens* sprung from the elaborate revenge plot of Crake whose father had been killed by the private security henchmen of a powerful transnational corporation.[10] On a larger scale, the catastrophe emerges from a system of exploitation and mismanagement. While scientific efforts focused on the maintenance of health, beauty, youth, and immortality for the privileged, the planetary environment had been altered to a new hostility:

> [...A]s time went on and the coastal aquifers turned salty and the northern permafrost melted and the vast tundra bubbled with methane, and the draught in the midcontinental plains regions went on and on, and the Asian steppes turned to sand dunes, and meat became harder to come by, some people had their doubts. (*Oryx and Crake* 24)

The human survivors of the first wave of the engineered virus infections kill each other, fall prey to new hybrid breeds of predators such as wolvogs and pigoons, or perish without the elaborate technological apparatus of life-

[10] The father's death in a car accident had been staged after he had found out that the company lucratively marketed pharmaceutical products as remedies to diseases which had been artificially created and introduced into the general population (cf. *Oryx and Crake* 211/12).

support that had made life comfortable despite pollution and radical climate change. Incapacitated by its blind trust in its own ability to address risk as quantifiable, calculable, and containable, human civilization fails.

Oryx and Crake depicts a modernity where "quantitative description and manipulation displaces qualitative discourse, a disastrous development the novel captures precisely in the relative valuation of 'word' and 'numbers' people" (Dunning 86). The novel extrapolates the consequences of risky behavior, technoscientific hubris, and neglect of sustainability. A reliance on quantification and statistics, which permeates the social system throughout formerly separate sectors of scientific knowledge production (such as university education and research) down to individual lives, appears in the light of an event that was deemed highly unlikely but proved detrimental in its consequences.

And indeed, the novel's presentation of processes of individual and collective decision-making and of the dynamics that drive transnational corporate actors problematizes such a paradigm more effectively than any anticipatory admonitions ever could. It structurally foregrounds one of the most important operative devices of modern risk society: it projects the outcome of certain forms of behavior in the modeled environment of a hypothetical social situation. By establishing a narrative voice that tells the story of the disaster in retrospect, the novel confronts us with a society in which safety is perceived as a marketable commodity,[11] and what appears to be a free-market dynamic reveals itself as surprisingly irrational behavior devoid of prudence and foresight. As improbable risk turns into catastrophe, the novel's crossing of the "Katastrophenschwelle" as a device of extremity overrides, suspends, and effectively voids any previous logic of systemic risk and situation assessment as a basis for decision-making.[12]

---

11 In the novel's world a substantial portion of corporate profit is generated by the privatized military-industrial complex, and CorpSeCorp, a private security franchise, has taken over important parts of police-work. While the impoverished Pleeblands seem practically outside legal control, the suggested safety of gated enclaves beckons to higher income employees, whose loyalty and attachment corporations seek to secure by disseminating disproportionate fears of the outside and an (equally exaggerated) sense of security on the inside (cf. *Oryx and Crake* 26-28). Indistinct fears of disease, death, or merely loss of youth serve to lucratively market preventive biomedicine, cosmetics, and an extensive spa-culture (cf. *Oryx and Crake* 248-51). A profit-driven economy of security and fear diverts attention from the fact that the actual societal behavior is highly risky.

12 Where these thresholds are located is culturally and historically specific: Systems of evaluation generally seek to base processes of decision-making on calculations of potential outcome. If we picture the disaster threshold as a significant discontinuity in the ascending curve of the relation in which expectations of use and profit are weighed against expectable risk, the pattern of location, nature, and cause of this discontinuity depends on and must be characteristic to the respective social system (cf. Luhmann 2f).

Along the temporal divide of an ending, the posthuman novel displays the catastrophic as contingent but not arbitrary, extrapolated within a narrative order of catastrophe. With Snowman as survivor and human focalizer placed on the other side of the catastrophic threshold, both heterodiegetic narrator and, ultimately, the reader are cast in the role of a second-order observer—a role for which the protagonist is systemically too immersed. Such narrative perspectivation of primary and secondary observation presents the arrival of the unthinkable not as random perdition but as an escalation based on previous decisions which turn out to be wrong, dangerous, and negligent.

For the catastrophic threshold marks a potential event so extreme that regular procedures of dealing with and anticipating risk are no longer valid. Quantitative procedures of risk-assessment are unhinged once the expectable impact of the event approaches a certain degree of impending disaster perceived as critical. All calculations become void, once the possible outcome is categorized as catastrophic in effect. No matter how unlikely such an event, to take such as risk is generally regarded unacceptable.[13]

When such a non-negotiable limit is missing, as is demonstrated in the world of *Oryx and Crake*, risk-embracing behavior and the lack of a critical consensus to avoid the catastrophic threaten and ultimately disable previous systemic notions of normalcy and order. Immediately caused by a terrorist attack, the catastrophe foregrounds long-term conditions collectively produced by a society oblivious to the consequences of its actions and short-sighted to the imminent social and ecological dangers that put its existence at risk.

While Crake, Jimmy's brilliant and radical scientist friend, seems to offer an alternative point of view, a careful reading of the text's characterizations casts severe doubt on both his methods and insights. Crake's eco-guerilla agenda rebels against corporate culture and the planet's exploitation for economic profit, but his world-view is radically aleatory;[14] yet he seeks to implement the systemic randomness of evolution's micro-processes by human "authorship," and implants his own design to launch a severely altered and improved post-human species, through his Paradice-Project. In Crake the reader recognizes the utilitarian materialism of a scientist to whom the progressive dynamics of discovery and feasibility are uncoupled from the ethical responsibilities within a social contract. Jimmy, on the other hand,

---

[13] As Luhmann points out to illustrate socially inscribed risk-aversion, whether societies have developed a highly sophisticated (and highly sensitized) apparatus of administration or whether tribal societies invest a relatively high proportion of energy and semantic effort into a symbolic and mythological apparatus to generate promises of stability and certainty under pressures of survival – these systems will make high investments into preserving a normality covertly thought of as precarious (1-2).

[14] The novel illustrates his views typically in sequences of dialogue with Jimmy, such as when the two friends controversially discuss the concepts of art and romantic love as evolutionary functions (cf. *Oryx and Crake* 166-68).

stubbornly clings to the remnants of a belles lettres-humanism declared obsolete by a rampantly capitalist society.

And yet Crake is set up as an attractive character: Endowed with a brilliant and daringly independent mind, he appears socially detached but amiable enough and, at times, a good friend to Jimmy, whose perception of him displays the ambiguous shades of their longstanding and incongruous relationship. Crake's scientific genius launches his career early, and he wins the reader's sympathy by his willingness to take Jimmy, who has no comparably marketable talent, along on the ride. Yet his contempt for Jimmy's education, line of work, or the arts in general, is barely veiled and an integral part of his disdain for the inefficiency and evolutionary shortcomings of humanity as a species. Crake's approach is rationalistic, game-like, without detectable affect or empathy, and without belief in either God or Nature "with a capital N" (206). His view of the world as one "vast, uncontrolled experiment" (228) categorically displaces humanity from its self-proclaimed centrality; his radical posthumanism seeks to put an end to the damage done to the planet's eco-system by replacing humanity with a species better suited for sustainable co-habitation—ridding, to put it with Kojève, the animal of the fatal disease called humanity (in Agamben 12).

Interestingly, *Oryx and Crake* withholds explicit moral judgment at this point and refrains from resorting to the identificatory technique of simply showing a sympathetic Jimmy pitted against the villainous mad scientist. Instead, it depicts Jimmy as a character deeply entangled in self-interest and a compromised system. True to its posthuman topos, the novel utilizes the critical potential structurally inscribed into a postapocalytic vantage point to not pass explicit judgment on Crake's ideological position but draw the reader's attention to a blind-spot in Crake's paradigm.

For, all too similar to the system he seeks to destroy, his quantitatively oriented grasp of the world leads to what the novel implicitly criticizes as human delusions of grandeur, control, and the fallacy of a genesis amnesia. He forgets that his assumptions and estimates of a future outcome rely on the hypothetical operation of closure of a factually open system. Certain predictions about the future consequences of our actions are impossible, given the infinite complexity of the system. Yet they are brought into the realm of the imaginable by limiting the factors through an operation of fictional systemic closure. Empirically a successful and practicable method for everyday processes of decision-making, this operation becomes unstable as the system grows in scale and complexity and highly problematic once the hypothetical character of its model is forgotten.

While the novel's different layers of criticism are of course aimed at a broad number of aspects, the narrative construction of the temporal caesura of an ending functions in similar ways: The arrival of the catastrophic explodes the logic of risk and debunks a credo of security and risk aversion as indeed highly risk affinitive. Construing a reliable common denominator in its readership on a level of second order observation, the novel employs the "Katastrophenschwelle" as an operative device which creates a strong critical edge, as it foregrounds a non-negotiable discrepancy between reader and diegetic world. The novel generates a critical dynamics which stages humanity as an endangered and self-endangering species; it hopes to cast literary fiction in the role of a "self-defeating prophecy" (Beck 2007: 30), which hopes to serve as a means of preservation to the catastrophe it speculatively enacts.

III. Intimate Caesura and Precarious Humanity

In *Oryx and Crake*, the figure of the end functions as a central divide, which structures binary oppositions of pre- and post-catastrophe; it co-aligns man and animal, human and posthuman other, civilization and nature. With the end of human history, the "anthropogenic machine," (26) as Agamben has called the operations which generate categorical consistency within the narrative of human exceptionalism, comes to a standstill through a catastrophe caused by power struggles over biopolitical control. Yet the mechanisms of inclusion and exclusion of human genealogy are still at work within humanity's last remainder, Snowman, and generate his central conflict. He experiences a variety of encounters with non- and posthuman species, under at times life-threatening circumstances, which call into question his notions of humanity. As we trace these encounters throughout the novel, we witness a fundamental shift in the distribution of power: while early encounters with animals are clearly structured by an asymmetry that casts the animal-other as subjugated and instrumental, postapocalyptic confrontations with the posthumans and with lab-sprung hybrids gone feral leave the protagonist in the position of an inferior minority (cf. eg. 235ff, 275f).

When his social, ideological, and material frames of reference collapse, Snowman realizes the high level of maintenance required for upholding boundaries historically constructed to divide off and suppress man's animality. He experiences the intricate mechanism of the anthropological machine and the precariousness of categorical boundaries. The end of human history calls into question its beginnings that were marked by the decisive "metaphysico-political operation" (Agamben 6) of *homo sapiens* declaring himself human and of excluding an animal other. It "defines a critical threshold, at which the difference between animal and human, which is so decisive for our culture, threatens to vanish" (Agamben 21). *Oryx and Crake* traces the crumbling of the epistemic constructions which produce the distinctive categorical difference meant to separate humanity from its animal other and which yet runs as an indelible and "intimate caesura" (Agamben 15) right through human subjectivity. When, as Atwood's novel explores, apocalypse drives a wedge into that "anthropogenic machine" and brings its apparatus to a sputtering halt, the caesura propels Snowman, the human subject, into becoming deeply precarious in his self-understanding as human.

Down to the structural level, the novel's double-stranded narrative layout marks the protagonist Jimmy/Snowman as divided, reflecting the schism in his name and history. After the catastrophe power-relations and predator-prey relationships are inverted, and Snowman finds himself in a subordinate rank of the food-chain. A far cry from the self-proclaimed exceptionalist position of a previously privileged humanity, he has become Snowman, abominable and other to his own perception, exposed to the elements (307) as well as to the derision of a vengeful history, which erases man like Foucault's proverbial face in the sand (387). Despite the fact that Snowman is part of the species that genetically engineered the Crakers, he retrieves no feeling of superiority from that. Confronted by a functioning posthuman community physically and psychologically so well adapted to the new post-apocalyptic environment, Snowman painfully feels the disparity and a sense of inferiority from his own otherness. Anticipating how the Crakers must view him and internalizing the sentiments he imagines the posthuman gaze must hold, he alienates himself to a point where he feels out of place in his human body and avoids exposing it to view (42).

What seems remarkable, and what I read as crucial to the novel's ethical agenda, is Snowman's ability to perceive a difference that runs contrary to his engrained viewing habits and that threatens to unhinge the order of anthropocentric binary oppositions Jimmy had grown up with. Only because he is capable of seeing beyond older category boundaries and revise his perception of self and other can he make the transition towards an empathetic relationship. Whereas Crake had presented the Crakers as a raw batch of genetic material from which he had created a work of art, the offspring of mere "floor models" (305), Snowman recognizes them as individual beings, the future inhabitants of the earth and successor to humankind. In the face of this new species, objects and outcome of genetic tinkering as they may be, he himself becomes the aberration and the relic. The physical incarnation of a social abject, Snowman lives in a tree by the village of Crakers, with the children coming to visit him to hear his stories and to covertly stare at him, "because he is so unlike them" (7):

> For the children – thick-skinned, resistant to ultraviolet – he is a creature of dimness, of the dusk. […] They never stand too close to him. Is that from respect, as he'd like to think, or because he stinks?
>
> (He does stink, he knows that well enough. He's rank, he's gamy, he reeks like a walrus – oily, salty, fishy – not that he's ever smelled such a beast. But he's seen pictures.) (6-7)

In fact, Jimmy has a marked history when it comes to perceptiveness and attitude towards his non-human other. One of his earliest childhood memories is witnessing a bonfire with his father which turns out to be the burning of animal cadavers culled on suspicion of a bio-attack on the live-stock of the corporate compound. While adult bystanders simply witness the spectacle, Jimmy is traumatized by a feeling of pain and guilt for not having saved the animals (14-20). Even as a child, Jimmy's animal encounters set him apart because of a deep sense of responsibility and the fact that he intuitively does not recognize the inter-species divide so fundamental to adult perception. As Jimmy's father repeatedly serves to demonstrate, the boundary between human and animal has long become the basis of a socio-economic system which relies on the economic exploitations of creatures that have been robbed of their status as living beings with rights to be considered. In another instance, Jimmy empathizes with the genetically engineered pigoons, which again sets him apart in a society that utilizes the social construction of human exceptionalism to reduce fellow species to the status of objects the treatment of which depends mainly on their property value, corporate research interest, and the potential for generating wealth.

In an ironic rendition of the classical Robinsonian tale, Snowman displays little of the romanticized qualities of Adamic and colonial *homo faber*. In the character of Robinson, who utilizes, subjects, and exploits the material opportunities of his environmental givens, survival ultimately testifies to the superiority of utilitarian reason and practical capabilities in the face of all adversity. Yet, the stranded Snowman has little practical prowess beyond his knowledge of obscure guides and self-help books (cp. 4-5, 245). Snowman's function is one of telling and bearing witness, possibly of care for the beginnings of the new posthuman species, but not one of rebuilding civilization and establishing human dominion. The function of world-building falls to Crake, a geneticist *homo faber* who believes in science but lacks faith in the benign and liberating forces of enlightenment and thus choses to build the next world without humans.

Jimmy, on the other hand, does not suffer from delusions of godlike grandeur. His world-designing capacities reside in narrative and imagination. In the aftermath of catastrophe, his humanity becomes precarious as the struggle for survival reduces him physically and psychologically to bare existence and leaves him bereft of human companionship, a communicable history, or a common encyclopedia of cultural memory:

> There is a distant, peaceful murmur from the village: human voices. If you can call them human. […] He feels excluded, as if from a party to which he will never be invited. All he'd have to do is step forward into the firelight and there'd be a ring of suddenly blank faces turned towards him. Silence would fall, as in tragic play

> of long ago when the doomed protagonist made an entrance, enveloped in his cloak of contagious bad news. (105-06)

At least in his imagination, his function as predecessor leaves him abject and repellent to the community, a suppressed collective memory of an uncomfortable genesis. Longing for companionship but isolated by history, Snowman feels denuded of his humanity as a property not essential and stable but social, relational, and dependent on recognition by others. Reading his situation through Agamben's critique of humanist genealogy, Snowman's sensation of intimate and threatening exposure gains a dimension of fundamental peril beyond any actuary logic. The imperilment to his humanity complements and strangely supersedes the physical and objective risks that endanger his naked life: "I'm your past, he might intone. I'm your ancestor, come from the land of the dead. Now I'm lost, I can't get back, I'm stranded here, I'm all alone. Let me in!" (106)

Snowman senses the caesura in himself, just as he suspects the Crakers feel the internal residual otherness of their human ancestry. His situation forces him to perform a complex double operation that, despite his empathetic capacities, taxes his self-comprehension to its limit. He must learn to recognize the caesura of elemental otherness as intrinsic to his own identity and, in a second step, find ways to bridge the gap towards the posthuman other in an act of caring and responsibility that remains selfless and without reciprocation in kind. In the process, he struggles to rid himself of the cognitive frame of the society in which he grew up as part of a perverse taxonomy of exploitation and othering, which provided the ideological and economic basis to a blinding consumerism and cast promises of eternal youth and sexual bliss as primary objectives of a pursuit of happiness.

Here, where catastrophe brings the genealogical apparatus of the anthropogenic machine to a near standstill, it enables the human subject to remember what he, Jimmy/Snowman had already suspected—that the separation between humankind and its animal other is an intimate caesura which cannot be expelled but runs through the very core of humanity itself. The recognition of this duality, only rendered abject by complex processes of 'civilisatory' sublimation of human animality, lies at the heart of Jimmy/Snowman's new identity:

> To them [the Crakers] his name is just two syllables. They don't know what a snowman is, they've never seen snow.
>
> It was one of Crake's rules that no name could be chosen for which a physical equivalent – even stuffed, even skeletal – could not be demonstrated. No unicorns, no griffins, no manticores or basilisks. But those rules no longer apply, and it's given Snowman a bitter pleasure to adopt this dubious label. (7)

By appropriating the name of a species located, like mermaids, pygmies, or wolf-children, on the fringes of human self-categorization, Snowman fractures his identity which he has comprehended as unified by fictions of homogeneity only. He painfully and deliberately makes himself other to humanity and posthumanity alike, but he also roots himself in the fantastically rich semantic history of biological taxonomy, creating a hybrid self that embraces the heteroclite nature a humanist genealogy could never erase:

> The Abominable Snowman – existing and not existing, flickering at the edges of blizzards, apelike man or manlike ape, stealthy, elusive, known only through rumors and through its backward-pointing footprints. Mountaintribes were said to have chased it down and killed it when they had the chance. They were said to have boiled it, roasted it, held special feasts; all the more exciting, he supposes, for bordering on cannibalism. (7-8)

At a time where mankind as a species seems to have ceased, the human protagonist, despite his desolate state, despite the hunger, disease, predators, and onsets of deprivation-induced madness, and despite the fact that this will not save him in any literal sense, shows the redemptive capability for recognizing this otherness in himself and acts from a deep feeling of responsibility towards a companion species. In the story of how Jimmy came to be the Abominable Snowman, we are confronted with the central ethical agenda of the novel, which, as Dunning puts it, demands "humility in the face of the other" (99).

IV. The Posthuman Novel: Fiction, Risk, and the Urgency of Storytelling

In many respects, the posthuman narrative of *Oryx and Crake* escalates what Atwood regards as key to her own understanding of novelistic writing: It emphasizes the instability of meaning, the erosion of categories, and the slipperiness of language—all the more at stake in *Oryx and Crake* because the rich complexity of its history, beyond pragmatic communication, depends on the grasp and failing memory of a sole speaker who combats the fading of a vocabulary that has lost its uses and referents. Just like the pieces of debris the posthuman children pick up on the beach and bring to Snowman—for him to identify like the archaeological artifacts of a vanished culture, too alien to fathom their function— much of Snowman's vocabulary has become semantic flotsam (cf. 39).

As Snowman clings to these words, the solace he derives from the struggle is not so much nostalgia for the lost, pre-cataclysmic world, but an attachment to a richer universe of cultural imagination and humanist education that had been cast aside by the late capitalist society Jimmy had lived in.[15] His efforts to guard the found-objects and words from a final loss of meaning heighten the reader's awareness of the novel's capacity for multi-layered ambiguity, and we struggle with the perspective and thought-processes, the often questionable judgment and memory of a protagonist, on whose perception and recollections we rely for information, but whose understanding of the events surrounding him is often challenged and incomplete. Above all, *Oryx and Crake* as a posthuman narrative intensifies the necessity and urgency of storytelling Atwood regards as crucial to the human condition. As she puts it in "Reading Blind," storytelling must have "the Ancient Mariner element, the Scheherazade element: a sense of urgency. This is the story I must tell; this is the story you must hear – [...told] with as much intensity as if the teller's life depended on it." (in Bouson 2010: 3)

In *Oryx and Crake*, both narrator and protagonist cannot help but talk and tell stories, addressed to themselves, to the Crakers, to an assumed, hopelessly hypothetical human audience, which the third-person narration seems to address despite the fact that, on the diegetic level, all human audience must have ceased with the extinction of the species. And it is this urgency of storytelling, a narrative voice which seems to survive even the possibility of an audience as its focalizing protagonists surpass the apocalyptic threshold of an end of mankind, which characteristically informs posthuman narrative in a way that I consider more striking and specific than any more thematic definition. Posthuman narratives face a radical insecurity of addressee; they verge on the desperation of a monologue spoken into an empty space beyond. Yet they also manifest the powerful potential of storytelling as an aesthetic mode which can not only thematically and thus explicitly formulate a critical agenda but which can structurally and implicitly foreground what may otherwise have slipped beneath the perceivable surface of habituated cultural and historical tradition. Highlighting fiction as a cultural technique of simulation, of building a systemic model, literary story-telling renders visible a structural and functional similarity between literary fiction and probabilistic assessment, which, as we have seen, the dominant logic of risk prefers to obfuscate.

Like all posthuman narratives potentially can, *Oryx and Crake* simulates the scenario of an ending as a temporally divisive line of before and after that creates a doubled world of diegesis reflected in the novel's two-tiered narrative structure. As Elena Esposito points out, narrative systems of fiction rely on operations of closure to generate observable and communicable

---

[15] To wit, Jimmy spent much of his time at college rescuing obscure books in the library's archive and committing to memory lists of vocabulary that had been shed from a contemporary language use informed by a logic of use-value. With technoscientific knowledge production valued exclusively, the Arts and Humanities were relegated to positions of handmaiden, merely generating net value by spinning ephemeral neologisms for purposes of product marketing (195).

fictional worlds (Esposito 7-14), and posthumanist narratives heighten and reflect this process by introducing the figurative threshold of an "ending" as integral part to its construction. Focusing on how a society deals with, explains, and communicates calamity, harm, or disaster—or fails to do so—the genre simulates crisis as a source of insight. By highlighting a situation of exceptionality as normalcy's other, the novel draws attention to basic operations of 'normality' and patterns of expectation as they are tested against concepts of disorder, chaos, or the catastrophic. Thus, *Oryx and Crake* aptly shows the genre's capacity for creating a fictional world which can serve as hypothetical model of social phenomena the novel chooses to explore. By doubling and splitting the world of its diegesis, and establishing a narrative point of observation and of story-telling from beyond the catastrophic divide, the novel foregrounds the problematic operations on which its catastrophe may be predicated: a humanity forgetful of its own limitations, which overrated its own grasp of the future just as it has chosen to forget the genealogy and taxonomic history of its own humanity. Beyond a mere extrapolation of the horrible things that may happen if human societies continue on their current path, Atwood's story of an ending throws into stark relief the world-making mechanisms of fiction, of systemic simulation, which are at the heart of both literary fiction and calculations of probability. Yet where the novel promotes self-reflexiveness and awareness of its own artefactual status, the basic operations of risk-calculations downplay their speculative character where high-risk decisions are involved and are blind to their own systemic limitations.[16]

As we have seen, the novel neither sets out to humanize the alterity of a posthuman future by transposing difference into sameness, nor does it provide the comforts of closure, but it instead opens up a sense of radical contingency. Constructing the ending as simultaneously a caesura and a temporal threshold, posthumanist narrative deconstructs traditional notions of world- and sense-making by opening up the framework of anthropocentric emplotment. For posthumanist narratives such as *Oryx and Crake* self-reflexively render visible systemic operations of closure and highlight their constructedness, provisionality and contingency; they create a fictional framework which allows to confront and thus engage in the ongoing humanist debate on human, inter-species, and environmental issues on a new footing. Ultimately, like the "human footprint in the sand" (372), the solitary voice of a narrative beyond the end tells a story that seeks to find an audience and that struggles against a fading of historical memory that may well endanger the future of humanity.

[16] On the problem of systemic blind spots in operative systems see for instance Luhmann's chapter on "The Risk of Observing and the Coding of Function Systems", 73-82.

Works cited

Agamben, Giorgio. *The Open: Man and Animal*. Trans. Kevin Attell. Stanford: Stanford University Press, 2004. Print.

Atwood, Margaret. *Oryx and Crake*. New York: Anchor/Random House, 2003. Print.

---. "Writing *Oryx and Crake*." *Moving Targets: Writing with Intent, 1982-2004*. Toronto: House of Anansi Press, 2004. 328-330. (2004a). Print.

---. "*The Handmaid's Tale* and *Oryx and Crake* 'In Context'." *PMLA* 119.3 (May 2004): 513-517. (2004b). Print.

---. "The Road to Ustopia." *The Guardian* Friday, October 14, 2011. Web. http://www.guardian.co.uk/books/2011/oct/14/margaret-atwood-road-to-ustopia.

Arias, Rosario. "Life After Man: Posthumanity and Genetic Engineering in Margaret Atwood's *Oryx and Crake* and Kazuo Ishiguro's *Never Let Me Go*." *Restoring the Mystery of the Rainbow. Literature's Refraction of Science*, Vol. 1. Ed. Valeria Tinkler-Villani and C. C. Barfoot. Amsterdam/New York: Rodopi, 2011. Print.

Badmington, Neil. "Posthumanism." *The Routledge Companion to Literature and Science*. Ed. Bruce Clarke with Manuela Rossini. London: Routledge, 2012. 374-384. Print.

Beck, Ulrich. *Risk Society: Towards a New Modernity*. Trans. Mark Ritter. London: Sage, 1992. Print.

--- . *Weltrisikogesellschaft: Auf der Suche nach der verlorenen Sicherheit*. Frankfurt/M.: Suhrkamp, 2007. Print.

Bosco, Mark. "The Apocalyptic Imagination in *Oryx and Crake*." *Margaret Atwood. The Robber Bride, The Blind Assassin, Oryx and Crake*. Ed. J. Brooks Bouson. London: Continuum, 2010. 156-171. Print.

Bouson, J. Brooks. "Introduction: Negotiating with Margaret Atwood." *Margaret Atwood. The Robber Bride, The Blind Assassin, Oryx and Crake*. Ed. J. Brooks Bouson. London: Continuum, 2010. 1-22. Print.

---. "'It's Game Over Forever': Atwood's Satiric Vision of Bioengineered Posthuman Future in *Oryx and Crake*." *The Journal of Commonwealth Literature* 39.3 (2004): 139-156. Print.

Clarke, Bruce, and Manuela Rossini, eds. *The Routledge Companion to Literature and Science*. London: Routledge, 2012. Print.

Dunning, Stephen. "Margaret Atwood's *Oryx and Crake*: The Terror of the Therapeutic." *Canadian Literature* 186 (2005): 86-101. Print.

Esposito, Elena. *Die Fiktion der wahrscheinlichen Realität*. Trans. Nicole Reinhardt. Frankfurt/M.: Suhrkamp, 2007. Print.

Foucault, Michel. *The Order of Things: An Archaeology of the Human Sciences*. New York, NY: Vintage Books, 1973. Print.

Fukuyama, Francis. *The End of History and the Last Man*. London: Penguin, 1992. Print.

---. *Our Posthuman Future: Consequences of the Biotechnology Revolution*. New York: Farrar, Straus, and Giroux, 2002. Print.

Giddens, Anthony. *Modernity and Self-Identity. Self and Society in the Late Modern Age*. Cambridge: Polity Press, 1991. Print.

Gray, Chris Hables, et al., eds. *The Cyborg Handbook*. New York: Routledge, 1995. Print.

Griffiths, Anthony. "Genetics According to *Oryx and Crake*." *Canadian Literature* 181 (2004): 192-195. Print.

Haraway, Donna. "A Manifesto for Cyborgs: Science, Technology, and Socialist Feminism in the 1980s." *Socialist Review* 80 (1985): 65-107. Print.

--- . *The Companion Species Manifesto: Dogs, People, and Significant Otherness*. Chicago: Prickly Paradigm Press, 2003. Print.

--- . *When Species Meet*. Minneapolis: University of Minnesota Press, 2008. Print.

Hayles, N. Katherine. *How We Became Posthuman: Virtual Bodies in Cybernetics, Literature, and Informatics*. Chicago: University of Chicago Press, 1999. Print.

Hayward, Peter. "Media Watch: Margaret Atwood's *Oryx and Crake*." *The Lancet, Neurology*. 2 (2003): 580. Print.

Hengen, Shannon. "Moral/ Environmental Debt in *Payback* and *Oryx and Crake*." *Margaret Atwood. The Robber Bride, The Blind Assassin, Oryx and Crake*. Ed. J. Brooks Bouson. London: Continuum, 2010. 129-140. Print.

LeGuin, Ursula. "The Year of the Flood by Margaret Atwood." *The Guardian* Saturday 29 August 2009. Web. http://www.guardian.co.uk/books/2009/aug/29/margaret-atwood-year-of-flood.

Luhmann, Niklas. 1991. *Soziologie des Risikos*. Berlin: De Gruyter, 2003. Print.

--- . *Risk: A Sociological Theory*. With a new introduction by N. Stehr and G. Bechmann. New Brunswick: Transaction, 2002. Print.

Milburn, Colin. *Nanovision: Engineering the Future*. Durham: Duke University Press, 2008. Print.

Squier, Susan. "A Tale Meant to Inform, Not to Amuse." *Science* 302.5648 (2003): 1154-55. Print.

Stein, Karen F. "Problematic Paradice in *Oryx and Crake*." *Margaret Atwood. The Robber Bride, The Blind Assassin, Oryx and Crake*. Ed. J. Brooks Bouson. London: Continuum, 2010. 141-155. Print.

Wolfe, Cary. *Animal Rites: American Culture, the Discourse of Species, and Posthumanist Theory*. Chicago: University of Chicago Press, 2003. Print.

---, ed. *Zoontologies: The Question of the Animal*. Minneapolis: University of Minnesota Press, 2003. Print.

NICOLE MARUO-SCHRÖDER

"It's theoretically possible": Disaster and Risk in Contemporary American Film

In the opening sequence of *The Core* (2003), the crew of the space shuttle Endeavor is about to land when, due to an electronic fall-out, the navigational system fails and the shuttle approaches downtown L.A. instead of Houston, TX. Nobody knows what to do, except for Major Rebecca Childs (Hilary Swank), who suggests an alternative landing scenario based on her own manual calculations. Faster than the ground computer, she has come up with the L.A. River as a potential landing site for the shuttle. When, finally, the computer has calculated the risk of such a landing maneuver, it projects a possible fail scenario; asked by the flight director on ground Dr. Talma Stickley (Alfre Woodard) whether that would work, the technician simply shrugs and says "It's theoretically possible." Despite this rather bleak assessment, Stickley gives the shuttle crew her go-ahead and, after a couple of near collisions with the river bridges, the shuttle lands more or less safely, proving Childs right.

This sequence highlights a number of aspects that dominate the genre of disaster film. First of all, technology is shown to be unreliable, a potential risk, which may lead to a catastrophe: the navigational system failed and the computer calculations for the landing scenario were wrong. Secondly, the scene emphasizes the necessity to take a risk in order to avoid the disaster: ground and shuttle crew risk a potentially disastrous landing (and silently accept the sacrifice implied in it) and are rewarded. Finally, trust, particularly the trust in human capacities, is essential: the scene suggests that the potential failures of technology can and, indeed, must be compensated for by human creativity and intelligence. Once this is assured and technology is put – again – under human control, the risk is minimized and under control as well. Seen this way, disaster movies are not simply about disaster but also about risk and risk management, that is the ways in which risks can be contained and managed with the help of technology.

Hence, in the following, I will analyze how contemporary disaster movies represent risk and functionalize it as part of their narrative structure. As a number of theories point out, risk is not simply an objective category, an event whose likelihood can be calculated based on scientific data and facts but a culturally and socially constructed phenomenon (Lupton 28-33, Slovic et.al. 311, Zinn 6, 11-14).[1] Similarly, risk perception is not an objective assessment of facts but determined by a variety of socio-cultural as well as individual factors that influence a person's evaluation of risk. As Ursula Heise points out, "perceptions of ecological and technological risk scenarios are shaped by and filtered through narrative templates that manifest themselves in both visual and verbal artifacts" (Heise 122; see also 138-142). In other words, cultural texts can have a vital role in forming and perpetuating our understanding of the concept of risk and may influence both what we perceive as risk and how we act on this in a number of ways. Disaster movies can therefore be seen as an important part of such a discourse on risk, even more so because they are texts that circulate globally and thus have a far-reaching impact. A case in point is the film *The Day After Tomorrow* (2004), which had quite a huge impact on the discussion of climate change, even though it was accused of portraying it in an unrealistic way. Indeed, experts were divided on the question whether the film would have a positive or negative effect on the public perception of climate change (Leiserowitz 23, 25-26).[2]

The focus of this essay will be the visual and narrative patterns with which disaster movies present risk scenarios and the ways in which these risks are assessed and coped with. It is my contention that disaster films deal with the notion of risk in various contradictory ways: on the one hand, these films routinely turn risk scenarios into disasters that threaten to be of an apocalyptic, often also global scope, thus emphasizing the uncontrollable and 'random' nature of risk; on the other hand, the worst-case risk scenarios that have been conjured up during the movie are hardly ever fully transformed into film reality in the end, a plot device that somewhat paradoxically suggests that risks can be controlled and successfully managed after all. In this way, disaster movies can have it both ways: they visualize the catastrophic extent and consequences of high-risk scenarios and provide a happy ending at the same time. Technology as well as human ingenuity are vital for such a successful mitigation of disaster consequences and both are celebrated as indispensable tools in a variety of ways, even though (and maybe especially if) the disaster was caused by the misuse of technology in the first place. In consequence, risks are visualized as a highly dangerous and also contingent part of our daily lives, which – should they become reality – can nevertheless be controlled under certain circumstances that I will discuss in more detail further down. I will begin my discussion by highlighting some important general characteristics and patterns of the genre of disaster movies and how they interrelate with the concept of risk before I will illustrate my

1 For an excellent brief overview of various concepts of risk see, for instance, Renn. See also Heise (124-136) and Lupton.

2 A number of reception studies (in the U.S., the U.K., Japan and Germany) could show that the film sensitized most viewers regarding their perception on climate change. For an overview of the five different reception studies on the movie see Weik von Mossner.

points with disaster films that were released during the last two decades. I will close my paper with a brief analysis of *Contagion* (2011), a recent film that provides a counter example to the typical pattern of the disaster genre and hence, as I will show, a different approach to the notion of risk.

The Concept of Risk and the Genre of Disaster Movies

Like other (film) genres, the disaster genre cannot be neatly distinguished from other genres as it shares a variety of features with them and thus, most disaster films could be categorized under different labels as well, notably as action (*Volcano*), thriller (*The Sum of All Fears*), drama (*Titanic*), science fiction (*Independence Day*) or even war films (*Battle Los Angeles*).[3] For my purposes here, I will understand the disaster film as being centrally about a disaster (Roddick 246), which means that the disaster, which can be either global or local in scale, influences the plot in a decisive way. In other words, the films' focus lies on both the scale and impact of the disaster as well as on how the disaster is dealt with. Thus, they either portray the protagonists' attempt to avert the disaster, which, as discussed in more detail below, means to prevent its worst extent, as for example in *Armageddon* (1998) or *Godzilla* (1998), or they deal with how the protagonists cope with a disaster that they cannot do anything about, for instance the sinking ship in *Poseidon* (2006) or the flooding of major parts of the earth in *2012* (2009).[4] For both types of movies, risk plays a role in two distinct but related ways. In the first part of the narrative, risk is the starting point as it serves as a foreshadowing of the future, an anticipation of the nature and scope of the disaster that threatens to disrupt everyday life. Thus, risk is connoted clearly negatively with danger, loss, and destruction. Once the predicted risk starts to become reality and the actual disaster unfolds, risk again plays a significant role, determining how the protagonists deal with the disaster and its consequences. Here, risk is portrayed as a necessary coping strategy for both the aversion of the worst-case scenario and the survival of the catastrophe. Like courage and sacrifice, the willingness to take risks is one of the distinguishing qualities of the films' (mostly male) heroes. To risk one's life, for example, is a high-risk stake that usually pays (at least for the main protagonist) and hence, risk becomes positively connoted with hope and success.

---

[3] For overviews and definitions of the disaster genre see, for instance, Keane (Introduction), Yacowar, Roddick.

[4] The lines between these two 'types' of film are, of course, fuzzy – averting the worst extent of a catastrophe necessitates survival while the mere survival of a catastrophe, whose extent cannot really be influenced, means arguably that its worst extent (death of the protagonists) can be averted.

It is important, then, to differentiate between risk and the disaster itself. As Ulrich Beck points out, "[r]isk means the anticipation of the catastrophe," a future scenario that is not merely speculative but possible and controversial. Put differently, for the concept of risk to apply, the disaster has to remain a possibility because "[t]he moment risks become real, […] they become catastrophes. Risks are always future events that may occur, that threaten us" (9) and therefore, they have an enormous influence on our present and future lives.[5] While being a possible, if not necessarily likely, threat in the future (and it is important to note that Hollywood movies frequently use rather fantastic and improbable risk scenarios), a risk is still controversial; to some extent it is uncertain whether a risk will become reality or not, otherwise it would simply be a danger. Moreover, Jens Zinn emphasizes that "[t]he concept of risk is tied to the possibility that the future can be altered – or at least perceived as such – by human activities" (4). Risk implies that something can actually be done in order to prevent the worst from happening. For this paper, I will therefore not consider films in which neither the extent of the disaster nor the survival of those affected can be influenced by human action, as in *Knowing* (2009) or *Melancholia* (2011). For similar reasons I will not consider post-apocalyptic disaster movies, in which protagonists have to deal with the consequences of a catastrophe that has already happened and cannot be reversed, such as *The Book of Eli* (2010) or *The Road* (2009).

The necessity to distinguish between risk and actual catastrophe renders the relationship between disaster films and the concept of risk somewhat complicated since the point of disaster movies is to let the disaster happen, at least to a certain extent. A disaster movie in which the disaster can be completely averted, in which the risk is not at least partly realized, would be 'pointless,' so to speak, since large-scale spectacular destructions, the "money shots" as Alexa Weik von Mossner rightly calls them (107), are a key characteristic of the genre both visually and with regard to their narrative structure (cf. Keane 78). In other words, disaster movies do not just invoke a (worst-case) risk scenario but turn it into film reality. In a sense, disaster films can be seen as what Ulrich Beck calls the "staging" of a risk – they actualize, make present a future risk scenario. However, in how far the films actually function as a warning to change the structures and conditions that lead to the disaster will be discussed below.[6] As Beck notes, "only by

[5] Beck emphasizes that the danger, which a risk imagines, "shapes our expectations, lodges in our heads and guides our actions," becoming "a political force that transforms the world" (10).

[6] In this context Beck also emphasizes that staging is not to be understood as "deliberate falsification of reality" (10). In this regard, the comparison between the staging of risk in disaster movies and Beck's notion of risk staging is somewhat stretched since the film genre is less concerned with likelihood, scientific accuracy, or realism than with a gripping storyline and impressive scenes of destruction.

imagining and staging world risk does the future catastrophe become present – often with the goal of averting it by influencing present decisions. Then the diagnosis of risk would be 'a self-refuting prophecy,'" something that will not happen precisely because it is imagined to happen (10). It is also important to note that the worst-case risk scenario is almost never completely realized in films and more often than not the most serious disaster consequences can be prevented. In this way, the danger and threat that the risk and the subsequent disaster pose to civilization can be emphasized while enough of the world is left to be saved and build a better future. Hope, as it turns out, is an essential part of the disaster narrative.[7] The fascination disaster movies exert on their audiences is therefore the 'safe' realization of risk, the playing out of a 'what if': From the safe vantage point of their cinema seats, viewers can watch (parts of) the world being destroyed all the while knowing that there will be a happy ending. Such a combination of thrill and reassurance is part of the films' entertaining and "therapeutic" (Ryan and Kellner 56), one could also say escapist, quality.

However, I would argue that the genre needs the disaster not just for entertainment purposes – although this is undoubtedly an essential point as the occurrence of ever bigger, more fantastic, and arguably more impressive, computer-generated disaster sequences in Hollywood movies indicates. As much as the disaster is about entertainment of the audience, it can also be seen as a warning, which is made more pressing by the visualization of its catastrophic consequences for the world 'as we know it.' In this sense, disaster movies, particularly those that envision apocalyptic end-of-world scenarios, appear to be modern-day, secularized variations of the jeremiad: they conjure up the end of the world while at the same time insisting on the possibility to turn things around just in time to survive.[8] Risk becomes connected to the notion of hubris, and the actual disaster doubles as warning and punishment for a careless society that has deviated too much from standards of morality.[9] Depicting a world disrupted by catastrophic events, disaster movies provide in one sense a 'tabula rasa' from which to start anew. Nevertheless, their endings often confirm traditional norms and values: "Order is reasserted" as Maurice Yacowar so aptly observes (288). Seemingly about change and new beginnings, disaster movies are deeply conservative and Nick Roddick's contention that disaster movies of the

---

7 Cf. Greg Garrard, who writes that "only if we imagine that the planet *has* a future, after all, are we likely to take responsibility for it" (107).

8 The frequent use of religious symbolism and narratives that can be found in many disaster movies underlines this point and I am grateful to Antje Kley for drawing my attention to it. *I am Legend* (2007) is an excellent example for this as its ending imagines a new beginning in the form of a small, religious community that is reminiscent of 17th century Puritan settlements.

9 For a more detailed discussion of the use of end-of-world rhetoric and biblical images see Schröder.

1970s are "'reactionary culture' par excellence" (245) is still true for today's movies, even if to a lesser extent. Somewhat paradoxically, the genre uses the disaster as a warning while frequently leaving the 'risky' structures that caused it in place.

This intricate interdependence between disaster and risk leads to several narrative patterns that I find significant: First of all, the risk scenario – a disaster that is in most cases quite fantastic and improbable – is contrasted with the risk management, the rescue mission which is equally fantastic and unlikely. In other words, one risk narrative (the risk of the future disaster) is balanced with another (the risks involved in the management of the disaster). Secondly, and connected to the first point, most films visualize the catastrophe as nature out of bounds regardless of the cause or origin of the catastrophe, whereas the disaster management, the rescue mission, is clearly set in the realm of culture and technology. Thirdly, although the disasters are visualized as spectacles of an impressive destructive force, they can nevertheless be partly averted and survived; even films in which the catastrophe actually takes place have a happy ending, and it is frequently a happy ending that insists on the superiority of technology vis-à-vis nature and serves to promote trust in the self-healing forces of both nature and culture.

"Against All Odds and In the Face of Tremendous Adversity": Controlling the (Risk of) Disaster

I will begin my analysis with the first pattern, the opposition of the disaster on the hand and the rescue mission on the other. Despite their (visual) verisimilitude through computer-generated images and the elaborate scientific explanations and facts that disaster movies use to construct their risk scenario, it is not the concrete risk that these films are interested in but rather, how people react in the face of its realization (cf. Hofmann 191). Basically, disaster movies routinely turn a rather improbable risk scenario into (film) reality and, moreover, following the logic of the genre, show a just as improbable solution to be successful. In both *Deep Impact* and *Armageddon* (both 1998), for instance, the rather unlikely event of a meteor hitting the earth with fatal consequences for the whole planet becomes real. In *2012* the earth's core is heated up by unprecedented amounts of solar radiation causing tectonic shifts and the flooding of the whole planet, whereas in *The Core* the earth's core stops rotating causing the atmosphere to become unstable, again with fatal consequences for the whole planet. In *Godzilla*, nuclear tests cause a saurian to mutate and turn into a monster, which destroys NYC. In *Independence Day* (1996) and, more recently, *War of the Worlds* (2005), *Cloverfield* (2008), *Battle L.A.* (2010), and *Battleship* (2012) aliens invade planet earth to exploit its resources. Even movies that take more realistic or likely risks as their topic, such as *The Day after Tomorrow*, stage them in ways, to use Beck's term, that highlight the fantastic and extraordinary. Thus, one could say, that even and maybe especially risk scenarios that are highly unlikely if not impossible in our real world are realized. In a way this mirrors the fact that people are more concerned about risks that – if realized – "have catastrophic effects on humans and the environment" than about 'low-impact' risks, even though the former might have a much lower probability (Renn 55; see also Slovic et.al. 320). On a more symbolic level, this impossibility underlines the random and unexpected nature of the disaster that hits earth. Serving the blockbuster quality of the movies, it also indicates that the nature of the disaster or a realistic assessment of its causes and effects are not that important. Instead, the movies highlight its symbolic quality as both punishment and purge and its function as a test in the face of which humans have to react and prove themselves.

This is where the rescue missions that are attached to the various disaster scenarios become significant: they are just as fantastic (and fantastically unlikely) as the disaster and serve as 'playground' to put humans to a test. Their dangerous and audacious character turns them into highly risky affairs both with regard to their likelihood to succeed and for those who carry them out. Frequently, lives are lost in the course of action and sacrifices need to be made for a positive outcome. In other words, the risk scenario and the subsequent disaster are matched and balanced by a risk management that is also characterized by a high risk, and death plays a major role in both. While the majority of people simply die in order to illustrate the scale and danger of the catastrophe, death has also a symbolic function within the films. Generally, and in line with the genre characteristics, the disaster can be seen as a form of punishment, something that purges a society that has grown corrupt and immoral and now has to 'pay' for its sins. The idea of the disaster as punishment is frequently taken up in the form it takes. The giant wave in *The Day after Tomorrow* and *Deep Impact* (1998) is reminiscent of the deluge, for instance, and in both cases New York City, a pars pro toto for metropolitan lifestyle and society, is literally and metaphorically cleansed. Similarly, the volcano eruption in *Volcano* (1997) can be read as a purgatory, cleansing and renewing L.A., which is marked at the beginning of the movie as morally corrupt. This idea of the catastrophe as punishment relates to the fact that sacrifice is often part of the rescue mission.

Hence, people frequently die as part of the sacrifices that have to be made in order to avert the catastrophe – such a heroic death becomes especially obvious and meaningful when main characters die. Sacrifice – originally a religious rite – is an act in which the sacrificial victim is exchanged for redemption. In her study on the function of sacrifice in Hollywood movies, Claire Sisco King explains that the "suffering and noble death [of the sacrificial victim-hero] allow for synecdochic figurations of the nation as traumatized and then recovered, lost and then found, ruined and then repaired" (15). More specifically, in disaster movies a seemingly lost or ruined world can be saved in time through the (mostly male) hero's sacrifice of his own life. In *The Core*, for instance, most of the characters on the rescue team sacrifice themselves to ensure the success of the mission, thus making up for technological shortcomings some of them are responsible for. The shuttle crew in *Deep Impact* dies for the same reason and in *Armageddon*, main protagonist Harry Stemper decides to give up his own life in order to save the world.

While such a sacrifice means the end of the hero's life, it ensures mission success and thus, it is symbolically a reconstitution of life. It 'repairs,' as it were, a society that has been fragmented and destroyed by the disaster. As Claire King puts it, "sacrifice redresses a crisis or breach within a community through expiatory substitution wherein the sacrificial object takes on and atones for the imperfections of the larger social body" (15). It also helps to impart a quasi-religious aura to the dead hero and thereby reinforces notions of traditional masculinity and male heroism (King 37, 41). By extension, the sacrifice likewise helps to reinstate control over a world that has gone out of bounds so that humans become the rulers of their own fate again. A case in point can be found in *I am Legend* (2007), which shows a post-apocalyptic world in which a virus has either killed humans or turned them into so-called "darkseekers," human-like creatures that avoid daylight. Main protagonist Robert Neville sacrifices his life in order to ensure that the cure he found against the virus can be brought safely to a community of not yet infected survivors. Not only does his death turn him into a martyr-like figure, a reading that is reinforced by the religious imagery that can be found throughout the film, it also ensures control over a disease that was generated by humans in the first place. Life is sacrificed in order to contain the disaster, that is to minimize risk (again), reinforcing trust in human institutions and structures while at the same time also (seemingly) diminishing the risk they carry. In short, not only is risk-taking required to contain the consequences of the disaster; sacrifice as well often helps to both justify and contain risk in these movies.

Culture's Other: Disaster as Nature out of Bounds

Discussing Max Weber's argument that the disenchantment of the world led to a replacement of magic by technology and rationality as means of mastering the world, Jens Zinn points out that "[r]isk implies that an uncertain future can be made available to human action foremost with the help of positivist science and technique" (10). This is mirrored in the ways many movies contrast the disaster and how it is 'managed': While the disaster as such is mostly visualized as a disruptive force of nature, which invades the space of culture to destroy it, the containment of the disaster – its (partial) reversal – is very much connected to the realm of science and technology. Put differently, the ways in which many of these films visualize their risk scenarios does not so much highlight the cause of the catastrophe than its consequences: whereas the catastrophe is linked to nature (even in cases where its origin is anthropogenic), its containment is connected to culture and, more specifically, technology. In *The Core*, for example, the disaster is triggered by a secret weapon, which leads to a destabilization of the earth's core; the disaster itself, however, is pictured exclusively as a natural catastrophe of global scope. Nature stops behaving according to natural laws and takes revenge on humans by causing electronic gadgets to become dangerous for those who use them.[10] It appears to be out of bounds destroying famous landmarks and cities around the globe. The destruction of Rome, for instance, is pictured as apocalyptic thunderstorm that destroys the city, which can be taken to symbolize both cultural achievements and moral degeneration. Despite the technological cause for the disaster, nature is visually blamed for the catastrophe. Along the same lines, both *Godzilla* and *The Day After Tomorrow* picture the catastrophe as nature invading human space: while in *Godzilla* the eponymous creature wreaks havoc in New York City, in *The Day After Tomorrow* a giant wave floods the city.[11]

Such natural disaster sequences are almost invariably contrasted with scenes of the rescue mission, which foreground the role that science, technology, and human effort play in the aversion of the apocalypse. To stay with the present examples, in *The Core* the saving of the world is made possible by the latest (military) technology. The sequence in which the protagonists prepare for their rescue mission is a parade of state of the art technology. It is accompanied by military music as well as the voice-over of its hero, scientist Dr. Josh Keyes (Aaron Eckhart), who explains the technological details of the endeavor and comments that "With luck, irony will break for the good guys for once and the world's biggest weapons of mass destruction will help save the world," adding an ironic twist to the sequence. Indeed, the whole preparation for the world-saving endeavor is a rather obvious celebration of technology and human ingenuity, which borders on parody.[12] However, this (exaggerated) emphasis on technological

---

[10] At the beginning of the film, people die because their pacemakers stop working while later on, in the sequence discussed here, people are hurt using things like an espresso machine or a TV.

[11] On second glance, however, *Godzilla* provides a more ambiguous reading as it is the military that causes most of the destruction in its pursuit of the monster.

[12] In his study of the relation between the genre of disaster movies and the concept of camp, Ken Feil reads *The Core*'s self-ironic humor and parodic elements as a "replay of 1990s disaster movie discourse" (134) with its pleasure in destruction. He also sees it as an attempt to get away with reveling in scenes of large-scale destruction without conjuring up unwanted associations with the real disaster of 9/11, an incident that

achievements is typical for the genre and also characterizes the entire rescue mission to the core: despite immense obstacles, technology saves the day in the end, helping to control nature and to put her (back) in her place. In a similar manner, in *Godzilla* fighter jets help to destroy the monster's nest, and in *The Day After Tomorrow*, military helicopters descend angel-like onto New York City to rescue the survivors. Slightly less obvious is the role of technology in *I am Legend*, in which the hero Robert Neville uses technology both to survive and to find the cure for the fatal virus. Yet, here, too, it plays a vital role: his home, equipped with a number of automatic defense-mechanisms, and especially his laboratory serve as a technological enclave in a world that has deteriorated into a dangerous wilderness. Such successful endings of the missions suggest that it is the people, not technology, that pose a risk, namely the risk of abuse. Risk, thus, becomes tied to the taking of action (cf. Renn 50) rather than to technological errors. In this way, most disaster films emphasize that technology, provided that it is put in the right hands, is indispensable and can – and should – be trusted.

Nevertheless, even the latest technology together with seemingly limitless material and financial resources cannot always guarantee the success of the mission.[13] Again a typical feature of the genre, the plan to avert the catastrophe is audacious and requires certain human characteristics such as courage, resourcefulness, and the ability to make judgment calls in the face of danger. In addition to the trust in technology as well as the willingness to sacrifice oneself, another human quality becomes vital: many of the decisions that are made as part of the risk management are based more on emotions than on rationality. Frequently it is "gut feeling" rather than purely scientific considerations or calculations of probability that lead to decisions that turn out to be successful. Indeed, frequently such an emotional assessment of risk is shown to be (more) accurate and reliable, something which relates to how risk seems to be assessed in real life. As Paul Slovic et.al. argue, in people's judgments of risks affect and emotion are at least as important as rational calculations, particularly if complex situations are judged (Slovic et.al. 315). The above-mentioned shuttle landing in *The Core* is a case in point: Major Childs' calculations and her trust in the

makes any pleasure in destruction seem perverse. In the face of its box-office failure, however, he reads it as an attempt that was not successful (140).

13 Interestingly enough, money is never tight in the realization of even the most expensive and large-scale rescue missions; neither are material resources or man-power. In *2012*, to give a recent example, the money to put the fantastic plan of building eight giant arks to survive the flood into reality comes from tickets (1 billion Euro each) sold to those who can afford it. The work is – quite ironically – provided by Chinese labor. When in *The Core* scientist Dr. Brazzleton (Delroy Lindo) is asked what he would need to realize his plan of building his specially modified rescue vessel he answers "Fifty Billion dollars". General Purcell (Richard Jenkins) simply asks whether he would take a check.

commander's ability to fly the shuttle prove more accurate than a 'rational' computer calculation – lives can be saved not despite but because of what one could call the 'human factor' within risk assessment. While experience and expert knowledge often provide the basis for such decisions (so that they are based on rationality to a certain extent), the films take care to emphasize that the heroes (less often heroines) make their decision against the odds and use their personal judgment in order to come to the right decision. Thus, in addition to state-of-the-art technology, both the willingness to take risks and a partly 'emotional' assessment of risks become central ingredients for the containment of the catastrophe and the movies' happy endings.

It's (not) the End of the World as We Know It: Spectacular Catastrophes and Happy Endings

The contrast between the risk scenario – the natural catastrophe – and the risk management – the technologized rescue mission – finds a parallel in the opposition of the disaster as a disruptive spectacle of considerable size and the happy ending, which promises order and containment. While disasters are usually visualized in dimensions that emphasize their nature as extremely dangerous events that have far-reaching consequences, their actual effects as suggested by the films' positive outcome are relatively short lived and can be quickly overcome. Film disasters (even the local ones) are awe-inspiring spectacles because of sheer size and destructive force – nothing is small or subtle about these catastrophes. This underlines the size and terror with which the catastrophe threatens humanity and thus emphasizes the idea of a sublime nature, which is completely unaffected by any human concerns. These spectacles of destruction are also characterized by a certain beauty, an "aesthetics of destruction" as Susan Sontag calls it (213), so that they are spectacularly beautiful sights as well. Moreover, it is enjoyable to watch the destruction itself as Geoff King explains: "Part of this pleasure may be rooted in a general delight sometimes taken in the imaginary destruction of familiar landscapes or cultural edifices. There is a certain carnivalesque appeal in this licensed enjoyment of destruction" (162).[14]

The wave in *The Day After Tomorrow* is indeed both big and beautiful – it is a spectacle of enormous proportion, which, like the biblical deluge, does not just destroy but also purify the city thus making possible a new beginning. Similarly, the wave in *Deep Impact* as well as the meteor impact in *Armageddon* are spectacles both beautiful and terrifying. Moreover, these

[14] Cf. Ken Feil, who argues that especially the films of the 1990s "perfect the art of pleasurable destruction," which stands in contrast to the sympathy they evoke for the characters affected by the disaster (68). Stephen Keane speaks of the "postcard theory" of disaster movies and maintains that "if a building or city is not instantly recognizable it's not worth destroying" (83).

catastrophes are also technological spectacles, impressive feats of computer-generated imagery, which helps to visualize the unimaginable.[15] Here also lies another ambiguity of these spectacles: while size and destructive force serve to impress the danger of the uncontrollable destructive force of nature on the viewer, the technology which brings it to the screen, suggests the opposite: CGI controls nature in the sense that it can make nature do what we want. Furthermore, the catastrophe's visual character, exaggerated and hyper-real at the same time, turn it into a theme-park ride, a short-lived spectacle of destruction that can be enjoyed without any consequences.[16]

The ways in which film disasters are staged suggests that they are short-lived affairs as they are reduced to one or, at most, very few climactic moments; long-term consequences are simply not part of the narrative and, in fact, blended out by the positive imagery that their typical narrative structure provides, the happy ending. Despite large scale destruction and any hopelessness and despair that the catastrophe might have brought about humanity, in the end, civilization prevails and, even more importantly, culture's dominance over nature is re-established. Even in films, in which a global catastrophe actually happens, a happy ending seems to reverse its terrifying impact on human civilization. While *Armageddon* ends with multiple marriages, reinforcing the idea of a new beginning on a social level, *The Day After Tomorrow* ends with the iconic image of the blue planet seen from space by an astronaut who comments that "the air has never looked so clear." Similarly, in *The Core* the beginning disintegration of earth can be stopped and "earth is healing itself" as one of the characters observes at the end. The ending of *I am Legend* is a variation of this theme of peaceful nature as it closes with the image of domesticated wilderness, an idyllic, pre-modern, self-sufficient village that brings to mind 17th century Puritan New England. In a way, the film's ending is reminiscent of the "pastoral countermodel," which is, as Ursula Heise argues, frequently evoked as part of an environmentalist rhetoric that Lawrence Buell has called "toxic discourse" (140).[17] In *I am Legend*, the toxic pollution would be the man-

---

15 Referring to Michael Allen, Pam Cooke and Mieke Bernink, Stephen Keane points out that "contemporary special-effects technologies represent the next justified step in a longstanding and ongoing cinema of spectacle" (78).

16 However, see also Alexa Weik von Mossner's discussion of *The Day After Tomorrow* and her argument that it is the "*visceral* effect" of the film's spectacular disaster sequences that influenced viewers and generated the film's impact on the public discussion of climate change (98).

17 This image of a rural community is actually complicated by the film's plot, which contrasts 'us' (the humans) and 'them' (the so-called darkseekers). Although during the film these darkseekers are mostly pictured as less than human, there are moments when it becomes clear that they are capable to think, act, and feel like humans. The peaceful Puritan village, whose most prominent features are a church and fortified wall, turns into a gated (religious) community, a protected area which excludes the different 'other' (the name of the darkseekers here also attains religious connotations).

made virus while the pastoral is here not just evoked as a countermodel but, in fact, realized at the ending of the movie as the de-facto future of the survivors.

Such happy endings tend to take away most of the terror or anxiety that the risk scenario, which is visualized as an impressively 'real' event of breathtaking magnitude, might have. This is underlined by the rather short-lived nature of the catastrophe, which is visualized as a climactic moment rather than an ongoing process. Therefore, it is not so much the consequences of the catastrophe that are emphasized as the possibility of a new beginning and with this the realization of a 'better' world. As Heise so aptly points out in her discussion of risk and narrative, "[i]n the apocalyptic perspective, utter destruction lies ahead but can be averted and replaced by an alternative future society; in the risk perspective, crises are already underway all around, and while their consequences can be mitigated, a future without their impact has become impossible to envision" (142).[18] Paradoxically, in their visualization of risk scenarios, disaster movies seem to erase the risk to a certain extent: With the realization of the catastrophe, the risk seems to be over and contained and its consequences are no longer relevant.

The Risk of *Contagion:* The Invisible Catastrophe

As I have argued, the spectacular quality of the visualization of the catastrophe in contrast to the happy ending as well as the related opposition of nature (disaster) and culture/ technology (rescue) are essential aspects of the ways in which the concept of risk is usually visualized in the disaster film genre. Such patterns and their influence on the notion of risk become even clearer if one takes a closer look at a recent film that does not adhere to these typical genre characteristics. Steven Soderbergh's aptly named *Contagion* (2011) is a film about a pandemic which is caused by a mutated, highly contagious and potentially fatal virus that travels around the world in a matter of days. The film has variously been reviewed as an "international thriller" (Denby n.p.), a "medical thriller" (Benson-Allott 14), a "bio-threat suspense film" (Covert n.p.), an "outbreak film" (Yamey and Hwang 850) as well as a disaster film (Longworth n.p.), a mixed classification that points to *Contagion*'s hybrid character in terms of its genre.[19] Indeed one could argue that it is this hybridity that allows the film to explore a different approach to the disaster genre and undermine some of its conventions and implications

---

[18] Heise sees apocalyptic narratives as a form of risk perception but points out that they envision the future in different ways than theories of risk or risk narratives (141).

[19] In a phone interview, Steven Soderbergh has explained that he wanted to avoid "all the traps and tropes of the typical disaster movies. We don't go places our characters haven't gone; no shot of Paris where a bunch of extras we haven't met are dying. No scenes with the president. No helicopter shots floating over the city" (Covert n.p.).

for the notion of risk.[20] While thrillers are also concerned with issues of risk and potential catastrophes, they tend to take on a more 'realistic' approach, which is particularly true for medical thrillers with their focus on medical and scientific details. Thus, these films emphasize the everyday character as well as the high probability of risk, which distinguishes them very much from the 'typical' disaster film with its (visual and narrative) focus on the extra-ordinary.

Thus, in contrast to most examples of the genre, *Contagion* chooses a risk that is possible, even probable and stages its realization in a quite realistic way.[21] For instance, the catastrophe is not visualized as a climactic spectacle but rather as an ongoing process throughout the film. In a certain sense the catastrophe is not visible at all as the virus and the ways in which it is transmitted are invisible. And although it is of natural origin, the pandemic is not characterized as a natural catastrophe but in fact, rather closely linked to social and economic structures. And while the ending certainly provides closure, it is not necessarily an overly 'happy' one that counters or even ignores the consequences of the catastrophe. All of these characteristics influence the notion of risk, as it emerges in *Contagion*, in decisive ways.

The film opens with a black screen and the sound of coughing, which is, as it turns out, one of the symptoms of the disease, before we see Beth Emhoff (Gwyneth Paltrow) waiting for her connecting flight at Chicago's O'Hare airport. The black screen underlines the nature of the catastrophe we are about to witness, the spread of an infection that is largely invisible and goes unnoticed. Being one of the first infected people, Emhoff has just carried the virus from Hong Kong to the U.S., where she will die very soon after this scene. Without a long exposition that prepares the viewer (and protagonists) for the upcoming disaster, the film starts right at the beginning, if not the middle, of the catastrophe. Moreover, instead of one linear storyline, which leads to a climactic disaster sequence, the film offers a number of not always intersecting plotlines, a decentralization that is continued into the visualization of the catastrophe itself. Rather than one spectacular, highly visible catastrophic climax, *Contagion* features a catastrophe that is ongoing and, what is more, largely invisible.[22]

This invisibility of the catastrophe necessitates a deviation from the typical visual politics of the disaster genre with its emphasis on highly visible

---

[20] I would like to thank Alexa Weik von Mossner for helping me to develop this point.

[21] In contrast to most disaster movies, *Contagion* has frequently been praised for its scientific accuracy. Yamey and Hwang, for instance, praise *Contagion* as "smart, true to life, and informative without being dull" (850) in their review published in the *British Medical Journal*. Similarly, in *Science* Kristen Mueller calls the film a "gripping yet refreshingly accurate warning" about a potential pandemic (1064).

[22] Cf. Caetlin Benson-Allott, who argues that *Contagion* emphasizes the "limits of visibility" and therefore goes against the "hypervisibility" that CGI makes possible, namely the "convincing depictions of things impossible to see in everyday life" (14).

and spectacular scenes of mayhem and destruction. Instead of such visual spectacles, *Contagion* utilizes characteristics that are typical for the (medical) thriller: the narrative focuses on a mysterious disease, pictures a mission that is structured as a race against time, and highlights the significance of (mis-)information for instance. In fact, it is the absence of visual spectacles and, arguably, the invisibility of the virus that contribute to the realistic atmosphere of the film, which focuses on the consequences of the quickly spreading and highly fatal pandemic instead: empty streets, supermarkets destroyed by looting, and, finally, sick patients that are dying (alone) in public places that have been turned into make-shift hospitals.[23] Moreover, the invisibility of the virus also emphasizes the risk of infection since it can potentially be everywhere. Accordingly, the film focuses on the various ways in which the virus can spread and draws our attention to doorknobs, elevator buttons, glasses, (finger) food, the shaking of hands, coughing and the like; it also makes visible how often we perform these simple actions every day, again highlighting the risk of infection. As a logical consequence, the virus spreads very quickly around the globe, killing people before they really know what is going on.

Moreover, the film underlines that the pandemic cannot easily be cured – indeed, the film emphasizes the length of time it takes to first of all identify the virus and the ways in which it spreads and then find a possible cure or vaccine. In other words, science and technology – finding a solution as well as attempting to contain the catastrophe – are not (immediately) successful. Rather, the film portrays a society that tries to save itself by social isolation, which rapidly turns into selfish egoism, so that the movie's taglines – "Nothing spreads like fear" and "Don't talk to anyone. Don't touch anyone" – are aptly visualized. In contrast to other movies, it is not so much nature that is the problem here; instead, the catastrophe is characterized as a social and cultural one. The film suggests that the mutation of the virus is ultimately caused by "the destructive power of corporate globalization" (Benson-Allott 15): the demolition of a forest in Macao leads to the accidental meeting of an infected bat with a pig, which is subsequently sold to a chef in Hong Kong, who in turn infects an American business woman by shaking her hand. It is people themselves, via the various routes of global economy, who help spread the virus literally in a matter of hours around the globe, thus killing large numbers of people. Furthermore, an essential part of the catastrophe lies also in the breaking down of the social systems, from the medical facilities, which quickly become dysfunctional because of the huge number

[23] John Wirt, for instance, writes that "*Contagion* depicts its devastating, plausible scenario with urgency and style" (n.p.). Similarly, David Denby points out that "*Contagion* confronts reality head on; it's a brief against magical thinking" (n.p.), and Colin Covert claims that the film is "a reality-show approach to the end of the world" (n.p.).

of sick and dying people, to the problem of riots and looting, which endangers the basic supply of necessary goods.

Finally, although the ending could arguably be called happy – after all, a vaccine has finally been developed – it does not necessarily seem that way.[24] Rather than with a hopeful shot of the world saved in time, *Contagion* ends literally where it began: with the infection. It traces the way the virus was accidentally created ("Somewhere in the world, the wrong pig met up with the wrong bat" as Dr. Ally Hextall (Jennifer Ehle) explains) and then ends with a photo of its first victim Beth Emhoff, which shows how she got infected by a coincidental handshake. Framing the movie with images of the infection does not so much suggest a happy ending than foreshadow a possible repetition of the events: a mutated virus just like this one can start any time anywhere, underlining the contingent and uncontrollable nature of such a catastrophe. Again, the narrative deviates from the typical pattern found in the disaster genre, utilizing characteristics of the thriller instead. In consequence, the notion of risk appears very differently in this movie: Here, the risk is not easily controllable with sufficient knowledge and technology or even through courageous and selfless behavior, just as the catastrophe itself cannot simply be stopped or reversed.[25] While in *Contagion* the catastrophe is visualized less spectacularly, it appears by no means less threatening, which holds also true for the way risk and risk-taking are portrayed. Through such a portrayal, the risk of infection, in fact, becomes a lot less controllable since it is everywhere rather than just concentrated in the realization of a brief catastrophic event. Moreover, the realized risk – the catastrophe – cannot easily be contained or stopped since the finding of the vaccine seems lucky rather than foreseeable and therefore does not provide a quick solution or happy ending.

Conclusion

Utilizing the generic characteristics of the (medical) thriller, *Contagion* goes beyond the conventions of the disaster genre, a 'deviation' that results in a more realistic approach to the portrayal of the disaster. In consequence, the film's unusual patterns seem to highlight a notion of risk that is characterized by its random, contingent, and uncontrollable nature, which stands in

[24] It takes months until the vaccine is developed and it takes even longer to produce it in sufficient amounts and to distribute it around the globe. This time period underlines the 'anti-climactic' visualization of the catastrophe by emphasizing the consequences of the global pandemic rather than offering a quick solution.

[25] Dr. Erin Mears (Kate Winslet) of the Center for Disease Control tries to help contain the outbreak of the catastrophe. Although she is quite conscious of the fatality of the virus and careful with regard to how it can be contracted, she is soon infected and dies a quite unheroic death despite her selfless commitment.

contrast to the idea of risk as it can be found in typical examples of the genre. The thrill of disaster movies lies in making real the most unlikely risk scenarios and also those that are most destructive – part of their appeal is their visualization of the disaster as extraordinary event, a spectacle that serves as a substitute for the disaster's invisible causes (Keane 101). This spectacle – formally a feat of technology – is a celebration of both large-scale destruction and human resilience and it is more often than not staged as an uncontrollable force of nature that invades culture's space. This spectacularly visualized risk scenario is countered by a risk management that glorifies human achievements (technology) and qualities (endurance, courage, resourcefulness). It is a technological spectacle that helps to gain back control over nature and to re-establish confidence in technology. Moreover, a successful handling of the catastrophe requires that further risks are taken so that risk and risk-taking actually attain positive qualities. Significantly, it is not so much scientific probabilities and facts that play a role in the evaluation of these risks but rather factors such as gut-feeling, guesswork, and plain luck. Therefore, despite the staging of risk as a catastrophe of enormous proportions, the successful rescue mission seems to suggest that it is both calculable and containable, an aspect that is underlined by the short-lived character of the catastrophe and the happy ending, that is by both visual and narrative patterns of the genre.

As a genre, then, disaster films participate in western risk discourses in a number of interesting ways. Staging highly devastating but rather unlikely risk scenarios, the films not just correspond to but exaggerate the types of risk most people actually fear: high-impact, low-probability risks as well as risks that lie beyond the control of the individual. This exaggerated nature of the film disasters propels them safely into the realm of the fictional, which makes the films so enjoyable and entertaining. Moreover, while such a focus on the extra-ordinary at the expense of what one could call everyday risks emphasizes the dangerous, contingent and uncontrollable nature of risks, the technology-oriented solutions that are offered as part of the disaster mitigation stand in contrast to this: they serve to instill a sense of control and safety, thus promoting a notion of technology and science as unfailing and all-powerful. As apocalyptic narratives in Heise's sense, disaster films paradoxically stage risks that threaten to annihilate the world as we know it only to end up with a world, in which the consequences of the disaster are not really relevant. Thus, rather than being self-refuting prophesies à la Beck, the narrative templates of most disaster films encourage an almost limitless confidence in human technology and progress precisely by visualizing worst-case scenarios. Hence, although contingent and dangerous at first glance, our environment is ultimately shown to be controllable and foreseeable as technology and humans work together to regain control over nature – which in most disaster movies turns out to be the real risk that needs to be contained.

Works Cited

Balmford, Andrew, et al. "Hollywood, Climate Change, and the Public." *Science* 305 (17 September 2004): 1713. Web. 19 September 2007 <sciencemag.org>.

Beck, Ulrich. "Introduction: Staging Global Risk." *World at Risk.* Transl. Ciaran Cronin. Cambridge: Polity Press, 2009, 1-23. Print.

Benson-Allott, Caetlin. "Out of Sight." *Film Quarterly* 65.2 (Winter 2011): 14-15. Print.

Covert, Colin. "Something in the Air in *Contagion.*" *Star Tribune.* (5 September 2011). Web. 19 March 2013 <http://www.startribune.com/printarticle/?id=128937628>.

Denby, David. "Call the Doctor." *The New Yorker.* (19 September 2011). Web. 19 March 2013 <http://www.newyorker.com/arts/critics/cinema/2011/09/19/110919crci_cinema_denby>.

Feil, Ken. *Dying for a Laugh: Disaster Movies and the Camp Imagination.* Middletown: Wesleyan University Press, 2005. Print.

Garrard, Greg. "Apocalypse." *Ecocriticism.* London: Routledge, 2004. 85-107. Print.

Heise, Ursula K. *Sense of Place and Sense of Planet: The Environmental Imagination of the Global*. Oxford: Oxford University Press, 2008. Print.

Hofmann, Wilhelm. "Nichts ist so unterhaltend wie der Untergang der Welt: Überlegungen zur Risikokommunikation in Katastrophenfilmen." *Sinnwelt Film: Beiträge zur interdisziplinären Filmanalyse.* Ed. Wilhelm Hofmann. Baden-Baden: Nomos Verlagsgesellschaft, 1996. 159-193. Print.

Keane, Stephen. *Disaster Movies. The Cinema of Catastrophe.* London: Wallflower, 2001. Print.

King, Claire Sisco. *Washed in Blood: Male Sacrifice, Trauma, and the Cinema.* New Brunswick: Rutgers University Press, 2012. Print.

King, Geoff. *Spectacular Narratives: Hollywood in the Age of the Blockbuster.* London: I.B. Tauris, 2000. Print.

Leiserowitz, Anthony A. "Before and After *The Day After Tomorrow*: A Study of Climate Change Risk Perception." *Environment* 46.9 (November 2004): 22-44. Web. 30 January 2013 <http://www.upf.edu/pcstacademy/_docs/200411_environment1.pdf>.

Longworth, Karina. "Steven Soderbergh Says We're Killing Ourselves in *Contagion.*" *The Village Voice* (7 September 2011). Web. 19 March 2013. <http://www.villagevoice.com/2011-09-07/film/steven-soderbergh-says-we-re-killing-ourselves-in-contagion/>.

Lupton, Deborah. *Risk.* London: Routledge, 1999. Print.

Mueller, Kristen L. "Nightmare of an Exploding Pandemic." *Science* 334.6059 (25 November 2011): 1064. Web. 23 February 2012 <http://www.sciencemag.org/content/334/6059/1064.1.full>.

Renn, Ortwin. "Concepts of Risk: An Interdisciplinary Review. Part I: Disciplinary Risk Concepts." *GAIA* 17.1 (2008): 50-66. Web. 30 November 2012 <http://www.ingentaconnect.com/content/oekom/gaia/2008/00000017/00000001/art00013>.

Roddick, Nick. "Only the Stars Survive: Disaster Movies in the Seventies." *Performance and Politics in Popular Drama: Aspects of Popular Entertainment in Theatre, Film and Television 1800-1976.* Ed. David Bradby. Cambridge: Cambridge University Press, 1980. 243-69. Print.

Ryan, Michael, and Douglas Kellner. "Crisis Films." *Camera Politica: The Politics and Ideology of Contemporary Hollywood Film.* Bloomington: Indiana University Press, 1988. 49-75. Print.

Schröder, Nicole. "Framing Disaster: Images of Nature, Media, and Representational Strategies in Hollywood Disaster Movies." *Local Nature, Global Responsibilities: Ecocritical Perspectives on the New English Literatures.* Ed. Laurenz Volkmann, et al. Amsterdam: Rodopi: 2010. 289-306. Print.

Slovic, Paul, et al. "Risk as Analysis and Risk as Feelings: Some Thoughts about Affect, Reason, Risk, and Rationality." *Risk Analysis* 24.2 (2004): 311-322. Web. 30 November 2012 <http://onlinelibrary.wiley.com/doi/10.1111/j.0272-4332.2004.00433.x/pdf>.

Sontag, Susan. "The Imagination of Disaster." *Against Interpretation and Other Essays.* New York: Farrar, 1969. 209-25. Print.

Weik von Mossner, Alexa. "Facing *The Day After Tomorrow*: Filmed Disaster, Emotional Engagement, and Climate Risk Perception." *American Environments: Climate – Culture –Catastrophe.* Ed. Christof Mauch and Sylvia Mayer. Heidelberg: Winter, 2012. 97-115. Print.

Wirt, John. "Soderbergh's Latest, *Contagion*, a Fall Winner." *The Advocate* (2011). Web. 19 March 2013 <http://theadvocate.com/csp/mediapool/sites/Advocate/assets/templates/FullStoryPrint.csp?cid=793901&preview=y>.

Yacowar, Maurice. "The Bug in the Rug: Notes on the Disaster Genre." *Film Genre Reader III.* Ed. Barry Keith. Austin: University of Texas Press, 2003. 277-95. Print.

Yamey, Gavin and Jimee Hwang. "An Outbreak of Scientific Accuracy." *BMJ* 343 (2011): 850. Print.

Zinn, Jens O. "Introduction: The Contribution of Sociology to the Discourse on Risk and Uncertainty." *Social Theories of Risk and Uncertainty: An Introduction.* Ed. Jens O. Zinn. Malden: Blackwell Publishing, 2008. 1-17. Print.

Films:

Armageddon. Dir. Michael Bay. Perf. Ben Affleck, Bruce Willis. Touchstone Pictures, 1998.

Battle Los Angeles. Dir. Jonathan Liebesman. Perf. Aaron Eckhart, Michelle Rodriguez. Columbia Pictures, 2011.

Battleship. Dir. Peter Berg. Perf. Taylor Kitch, Brooklyn Decker. Universal Pictures, 2012.

The Book of Eli. Dir. Albert and Allen Hughes. Perf. Denzel Washington, Gary Oldman. Alcon Entertainment, 2010.

Cloverfield. Dir. Matt Reeves. Perf. Mike Vogel, Jessica Lucas. Paramount Pictures, 2008.

Contagion. Dir. Steven Soderbergh. Perf. Matt Damon, Kate Winslet. Warner Bros. Pictures, 2011.

The Core. Dir. Jon Amiel. Perf. Aaron Eckhart, Hilary Swank. Paramount Pictures, 2003.

The Day After Tomorrow. Dir. Roland Emmerich. Perf. Jake Gyllenhall, Dennis Quaid. Twentieth Century Fox, 2004.

Deep Impact. Dir. Mimi Leder. Perf. Robert Duvall, Téa Leoni. Paramount Pictures, 1998.

Godzilla. Dir. Roland Emmerich. Perf. Matthew Broderick, Jean Reno. Centropolis Film Productions, 1998.

I am Legend. Dir. Francis Lawrence. Perf. Will Smith, Alice Braga. Warner Bros. Pictures, 2007.

Independence Day. Dir. Roland Emmerich. Perf. Will Smith, Jeff Goldblum. Twentieth Century Fox, 1996.

Knowing. Dir. Alex Proyas. Perf. Nicholas Cage, Chandler Canterbury. Summit Entertainment, 2009.

Melancholia. Dir. Lars von Trier. Perf. Kirsten Dunst, Charlotte Gainsbourg. Zentropa Entertainments, 2011.

Poseidon. Dir. Wolfgang Petersen. Perf. Richard Dreyfuss, Kurt Russell. Warner Bros. Pictures, 2006.

The Road. Dir. John Hillcoat. Perf. Viggo Mortensen, Kodi Smit-McPhee. Dimension Films, 2009.

The Sum of All Fears. Dir. Phil Alden Robinson. Perf. Ben Affleck, Morgan Freeman. Paramount Pictures, 2002.

Titanic. Dir. James Cameron. Perf. Leonardo DiCaprio, Kate Winslet. Twentieth Century Fox, 1997.

2012. Dir. Roland Emmerich. Perf. Chiwetel Ejiofor, John Cusack. Columbia Pictures, 2009.

Volcano. Dir. Mick Jackson. Perf. Tommy Lee Jones, Anne Heche. Donner/Shuler-Donner Productions, 1997.

War of the Worlds. Dir. Steven Spielberg. Perf. Tom Cruise, Dakota Fanning. Paramount Pictures, 2005.

Colin Milburn

Green Gaming: Video Games and Environmental Risk

Up front, it may seem perverse to write of green gaming—to present the word "green" in the context of video games. After all, the video game industry right now would seem to be a significant factor, a prime suspect, in the intensification of certain environmental problems, especially those associated with the worldwide production and disposal of consumer electronics. If we understand the video game, broadly speaking, as a particular assemblage of hardware and software, a media technology that depends not only on the constant innovation and dissemination of powerful computational devices but also on the expansion of the energy economy that enables these devices to operate, we therefore cannot speak of the video game without also conjuring a vocabulary of pollution, carbon footprints, greenhouse effects, habitat depletion, extinction: in short, the volatile language of environmental risk.

To be sure, a penumbra of environmental hazard surrounds the video game, from cradle to grave and beyond (Dyer-Witheford and de Peuter, 222-224; cf. Maxwell and Miller; Taffel; Bozak). For instance, the metallic ore columbite-tantalite, or coltan, is required for making the capacitors of many common electronic devices, such as cell phones, DVD players, computers, and video game consoles. Mined in several different countries—including Australia, Brazil, Canada, China, Ethiopia, and the Democratic Republic of Congo—coltan ore is processed into tantalum powder and then sold to high-tech developers all over the world. As consumer appetites for all manner of electronic technologies have been steadily growing in recent decades, the industrial market for tantalum has likewise kept apace. This situation poses serious environmental and geopolitical concerns.

The so-called "PlayStation War," for example, fueled in part by the mineral resources of central Africa, has become emblematic of the unforeseen dangers brought on by the expansion of digital technologies (Hari; Lasker; Freccia). The worldwide launch of the Sony PlayStation 2 in 2000 required the rapid production of an unprecedented number of capacitors. But Sony could not meet the astonishing demand for its machine, due to a shortage of tantalum on the open market. The price of tantalum powder skyrocketed. In response, coltan mining in the rebel-occupied eastern region of the Congo began to escalate, directly financing the invading forces from Rwanda and Uganda. Illegal coltan mining and smuggling has continued to support military conflicts in the region, even as some Congolese have come to see the ore as symbolic of their country's crucial function in the digital age (Montague; Mantz; Smith). Among the various human costs of the coltan operations, prisoners of war and children have been forced to work in the mines. As the former British Member of Parliament Oona King put it: "Kids in Congo were being sent down mines to die so that kids in Europe and America could kill imaginary aliens in their living rooms" (quoted in Hari).

In response to the mounting public unease about "blood coltan," Sony announced that it long ago stopped acquiring any tantalum from illegal Congolese sources. However, it seems unlikely that the quantity of PlayStation 2 and later PlayStation 3 units distributed around the world could have been produced without some percentage of tantalum derived from Congolese coltan, whether Sony is aware of it or not (Wakabi; Lasker; Dyer-Witheford and de Peuter, 223; Mantz). Considering the complex international networks of transportation, processing, and brokerage that constitute the coltan trade, the number of intermediaries involved from the time ore comes out of the ground to the time tantalum powder and wires arrive at a manufacturing facility, global tech corporations are not always able to verify the specific source of these components, the origin of each atom of tantalum—and meanwhile, everyone else remains completely mystified (Smith and Mantz).

The political and economic dimensions of coltan mining are inseparable from its environmental dimensions, whether in conflict zones or in more peaceful regions. There are many ecological impacts associated with mining in general, of course, including the devastation of wildlife habitats due to deforestation, surface removal and erosion, as well as the pollution of water sources with runoff from the mining operations. Polluted water sources can cause negative effects all along the food chain. But coltan mining in the Democratic Republic of the Congo has introduced particular ecosystem risks, as well. For instance, coltan miners have expanded into protected wildlife areas and national parks, not only disrupting habitat features but also hunting animals in the area. The miners and the militia groups, far removed from their normal food supplies, often eat the local "bushmeat"—including endangered elephants and gorillas. Coltan regions have suffered a devastating depopulation of several species, such as the Grauer's gorilla, now at high risk of extinction. According to a 2001 report on the coltan boom published by the Dian Fossey Gorilla Fund and the Born Free Foundation: "The magnificent Grauer's gorilla will become the first great ape to be driven to extinction—a victim of war, human greed and high technology" (Redmond, 4; see also Glew and Hudson).

These are just a few examples of the environmental risks and humanitarian dilemmas involved in manufacturing video game hardware and other digital devices. On the opposite end of the product lifecycle, we have the escalating problem of e-waste, the mountains and oceans of electronic trash spreading in Asia, Africa, Latin America, and elsewhere. Castoff computers, cell phones, and game consoles from around the world are shipped on enormous cargo barges—themselves a tremendous source of carbon emissions—and piled up in vast landfills, leaching toxic chemicals into soil and the water table, sometimes set on fire, melted down, streaming pollutants into the atmosphere (Grossman; Gabrys). And so on.

Even between the cradle and the grave, the video game presents various environmental perils. Because consoles such as the Microsoft Xbox, the Nintendo Wii, and the Sony PlayStation are such powerful computational devices, they suck a tremendous amount of energy. In 2008, a report by the U.S. Natural Resources Defense Council found that video game consoles consume around 16 billion-kilowatt hours per year, which is equivalent to the total energy usage of a very large city (Horowitz et al.). Responding to such critiques, Sony, Microsoft, and Nintendo have since issued redesigned firmware upgrades to improve the energy efficiency of their devices, but this proves only a partial solution, especially considering the number of devices involved.

This issue of scale is emphasized by a 2007 Greenpeace machinima video called *Clash of the Consoles*. In the video, three iconic game characters—Mario (Nintendo), Master Chief (Microsoft), and Kratos (Sony)—confront the risks posed by the manufacture and disposal of game consoles: "Three great heroes of the video game universe come together to battle the worst threat their world has ever known. Themselves." Kratos, star of the *God of War* series, scoffs at a PS3 unit in his hands: "How's one little box so dangerous? I'm here to battle, I'm the friggin' God of War!" The narrator responds: "One console may not sound like a threat, but try sixty million." The heroes tremble as they face an enormous crumbling mountain of consoles. It begins to topple as the heroes dash off, in search of a better solution: "With no safe way to dispose of or recycle these toxic video game systems, the only way these heroes can survive is to race for the greenest video game console ever." Yet even as Mario, Master Chief, and Kratos catch a glimpse of a glowing green console off in the distance, racing through a wasted landscape in pursuit of this chimera, the towering heap of discarded machines comes crashing down, rocking the earth while their backs are turned.

In this light, the term *green gaming* would appear oxymoronic, a mystification of its own material context. But even in this light, I want to reconsider how gaming might afford, motivate, provoke, or engender a cultural politics of green (Chang). I do not simply mean whether or not game manufacturers might continue to improve the environmental profiles of their products—which they no doubt can and perhaps will, even as more and more devices are produced. Rather, I am interested in the question of whether gaming can create the conditions of ecological awareness necessary to address environmental risk, as well as the risk that gaming itself represents.

A number of developers have experimented with green gaming: the possibility that games (a game, any game) might contribute to green politics, engaging players to recognize the precarious situation of our planet, and perhaps even providing the cognitive resources for actually doing something about it. Games with ecological themes have existed since the early days of the medium, certainly. But green gaming would be a specific form of gameplay and a narrative genre that posits the environment under threat, a conjectural state of imminent crisis, and tenders gaming itself as a meaningful response. Greening, in other words, as an affordance of gaming: a techno-political disposition enabled by games that speculate on the ecological risks of contemporary social practices and industrial infrastructures. By animating what Ulrich Beck has described as "the anticipation of catastrophe," vivifying the potential consequences of everyday pollution, wilderness depletion, and high-tech consumerism, these games would become sites of green action in themselves, digital laboratories for remediating ecological and geopolitical risks in advance (Beck, 9; Heise).

From a cynical perspective, the existence of such games might seem to be a simple case of greenwashing, something like a public relations effort to absolve the video game industry and video game players from whatever degree of responsibility they might have for the problems of e-waste, strip mining, carbon emissions, and so forth. But more optimistically, these games may contain in themselves the potential for change, or at least for hope. In this regard, I propose three distinct modes of green gaming, each featuring different capacities for the promotion of ecological thought: the games of environmental discipline, the games of environmental control, and the games of environmental responsibility.

Discipline

Although Michel Foucault situated the societies of discipline in the eighteenth and nineteenth centuries, formal elements of disciplinary society still persist, especially in the politics of securitization that have become ever more pronounced in recent years. Foucault described the societies of discipline as characterized by a conceptual infrastructure—an episteme—configured as a grid: a series of enclosures, both material and discursive, for shaping social organization, knowledge making, and the production of individual subjectivity. A logic of containment, manifested in specific institutions and architectural spaces, began to emerge or take on new determinate forms in the modern era: the clinic, the public school, the army barracks, the factory, and the prison. Disciplinary society formulates specific types of subjects, that is, subject positions created and reinforced by the bureaucratic organization of social order. Among these, of course, is the criminal as a type of person: abnormal, deviant, outside the social order, and yet also a category into which any normal person could risk sliding. Hence, the necessity of constant self-policing and self-surveillance. Foucault describes this condition of self-policing as the carceral function of modern society, the internalization of panoptic power: "He who is subjected to a field of visibility, and who knows it, assumes responsibility for the constraints of power; he makes them play spontaneously upon himself; he inscribes in himself the power relation in which he simultaneously plays both roles; he becomes the principle of his own subjection" (202-203).

A majority of the video games that address issues of environmental risk and crisis operate through the carceral function, for they typically situate environmental hazards under the category of criminal behavior: *crimes against nature*. These games ask the player to occupy two roles simultaneously, acting as the policing agent who discovers and confronts some illicit activity, which appears therefore as the source of all environmental risk, while simultaneously self-policing against the risk of falling into the category of eco-criminal. For example, in *Sonic the Hedgehog*, developed for the Sega Genesis/Mega Drive in 1991, the valiant hedgehog is pitted against the evil technologist, Dr. Robotnik, who is depicted as a gross polluter. *Captain Planet and the Planeteers*, a 1990 game for the Nintendo Entertainment System based on the U.S. cartoon show, puts the player in mortal combat against a rogues' gallery of professional eco-villains. In the 1992 Sega Genesis game *Ecco the Dolphin*, the courageous cetacean faces off against aliens from outer space. These aliens plunder the oceans, sucking up all the sea life in a totally unsustainable way, and only Ecco can stop them. More recently, the 2008 PC game *Eco Warriors* encourages the player to battle with ruthless pollution-robots, or necrobots. After containing the threat of these toxic machines, the eco warrior dutifully recycles their metallic remains.

While the Manichean structure of these games perhaps speaks for itself, pitting ecological crusaders and virtuous animals against evil others—overfishing aliens, dastardly polluters, necrobots—it is worth emphasizing the degree to which the games of environmental discipline portray the eco-criminal as beyond the natural order of things: inhuman, inorganic, not of this earth. By repudiating the eco-criminal, these games would tacitly immunize the game-playing subject against the risk of falling into the space of abjection.

The operations of environmental discipline even become the plotline of the 2002 game *Super Mario Sunshine*, developed for the Nintendo Game Cube. Mario, Princess Peach, and a few other friends from the Mushroom Kingdom go for a holiday on the Isle Delfino. This island country has the shape of a dolphin—a familiar icon of environmentalist thought—and its energy infrastructure is driven by "Shine Sprites," creatures of solar power. When Mario and the gang arrive, they immediately discover that the island has been contaminated with glowing toxic waste. Slicks of "icky, paint-like goop," pools of acidic sludge, and splashes of graffiti are everywhere. The horrible pollution has driven away the Shine Sprites, and the island is now falling into darkness. The islanders have seen a shadowy figure resembling Mario at the scene of each crime.

The police arrest Mario, accusing him of befouling the island. He is abruptly put on trial: "The accused is charged with polluting our beautiful home, and yes, threatening our very way of life." To the islanders, Mario represents a danger to the environment ("our beautiful home") and the social order ("our very way of life"), and he is not even allowed to defend his innocence. At this moment, the game represents the democratic system in a "state of exception": the extralegal suspension of the law as such in the name of public good, the failure of rules and procedures when the law faces an enemy of the nation, an enemy of natural order (see Agamben). On the evidence of his appearance alone, Mario is sentenced to clean up the island. The rest of the game involves Mario washing up the mess and trying to redeem his reputation. He eventually discovers that the son of his arch-nemesis Bowser is the real culprit, having disguised himself as Mario in order to frame him. Eventually, Mario trounces the monstrous Bowser and Bowser Jr., restores ecological purity to Isle Delfino, and returns to the status of hero, no longer tainted by association with the sinister shadow-Mario, the eco-criminal.

Super Mario Sunshine casts the eco-criminal as outside the natural and social orders: a figure who undermines society precisely by contaminating the environment. At the same time, in representing the act of environmental defacement through a parodic narrative of executive power and the legal system, it also makes visible the risk that anyone might fall into the trap of eco-crime, that anyone might inadvertently find themselves on the dark side. Hero and villain are thus represented as mirror images of each other. In this game, the legal system is incapable of securing true justice without the intervention of a virtuous plumber who actively polices against his shadow self. It presents a startling literalization of Foucault's carceral logic. Like other games of environmental discipline, it depicts environmental risk as the result of illicit behavior—a deviancy that likewise threatens the interiority of the good citizen-subject, the good gamer, who therefore must be self-disciplined. Such games body forth of the necessity of vigilantism, a form of policing beyond the rule of law: constant vigilance against pollution and the risk of self-pollution.

And yet, insofar as games like *Super Mario Sunshine* pivot on Manichean narratives, where mistaken identity might blur the distinction between hero and villain for a short while but never ultimately disrupt the sense in which the hero-avatar must stand for the forces of nature against the unnatural forces of desecration—where truth and justice are all sorted out correctly in the end—they ultimately affirm the game-playing subject as virtuous, clean, and nonpolluting. Though there may be a risk of becoming a polluter, or at least charged as one, the ecological condition of the game player is always upheld as pure and disciplined.

By positioning threats to environmental stability as beyond the subjective space represented by the playable avatar, the games of environmental discipline are actually incapable of addressing their own connections to circuits of pollution. As a mode, these games assume an ethics of proper behavior and proper relation to the environment. Yet in ordering the inside and outside, they exclude—and thus excuse—their own contributions to environmental risk and the problems of e-waste, energy consumption, and resource extraction represented by game technologies in general. By policing against the criminal other and, as it were, laying down the law, such games rely on a state of exception to their own normative frameworks: a law outside the law, a legal illegality of the games themselves.

In this respect, we might question the extent to which the games of environmental discipline could ever achieve an effective green politics, for any eco-crime they might commit themselves—as accessories to strip mining or toxic pollution, for example—is sanctioned by their own narrative apparatus. This narrative organization positions the origin of environmental risk beyond the *zone of interactivity or playability*, that is to say, outside the player's *zone of responsibility*. By conjuring eco-crime as irredeemably other and beyond legality, these games, in order to remain playable, must suspend the very laws that they have themselves posited. They must insist on a state of exception to their own green logic: eco-crime is not a crime, at least, if it is the condition of fun, or if it is, as they say, just a game.

Control

In his short essay "Postscript on the Societies of Control," Gilles Deleuze argues that the disciplinary formations of the modern era have been eroding away since the middle of the 20th century, replaced by mechanisms of control:

> We are in a generalized crisis in relation to all the environments of enclosure—prison, hospital, factory, school, family. . . . It's only a matter of administering their last rites and of keeping people employed until the installation of the new forces knocking at the door. These are the *societies of control*, which are in the process of replacing disciplinary societies. . . . [T]he different control mechanisms are inseparable variations, forming a system of variable geometry the language of which is numerical (which doesn't necessarily mean binary). Enclosures are *molds*, distinct castings, but controls are a *modulation*, like a self-deforming cast

> that will continuously change from one moment to the other, or like a sieve whose mesh will transmute from point to point. (3-4)

As we note in Deleuze's language of numerical systems and modulations, he sees the societies of control constituted under a general compliance to feedback regulation, that is, the logic of cybernetics, classically described as the science of control and communication (Wiener). Deleuze understands postmodern societies to operate through feedback, modulation, and tweaking, rather than disciplinary power. The individual is no longer contained in a specific subject position or architectural space, normal only to the degree of avoiding abnormality, but rather distributed among other elements of the social system, transformed into statistical data, algorithmic models, risk calculations, and online passwords. The individual, according to Deleuze, becomes "dividual": an assemblage of components each subject to the regulatory mechanisms of systematic control, whose prototype is the thermostat.

The thermostat functions to keep environmental conditions in dynamic equilibrium, oscillating around a fixed temperature. If the temperature in a house gets too cold, this information becomes input for the thermostat, which triggers the heater to warm things up; if this output now overshoots the set point, the information is once again input for the thermostat to turn the heater off or trigger the air conditioner, and so forth. A feedback cycle with no surveillance necessary, no sovereign or disciplinary power: it is autonomous, coordinated by the dumb mechanism.

Cybernetic logic now informs everyday discourse, everyday thought, to an astounding degree—to say nothing of politics or technics (Hayles; Galloway, *Protocol*). Certainly, the sciences of environmental systems—from evolutionary ecology to geo-engineering—rely on robust cybernetic models to comprehend the circulations and transformations of matter, energy, and information across different scales. And this is why so many video games, in addressing environmental risk, explicitly thematize processes and practices of feedback control. By locating environmental risk in the feedback loops between ecosystems, technological infrastructures, and the routines of everyday life, such games often present themselves as models of regulatory governance. They simulate the operations of socio-technical networks so as to train players to better inhabit such systems and administer them from the inside. Procedures of cybernetic management and informatic coordination inflect the narratives as well as the ludic mechanisms of these games, manifested in the playing. As Alexander Galloway has written: "Video games are allegories for our contemporary life under the protocological network of continuous informatic control. In fact, the more emancipating games seem to be as a medium, substituting activity for passivity or a branching narrative for a linear one, the more they are in fact hiding the fundamental social transformation into informatics that has affected the globe during recent decades" (*Gaming*, 106).

The imagination of control has certainly inspired a surge of energy awareness games, including *The Energy Balance*, *Energy Hog*, *Energyville*, *Stop the Guzzler!*, *Power Planets*, and *CityOne*. These games feature interactive simulations of petroculture, focusing on the electrical infrastructures of industrialized nations, the habits and demands of high-tech consumers, and the vampiric nature of domestic appliances. For example, in the 2010 Nickelodeon game *PowerHouse*, players are tasked with reducing the energy consumption of various rooms in a private home to more environmentally friendly levels: "This house has some major energy usage issues. But you can solve them, if you figure out where energy is being wasted. . . . Be creative! Stay strong! You have the power to save power!" The game's instructions make it clear that behavioral modification is the goal. In playing the game, we learn how to live more efficiently and save the world in the process: "Get every room's POWER METER in the green, and you and the planet are both winners!" It is, essentially, a game that turns the player into a thermostat.

A similar game, also called *The PowerHouse*, was designed in 2006 by Magnus Bang and his colleagues at the Interactive Institute in Sweden. It involves managing a household of seven people, trying to keep all of them happy while also balancing resource-usage to achieve a more sustainable lifestyle. It deliberately implements aspects of games like *The Sims* to motivate the player to keep playing, to learn the rules (the only viable solutions to energy reduction are those already programmed into the software) by spending more and more time at the computer. According to the developers: "Operant conditioning is a crucial component in almost every computer game. In *The PowerHouse*, we have applied different kinds of conditioning. Sound and visual effects attuned to the target group [teenage gamers] have been implemented to motivate users to stay at the computer. . . . The player also gets direct feedback in terms of bonus points immediately after executing a correct behavior in the game, for example when the microwave is used instead of the ordinary electrical oven. Naturally, the goal is to encourage players and direct them to perform the right actions" (Bang, Torstensson, and Katzeff, 128).

In asking players to optimize the domestic environment, discovering the rules of "correct behavior" and "right actions," *The PowerHouse* also narrates their subordination to the algorithm, oscillating within the parameters of better and worse choices. Programmed feedback and operant conditioning are part of the story, crucial to the winning experience. Indeed, the game features a Big Brother figure, modeled after a TV game show host, who watches over things and gives advice about how to proceed. Following the host's advice leads to rewards; ignoring it leads to less desirable outcomes. The player is in charge of the characters in the household, but success in the game means learning how to align the actions of characters with the advice of the host, who represents the rules of the energy economy, that is, the rules of the algorithm itself. Like other games in this genre, *The PowerHouse* persuades players to recognize, on the one hand, the cybernetic conditions of their own domestic spaces, and on the other hand, the possibility of a set of green practices that might modulate homeostatic conditions. It assiduously foregrounds our functionality as consumers in existing systems of energy production and distribution, vast networks that we engage only as end-users, adapting ourselves to the infrastructure in order to make it work more efficiently.

The decentralized regulatory mechanisms of these energy networks are made yet further evident in a prototype game created by Bang and colleagues called *PowerAgent*:

> The person playing *PowerAgent* has the role of a secret agent, and the mobile phone is the main agent tool. Via the phone, the boss, the mysterious Mr. Q, gives the player special missions to save the planet from the energy crisis. . . . [Each mission] contains a suggestion on how to act in order to be energy efficient in the upcoming real-world task, and it also holds information on how to influence family members. . . . Typical missions include (1) adjusting the heating in the house, (2) washing clothes, (3) cooking food, (4) switching off all stand-by appliances, and (5) minimizing the total household energy use for a day. . . . The mobile phone is connected to special equipment in the home that measures the use of electricity and heat water during the missions. In this way, it is possible for us to provide feedback on the success of the missions and reinforce behaviors that are appropriate from the standpoint of energy conservation. (Bang, Gustafsson, and Katzeff, 58)

PowerAgent draws attention to the ways in which power—in all its forms—now operates through self-regulating modalites. They are self-contained: the outside is already inside, an object defined by the program. Even the boss is nowhere but "in" the mobile phone—indeed, the boss is the mobile phone. The figure of social authority (boss, governor) appears as a terminal of the information network, a node in the computational architecture. What *PowerAgent* makes perfectly clear is the degree to which we are embedded in systems of control; we are mere accessories, invisible facilitators, *secret agents* of the power grid. We may be given specific tasks to improve functionality, or to keep things calibrated, but we are not ever outside—no more and no less than the boss. Our actions—the success of our missions, the reinforcement of our behaviors—may perturb the system, which eventually adjusts itself around the perturbation, resetting to new parameters, but they do not effect the formal dimensions of the system itself.

There is no outside imaginable, in the games of environmental control. Unlike the games of environmental discipline, which establish a space of criminality beyond their own playable standards of virtue, the games of environmental control body forth the conditions described by Deleuze, which culminate in the "conception of a control mechanism, giving the position of any element within an open environment at any given instant (whether animal in a reserve or human in a corporation, as with an electronic collar)" (Deleuze, 7).

Indeed, players of such games must concede to the rules of the algorithm and, in some cases, automated systems of surveillance. To play *PowerAgent*, you must install "special equipment in the home." Likewise, the 2011 *Power House* game developed by Stanford University, Kuma Games, and Seriosity requires players to register their home utility SmartMeter and sign an informed-consent agreement, allowing the game to access information from their monthly utility bills. The energy-usage data becomes the basis for the self-deforming and reforming gameplay experience.

Such games function according to logistics of infrastructure that cannot—or at least, this is how the societies of control perceive themselves—be radically changed, hacked, or reconfigured. They can only be modulated. This becomes especially clear in games such as *SimCity*, *Tropico*, and *Alpha Centauri*, which offer simulations of city planning or planetary engineering. These so-called "god games," which empower players to decide specific elements of socio-ecological organization—for instance, whether to use coal, nuclear, or solar energy—actually lay bare the structural limits on meaningful change under existing regimes of technoculture, even as we are given more and more choices for clean energy and efficient technologies. Each of these games allows modification of certain features or parameters as the simulation progresses, but the system (the simcity or simplanet) presents itself as self-adjusting to these choices, running out the effects of any given alteration without impacting the nature of the algorithm as such, the programmed rules of possibility. Even the 2013 version of SimCity, for example, which emphasizes the ecological consequences of industrial development and the benefits of alternate energy sources, nevertheless concedes to prevailing logistics of infrastructure, the path-dependences of inherited techno-social systems. As one player complains: "The new *SimCity* [only] allows people to create car-dependent 1950s-style developments: 1) No subways; 2) No bicycle infrastructure; 3) No mixed-use development to encourage walkability; 4) The allowed density of development is tied to the size of the road, which makes no sense. It's great that *SimCity* allows people to see the impact of pollution on their sims, but in terms of urban planning ideas, the new *SimCity* is stuck in 1950 suburban sprawl mode" (Gordon). Tweak the parameters, yes, but not the system itself. Greener, yes, but not quite green.

Responsibility

In contrast to the games of discipline and control, there are the games of environmental responsibility. These games do not correspond to an established form of social or epistemic organization. After all, societies of responsibility do not actually exist—not yet, anyway. They remain conjectural. But this mode of green gaming would render responsibility as a techno-political disposition, an emergent capacity. In her book *When Species Meet*, Donna Haraway writes: "Response, of course, grows with the capacity to respond, that is, responsibility. Such a capacity can be shaped only in and for multidirectional relationships, in which always more than one responsive entity is in the process of becoming. . . . [R]esponders are themselves co-constituted in the responding" (Haraway, 71).

The games of environmental responsibility animate our capacity to respond, to affect and be affected, to engage with others: other species, other people, and the otherness of our own planet. These games attend to their own involvement in the networks of the energy economy, while also drawing attention to players' culpability in enjoying media technologies that pose so many risks to the environment. So they represent a kind of counter-gaming, gaming turned against itself (Galloway, *Gaming*; Raley). In this regard, they rely on a certain subtlety, a certain faith in the power of irony. But their self-critical interventions are intensified by the interactive qualities of the video game as a medium. For immersive engagement, which is to say, playing, heightens the ironies of these games in ways that render responsibility *palpable*—shaped by systems of control, to be sure, and yet immanently transformable, open to the possibility that things could be otherwise.

A notable example is the game *Tasty Planet*, developed in 2006 by the Canadian company Dingo Games for Mac, Windows, and Linux and then later ported over to smartphones and touchscreen tablets. In this game, the player takes the role of an out-of-control nanotechnology blob—a gray goo. Originally invented as a bathroom cleaner, the goo proves to have unintended consequences. Indeed, it begins to devour the world. *Tasty Planet* is a game about consumption: the point is to consume everything on screen, absorb it, grow larger. The more the goo consumes, the more it can consume: the larger the goo, the larger the objects of its delectation. In the first levels, it can only eat molecules and microbes, but it soon progresses to higher organisms, cities, entire ecosystems, eventually growing so large that it can eat the Earth itself, all the planets in the solar system, and ultimately, the fabric of spacetime as such.

The game presents an allegory of technological consumerism and the environmental impacts of our cultural appetites, the desire to guzzle more and more resources in order to grow, develop, expand: a neoliberal fantasy turned nightmare. Indeed, the opening comic strip of the game presents the gray goo, our avatar protagonist—an antihero, certainly—as the product of technoscience gone wrong. A laboratory experiment to develop a more efficient way of cleaning our private, domestic environment ends up destroying the common, planetary environment. It is unleashed upon the world though an act of industrial misconduct: the scientists, realizing that their invention has gone out of control, simply flush it down the drain. The extent to which *Tasty Planet* presents an allegory of high-tech consumerism is sharpened in the sequel, *Tasty Planet 2: Back for Seconds*, in which the gray goo, prior to eating the whole planet, travels back in time. The bulk of the sequel is spent consuming dinosaurs and other prehistoric flora and fauna, fossilized remains of ancient biology now turned into energy supply for the ravenous goo. So it is a fairly straightforward commentary on petroculture, our fossil fuel dependencies that mobilize greater and greater levels of planetary exploitation.

The fun of the game is in the exuberance of consumption, the glee of eating everything in sight. The goo makes expressions of delight ("Yummy!"), and happy music plays in the background. We guide the goo along its path of destruction—and in this regard, in playing as the ravenous consumer, the game forces us to recognize our own responsibility. The goo can do nothing unless the player maneuvers it. So every act of consumption is caused directly by the player, even though there is no other choice if one wants to play. It also addresses our accountability as gamers—consumers of this video game, any video game—insofar as the goo is a figuration of the game itself: a high-tech medium of energy consumption, a *playable technology* taking over more and more of the world.

Online discussions of the *Tasty Planet* games among enthusiastic players frequently register an inherent ambivalence, namely, the fact that having fun with these games means taking responsibility for the destruction of the planet. The discourse of the players, self-conflicted and vacillating, indicates how interacting with the goo, responding to its insatiable behavior as it responds to commands, shapes a capacity for responsiveness and critical reflection. In these conversations, expressions of pleasure appear alongside discomfort, even grief. For example, one player writes: "the cat-eating levels are among my favorites, because the sad meowing cracks me up" (Dell). But another writes: "I feel so guilty for eating the cats!" (Joshalos). Indeed, consuming companion animals seems to upset a number of players: "i hate eating cats" (lewiss4455); "i have this empty feeling inside me after absorbing the cat" (Pandermatism); and so on. Such mixed feelings of pleasure and remorse extend to other species featured in the games, as well, including dinosaurs: "I made Rex chase his tail how adorable but after 20 seconds i ate him sad" (icicie).

Many players who participate in online forums seem especially keen to discuss the meanings of the final levels, where the goo must consume the planets in our solar system and then the whole universe. Some pretend to be apologetic: "Sorry guys, but I . . . Eh ate the Earth" (mysticicedragon3). Or:

"I felt bad for Pluto, as humans claimed it was not a planet anymore, so I tried to keep from eating it. One slip in my concentration, and I accidentally ate Pluto. I then imploded. I still feel bad for eating Pluto" (LittleFanGirl). The performance of emotional response is often a way of addressing and acknowledging the metaphorical aspects of these games: "And that kids is why we don't let untrained individuals experiment with the balance of nature . . . oh, never mind, we still do that" (Brogers44). Or: "cat eat mice, dog eat cat, blob eat everything and that's the food chain any questions yeah is it true yes because as we are speaking a blob is eating our planet" (kingsnake6666). Some see the *Tasty Planet* games as commenting directly on scientific responsibility: "unforturtanately [sic] the young scientists do not acknowledge that their series of actions can turn into such a catoshophy [catastrophe]" (FANBUSCUS). Or: "Well, Mr Scientist, it seems that your experiment went horribly right. It DID clean the Earth . . . From everything, but it cleaned the Earth. Just as planned?" (DarkraiPrince). Others see it as addressing even larger issues: "A good metaphor about capitalism. The more you grow, the more you want, no matter how many people under you you have to destroy, easily forgetting that you came from the streets in the beginning, and you had to eat shit and rats. At the end, Capitalism destroys the Earth" (DCervan).

To avoid this outcome, the only solution is to refuse to play by the rules, or to opt out entirely: "i quit before he ate the earth. So the goo did not eat the earth! i made history there!" (StarProgrammer). Another gamer, identifying with the goo, tries to behave responsibly—and loses the game: "I spared Earth just so they [the earthlings] would see me as their defender. They made me and thus it was my responsibility to show my gratitude. . . . [F]inally, after minutes of temptation to eat Earth, [I] devour Jupiter. Then I imploded. Nice, feel-good game!" (Merido). The sarcasm here foregrounds the double bind of the game (to win is to lose, to lose is to win) and its affective force.

In elevating environmental responsibility to the level of both theme and practice, *Tasty Planet* produces a communal field of affect—a complex of pleasure, humor, and discomfort. It brings players together, even in anonymity, to contemplate and work through what they have done. The game cultivates an ironic sense of accountability for the fate of the earth and its creatures by ludicrously amplifying the pleasures of destruction. Responsibility emerges in responding to the game, recognizing the lethal dimensions of having a good time. And so, for some players, the real game becomes how to play otherwise.

Shadow of the Colossus, a PlayStation 2 game developed in 2005 by the Japanese company Team Ico, further illustrates this point. In *Shadow of the Colossus*, we play as the wanderer, a young man who enters a mysterious land in hopes of resurrecting a dead maiden, Mono, sacrificed for some unknown purpose back in his own country ("She was sacrificed for she has a cursed fate"). He steals a magical sword—so he is marked from the outset as a criminal—and he travels to this land where he knows he might bargain with the god Dormin to bring the young woman, his love, back to life. The price of this bargain: to kill the sixteen colossi, gigantic beasts that seem to be manifestations of the environments in which they live—and indeed, when we slay them, they deteriorate into earth, stone, and mulch. As we wander the land searching for each colossus, it becomes clear that this is a world that has moved on. There are few animals at all—the occasional bird and lizard are the only vertebrates visible in this world—and while there are trees and grasses, most are dead, barren, or wasting. There are ruins of an old human civilization here, traces of another age. But now remain only the colossi, and the whole purpose of the game is to slaughter them.

With each death, Dormin—a god of inky darkness, oil and shadow—grows more powerful. Indeed, the colossi each contain a portion of this god's essence. When they die, geysers of black fluid and smoke erupt from their vast corpses, and the wanderer's body absorbs these organic energies. After the final colossus is killed, Dormin at last becomes capable of possessing the wanderer's body, highlighting the degree to which the wanderer has all along operated as an agent of this god whose dominion relies on extermination and extinction. Dormin is a figure of pure consuming power, taking far more energy and living essence than it returns to the world.

Shadow of the Colossus is a profoundly sad game, but a beautiful one. Many players comment on their discomfort with it, the evident narrative of environmental despoliation, and the difficulty of playing a character who ruthlessly destroys rare and wondrous creatures, not because he is malicious, but because he wants to save Mono, his love—which is to say, in order to play this game at all. To play the game means we must kill, and these deaths are our responsibility. As players of the wanderer, we are directly answerable for the extinction of the colossi. For example, one player has written:

> When I traversed these long stretches of scenery and the world, uninterrupted, I felt a greater sense of wonder and amazement; at the same time, I started questioning myself and the protagonist's journey. I was in doubt of myself. . . . . Every Colossus battle is unique in itself. Each holds its own personality, and some are completely harmless and docile. Which only comes back to reinforce the question of the morality of killing them. . . . My character, the very person I was playing, was the insinuator. I felt like a hunter of sorts, killing not out of necessity for my survival, but for the sake of my selfish goals and means. (wquach)

This is a common sentiment among players, strong remorse and, consequently, an active questioning of the meaning of the game. Indeed, in the elaborate fan discussions of this game, we see a kind of devotion emerge: a devotion to the game and its artistry, to the emotional experience that it provokes, and to the colossi themselves, their meanings, and the need for other players to be aware of these meanings even as the colossi pass from this world.

The sense of devotion is intensified for many players by a particular gameplay feature: namely, the wanderer's horse, Agro. The wanderer relies on Agro to carry him over great distances, to take him into battle with the colossi—and, at a pivotal moment in the game, to sacrifice himself. Players likewise develop a haptic and emotional relationship with Agro, in that maneuvering the horse with the PlayStation controller is a process of coaxing and constant care. It becomes the condition for love: a commitment to the nonhuman other, the algorithm that comes to stand for the nonhuman as such. As one player writes:

> It's no secret that I love *Shadow of the Colossus*. That game was an incredible experience for me, and I will never forget it. When I think about love being conveyed in a video game, I think about *Shadow of the Colossus*. . . . Agro is your trusty steed throughout the journey. He carries you wherever you need to go, as far as he can. . . . As I played the game, I came to care deeply about Agro.
>
> This connection that you have to Agro is facilitated by the game's controls. . . . When you are riding Agro you use the X button to kick your heels and go forward and use the left analog stick to steer left or right. . . . What this scheme does is it make you connect with Agro the way you would a real horse.
>
> You, the player, have to form a physical connection to Agro. . . . *Shadow of the Colossus* forces you to communicate with the controller in much the same way that Wander must communicate with Agro. . . . He's your only companion in this strange, harsh land, and you need him. You need him to survive. . . . I grew to love Agro. I could feel Wander's love for Agro, and I could feel Agro's love for Wander. . . . I hope to never forget. (Phillips)

The durable relationship with the horse that grows through playing *Shadow of the Colossus* concretizes various thematic dimensions of the game. The transspecies connection between the wanderer and Agro reproduces at a narrative level the physical connection between the human player and the gaming system. In this way, it highlights the profound sacrifices made in service to Dormin, in the name of love—a love not only for Mono or Agro but also for the game itself ("I love *Shadow of the Colossus*")—and our responsibility as players to the worlds in which we play:

> It is as the hero rides his horse to the final colossus' lair that the game begins to reveal its true genius. The hero is riding Agro across a bridge across a ravine when, suddenly, the ancient stone structure begins the crumble. In a desperate attempt to save her rider, the horse throws Wander to the other side before falling into the depths of the chasm. Years ago, when I had first watched Wander lean over the cliff edge and scream in despair, I honestly set my controller onto the floor and cried. . . .
>
> Wander, after suffering the loss of his horse, goes on to slay the final colossus. Upon doing so he returns to the temple, his body possessed by Dormin . . . At the same moment, Agro limps into the shrine with a broken leg, alive but unable to

> ever run again. The game ends with them finding the infant in the temple, an ending that had left me with an incredible feeling of remorse. After all, I did not merely observe the story's events unfold, I was responsible for them. I was the one who killed the colossi, revived Dormin, crippled my horse, destroyed my body, reduced myself to a child, and left my love stranded in an uninhabited land for the rest of her life. . . . It is a game about desperate love, self-sacrifice, tragic mistakes, and the friendship between a young man and his horse. For me, *Shadow of the Colossus* represents everything that games could be. (Higgins)

With the sense of what games could be—what they could be but are not yet, namely, instruments to improve the world rather than injure it—some players of *Shadow of the Colossus* come to realize that they simply cannot keep playing as if nothing had changed. For these players, to take the game seriously means acknowledging their own complicity—and refusing any longer to play by the rules, before it is too late: "I want the colossi to live, as the beautiful giants they are. The game sits on my shelf because I have no desire to stab these animal gods to death anymore, as they seem so harmless when left to themselves. I let them live by not playing, as little bits of code, unchanged" (Tornadosaurus Rex).

In the various experiences recorded by players of *Shadow of the Colossus*, as with other games of responsibility, we see emerging, in fits and starts, as a desire for a different game, a gaming of the game, a counter-gaming. It is, then, an opening of ecological awareness and a responsibility to act responsibly, not merely through techniques of discipline or control, not merely through heroic feats or virtuous activism, but rather through the capacity of games to touch us, to move us, and awaken our empathy.

Works Cited

Agamben, Giorgio. *Homo Sacer: Sovereign Power and Bare Life*. Trans. Daniel Heller-Roazen. Stanford: Stanford University Press, 1998. Print.

---. *State of Exception*. Trans. Kevin Attell. Chicago: University of Chicago Press, 2005. Print.

Bang, Magnus, Anton Gustafsson, and Cecilia Katzeff. "Promoting New Patterns in Household Energy Consumption with Pervasive Learning Games." *Persuasive Technology: Second International Conference on Persuasive Technology*. Ed. Wijnand IJsselsteijn, et al. Berlin: Springer-Verlag, 2007. 55-63. Print.

Bang, Magnus, Carin Torstensson, and Cecilia Katzeff. "*The PowerHouse*: A Persuasive Computer Game Designed to Raise Awareness of Domestic Energy Consumption." *Persuasive Technology: First International Conference on Persuasive Technology for Human Well-Being*. Ed. Wijnand IJsselsteijn, et al. Berlin: Springer-Verlag, 2006. 123-132. Print.

Beck, Ulrich. *World Risk Society*. Malden, MA: Polity Press, 1999. Print.

Bozak, Nadia. *The Cinematic Footprint: Lights, Camera, Natural Resources*. New Brunswick: Rutgers University Press, 2012. Print.

Brogers44. Comment in "Tasty Planet" thread. *Kongregate*. Web. 28 May 2012. <http://www.kongregate.com>.

Chang, Alenda Y. "Games as Environmental Texts." *Qui Parle* 19 (2011): 57-84. Print.

DarkraiPrince. Comment in "Tasty Planet" thread. *Kongregate*. Web. 12 December 2012. <http://www.kongregate.com>.

DCervan. Comment in "Tasty Planet" thread. *Kongregate*. Web. 11 December 2012. <http://www.kongregate.com>.

Deleuze, Gilles. "Postscript on the Societies of Control," *October* 59 (1992): 3-7. Print.

Dell, Mary. "Re: Tasty Planet." *Whateveresque*. Web. 9 September 2007. <http://whateveresque.com>.

Dyer-Witheford, Nick, and Greig de Peuter. *Games of Empire: Global Capitalism and Video Games*. Minneapolis: University of Minnesota Press, 2009. Print.

FANBUSCUS. Comment for "Tasty Planet: DinoTime" thread. *Kongregate*. Web. 8 December 2012. <http://www.kongregate.com>.

Foucault, Michel. *Discipline and Punish: The Birth of the Prison*. Trans. Alan Sheridan. Second Vintage Books edition. New York: Vintage Books, 1995. Print.

Freccia, Tim. "The PlayStation War: Battling for Coltan in the Congo." *Chronogram Magazine* 18.5 (2010). Web. <http://archives.chronogram.com>.

Gabrys, Jennifer. *Digital Rubbish: A Natural History of Electronics*. Ann Arbor: University of Michigan Press, 2011. Print.

Galloway, Alexander R. *Gaming: Essays on Algorithmic Culture*. Minneapolis: University of Minnesota Press, 2006. Print.

---. *Protocol: How Control Exists after Decentralization*. Cambridge, MA: MIT Press, 2004. Print.

Glew, L. and M. D. Hudson. "Gorillas in the Midst: The Impact of Armed Conflict on the Conservation of Protected Areas in Sub-Saharan Africa." *Oryx* 41, no. 2 (2007): 140-150. Print.

Gordon. Reply to Susie Cagle, "The New *SimCity*: Green Urbanist Dream, Gamer Nightmare." *Grist*. Web. 14 March 2013. <http://grist.org>.

Grossman, Elizabeth. *High Tech Trash: Digital Devices, Hidden Toxics, and Human Health*. Washington: Island Press/Shearwater Books, 2006. Print.

Haraway, Donna J. *When Species Meet*. Minneapolis: University of Minnesota Press, 2008. Print.

Hari, Johann. "Congo's Tragedy: The War the World Forgot." *The Independent* (London), May 5, 2006: 2. Print.

Hayles, N. Katherine. *How We Became Posthuman: Virtual Bodies in Cybernetics, Literature, and Informatics*. Chicago: University of Chicago Press, 1999. Print.

Heise, Ursula K. *Sense of Place and Sense of Planet: The Environmental Imagination of the Global*. Oxford: Oxford University Press, 2008. Print.

Higgins, Alex. "Shadow of the Colossus and the Unique Capabilities of Games for Storytelling." *Beta Fish Mag*. Web. 20 December 2012. <http://betafishmag.wordpress.com>.

Horowitz, Noah, Riley Neugebauer, Brooke Frazer, Peter May-Ostendorp, and Chris Calwell. *Lowering the Cost of Play: Improving the Energy Efficiency of Video Game Consoles*. NRDC Issue Paper. National Resources Defense Council, 2008. Print.

icicie. Comment in "Tasty Planet: DinoTime" thread. *Kongregate*. Web. 7 December 2011. <http://www.kongregate.com>.

Joshalos. Comment in "Tasty Planet" thread. *Kongregate*. Web. 12 February 2011. <http://www.kongregate.com>.

kingsnake6666. Comment in "Tasty Planet" thread. *Kongregate*. Web. 10 April 2011. <http://www.kongregate.com>.

Lasker, John. "Inside Africa's PlayStation War." *Toward Freedom*. Web. 8 July 2008. <http://www.towardfreedom.com>.

lewiss4455. Comment in "Tasty Planet" thread. *Kongregate*. Web. 24 August 2012. <http://www.kongregate.com>.

LittleFanGirl. Comment in "Tasty Planet" thread. *Kongregate*. Web. 24 December 2011. <http://www.kongregate.com>.

Mantz, Jeffrey W. "Improvisational Economies: Coltan Production in the Eastern Congo." *Social Anthropology* 16 (2008): 34-50. Print.

Maxwell, Richard, and Toby Miller. *Greening the Media*. New York: Oxford University Press, 2012. Print.

Merido. Comment in "Tasty Planet" thread. *Kongregate*. Web. 2 February 2011. <http://www.kongregate.com>.

Montague, Dena. "Stolen Goods: Coltan and Conflict in the Democratic Republic of Congo." *SAIS Review* 22 (2002): 103-118. Print.

mysticicedragon3. Comment in "Tasty Planet" thread. *Kongregate*. Web. 19 November 2011. <http://www.kongregate.com>.

Pandermatism. Comment in "Tasty Planet" thread. *Kongregate*. Web. 22 December 2012. <http://www.kongregate.com>.

Phillips, Henry. "Games and Love: *Shadow of the Colossus*." *Taufmonster's Log*. Web. 14 February 2012. <http://taufmonster.blogspot.com>.

Raley, Rita. *Tactical Media*. Minneapolis: University of Minnesota Press, 2009. Print.

Redmond, Ian. *Coltan Boom, Gorilla Bust: The Impact of Coltan Mining on Gorillas and Other Wildlife in Eastern Dr Congo*. Dian Fossey Gorilla Fund/Born Free Foundation, 2001. Print.

Smith, James H. "Tantalus in the Digital Age: Coltan Ore, Temporal Dispossession, and 'Movement' in the Eastern Democratic Republic of the Congo." *American Ethnologist* 38 (2011): 17-35. Print.

Smith, James H., and Jeffrey W. Mantz. "Do Cellular Phones Dream of Civil War?: The Mystification of Production and the Consequences of Technology Fetishism in the Eastern Congo." *Inclusion and Exclusion in the Global Arena*. Ed. Max Kirsch and June Nash. New York: Routledge, 2006. 71-94. Print.

StarProgrammer. Comment for "Tasty Planet: DinoTime" thread. *Kongregate*. Web. 7 December 2011. <http://www.kongregate.com>.

Taffel, Sy. "Escaping Attention: Digital Media Hardware, Materiality and Ecological Cost." *Culture Machine* 13 (2012). Web. <http://www.culturemachine.net>.

Tornadosaurus Rex. Response to Sean Beanland, "Shadow of the Colossus - I Feel So Sad." 5 February 2008. *Alethiometry*. Web. 11 October 2010. <http://seanbeanland.blogspot.com>.

Wakabi, Wairagala. "The Arms Smugglers." *New Internationalist* 367 (2004): 20-21. Print.

Wiener, Norbert. *Cybernetics: Or, Control and Communication in the Animal and the Machine*. 2nd ed. Cambridge, MA: MIT Press, 1961. Print.

wquach. "A Tribute to 'Shadow of the Colossus.'" *N4G*. Web. 11 September 2011. <http://n4g.com/user/blogpost/wquach/518464>.

Index

A Friend of the Earth (T.C. Boyle) *23, 76*
Acosta, Terese Paloma *15, 154*
Agamben, Giorgio *16, 163, 166, 172, 175, 206*
Alaimo, Stacy *104-105*
Amsterdam, Steven *14, 23, 59-78*
The Anatomy of Criticism (Northrop Frye) *124*
Animals *28, 48-49, 54, 71, 86-87, 92, 143, 147-148, 157, 171, 202, 205, 211, 213, 215, 217*; cadaver of *174*; and humankind *172, 175*
The Animals in That Country (Margaret Atwood) *152*
Antarctic *48, 54*
Anthropocene *21*
Anti-intellectualism *44*
Anticipation *13, 25, 144*; of catastrophe *15, 36, 102-103, 140, 143, 152, 204*; of climate change *139*; of crisis *60*; of risk *170*
Apocalypse *45-46, 48-49, 66-67, 92, 97, 122, 165, 177, 182, 185, 189, 193, 197*
Appadurai, Arjun *14, 61-62*
Atwood, Margaret *15, 16, 23, 141, 152, 155, 161-180*
Augé, Marc *64, 73*
Badmington, Neil *163-164*
Bang, Magnus *209-210*
Barad, Karen *104-105*
Beck, Ulrich *7, 8, 10-12, 15, 24-25, 32, 35, 59, 76, 82, 96, 102-103, 105, 108, 110, 119, 121-124, 126, 133-134, 139, 146-147, 157, 165, 172, 184-186, 197, 204*
Becquerel, Henri *92, 94*
Bildungsroman 30, 45-46, 48, 122
Biodiversity *139*
Bio-engineering *34*; genetic *121*
Black humor *125-127, 130-131, 133*
Body *74-75, 86, 101, 103-107, 109, 112, 215*
Boyle, T.C. *23, 76*
Bridges, James *15, 102*
Buell, Frederick *11, 13, 67, 70*
Buell, Lawrence *11, 13, 66-67, 192*
Cancer *52, 56, 84-86, 89, 91, 95, 103, 113-114, 120, 127, 129*
Carson, Rachel *9, 11*
Catastrophe *13, 25, 28, 39, 7, 103, 130, 132, 140, 148, 162, 168-170, 172-173, 175, 177, 189, 193, 214*; aftermath of *174*; anticipation of, see Anticipation of catastrophe; economic *156*; environmental *143-144, 146*; in film 183-*184, 186-187, 191-197*; future *67, 143, 145*; global *192*; narratives of *24, 26*; social *156*
Catch-22 (Joseph Heller) *126, 131*
Chernobyl *101*
Chicago Tribune 84, 88, 90
The China Syndrome (James Bridges) *15, 102-103, 106-110, 112, 114-115*
The Circle Game (Margaret Atwood) *152*
Clampitt, Amy *15, 141-142, 149-150*
Climate *40, 59*; and apathy *43, 46*; and catastrophe *29, 36*; multiple meanings of *36*; perception of *43*; and risk, see Risk of climate change; and scenario *59;* and scepticism *43, 50*; uncertainty about *51*
Climate change *10, 12-14, 21-25, 27-29, 31, 33-34, 36, 39-41, 43-44, 50, 54-57, 59, 65-66, 68-69, 76, 139, 169, 181*; anticipation of, see Anticipation of climate change; anthropogenic *23, 48, 50*; awareness of *57;* debates on *59;* denial of *29, 42-43, 48-50, 52, 54, 56*; discourse of *36*; knowledge of *43*; and religion *53-54*; and risk, see Risk of climate change; understanding *52*
Climate change fiction *40, 56, 60-61, 63, 76*
Climate change novel *23-24, 26-27, 35-36, 65*
Climate collapse *24*
Climate refugees *27, 33, 139-159*
Climate Refugees (Michael Nash) *140*
Climate science *29, 30, 32, 43, 60*
Comedy *120-122, 125-127, 131, 133*; in the age of uncertainty *121, 124*
Comedy of correction *124, 128-129, 133*
The Comedy of Survival (Joseph Meeker) *34*
Comedy of the absurd *15, 121, 123-124, 126, 129, 134*
Contagion (Steven Soderbergh) *17, 193-196, 183, 193, 195-196*
Control *121-122, 144, 146, 152-153, 155, 157, 165, 171, 207-211*; biopolitical *172*; over nature, see Nature, control over; of risk *186*
The Core (Jon Amiel) *181, 186-190, 192*
Cosmopolitanism *62, 76*
Crisis *45, 51, 59, 67, 70, 75, 193, 204-205*
Crossing into America (Teresa Paloma Acosta) *154-155*
Cultural toolkit *44-45*
Curie, Marie *83, 86, 88, 94*
Curie, Pierre *83-84, 90-92, 94*
Danger *8, 10, 28, 40, 45, 50, 57, 60, 103, 111, 145, 153, 184, 190-191*; and video games *201, 206*; ecological *170*; external *168*; global *96*; of radium *93-94;* of nuclear power *102;* sense of *110, 145*
The Day After Tomorrow (Roland Emmerich) *182, 186-187, 189, 191-192*
Deforestation *59*
Deleuze, Gilles *62, 207-208, 211*
DeLillo, Don *122*
Desertification *140*

Destruction *45, 143-147, 194, 213*; aesthetics of *191-192*; pleasures of *214*
Deterritorialization *60-64, 67, 69-71, 76*
Disaster *49, 55, 68, 110, 115, 121, 145, 169-170, 178, 181-200*; anticipation of *110;* environmental, see Environment and disaster; fear of *146*; in films *16, 181-200*; management of *186*; natural *49, 128, 189*; as nature out of bound *188-191*; and risk, see Risk and disaster
Disease *56, 91-92, 176, 194*
Douglas, Mary *11, 41, 139*
Dr. Strangelove (Stanley Kubrick) *109, 123, 126*
Dystopia *24, 26-31, 33, 162-166*
Eco-criminal *205-207*
Ecocriticism *46, 62, 67, 142*; African American *142*; Marxist *142*; post-colonial *142*
Ecological Politics in the Age of Risk (Ulrich Beck) *119, 121, 124, 139*
Ecology *28, 51, 153, 208*
Ecosystem *47, 153, 162, 165, 171, 202, 208*
Education *30, 50, 169, 171*
EisTau (Ilija Trojanow) *13, 40, 42, 48-49, 53-56*
Elegy *49*
Emotions *101, 104-107, 111, 115, 214, 216;* and affect *157, 212*; and assessment of risk *190-191*; effect of *102*
The End of History (Francis Fukuyama) *164*
Environment *30, 34, 36, 66-67, 104*; and apathy *50*; awareness of *67, 153*; and campaigns *59;* and catastrophe, see Catastrophe, environmental; changes in *75, 139-140, 142, 144, 148, 157*; control of *17, 167, 207-211*; and crisis *141-142, 146, 151, 154*; damage of *49, 97*; degradation of *122, 141*; destruction of *147*; and disaster *66, 145, 151*; and discipline *17*; domestic *209, 213*; and education *56*; of fear *165*; global *148, 154*; and hazard *54, 203-205*; and justice *29*; living *114*; local *60, 67*; and memory *141*; and migration *142*; and mourning *157*; and nature *139*; planetary *168*; and policy *32*; and politics *31-33, 204*; and refugees *140*; and resources *166*; responsibility of *17*; and threat *36, 207*; understanding of *63*; unfamiliar *153*
Environmental justice *9, 155*
The Environmental Imagination (Lawrence Buell) *67*
Environmental risk *8-9, 13-15, 17, 22, 24, 29, 35, 40-43, 45, 53-54, 56, 97, 103, 139, 142, 144, 146, 151-154, 157, 201-219*; awareness of *147*; global *10, 12, 147-148*; literary conceptualization of *156*; perception of *48, 153, 156-157*; sense of *150*
Environmentalism *9, 29-30, 45, 47, 54, 66*
Epic *46, 122*
Evernden, Neil *73*
Ewald, François *7*
Exceptionalism *162, 173*; American *44*; human *163, 172, 174*
Fear *8, 43, 52, 71, 103, 107-108, 110, 112-115, 144, 162*; of disaster *146*; religious *145-146*
Fifty Degrees Below (Kim Stanley Robinson) *13, 24, 27, 31*
Fleischmann, Doris E. 87-88
Flight Behavior (Barbara Kingsolver) *13, 24, 27-28, 33, 40, 42-43, 47-50, 54-56*
Flooding *39, 48, 56*
Forty Signs of Rain (Kim Stanley Robinson) *13, 24, 27, 31*
Foucault, Michel *204, 206*
From Apocalypse to Way of Life (Frederick Buell) *11, 67*
Frye, Northrop *124*
Fukushima *101, 116*
Fukuyama, Francis *164*
Gain (Richard Powers) *123*
Garrard, Greg *185*
Genre *15, 24, 45-46, 56, 66, 120, 122, 124, 127, 177, 193-194, 196-197*; and convention *33, 107*; and tradition *46*; and video games *204, 210*
Giddens, Anthony *7, 10, 67, 119, 123-124, 126, 139, 165*
Glaciers *49, 54-55*
Global Risk, see Risk
Global scale *59-60*
Global terrorism *25, 41*
Global warming *21, 27, 29-30, 33-34, 39-40, 42-43, 45, 47, 50-51, 54-55, 59-60*
Globalization *25, 57, 59, 61-62, 67, 195*
Gore, Al *140*
The Great Bay (Dale Pendell) 23
Green gaming *201-219*
Greenhouse gas emissions *10, 21-22, 32, 39, 59, 63, 201, 203-204*
Guattari, Félix *62*
Gulf current *33, 40*
Haraway, Donna *212*
Health *74, 85-86, 88-89, 95-96, 101, 120*; problem *127*; public *140*
Heise, Ursula *12-13, 40, 45-46, 48, 60, 62-63, 66, 69, 76, 122-123, 182, 192-193, 197, 204*
Heller, Joseph *126, 131*
Holmes, Oliver Wendell *87*
Hulme, Mike *22-23, 36, 41, 75*
I Am Legend (Francis Lawrence) *185, 188, 192*
Illness narrative *35*
Illness as Narrative (Ann Jurecic) *35*
"In a Clearing" (W.S. Merwin) *147*
An Inconvenient Truth (Al Gore) *140*
Individualism *44*
Information deficit model *40*
IPCC report 2013 *21*

Irony *30*
Irresponsibility *121-122, 124-125, 129*
"John Winthrop" (Nicole Cooley) *145*
Johns-Putra, Adeline *23*
Jurecic, Ann *35*
Kafka, Franz *123-124, 126*
Kafkaesque *15*
Katastrophenschwelle 16, 163, 166-172
The Kingfisher (Amy Clampitt) *141*
Kingsolver, Barbara *13, 24, 27, 36, 40, 42, 51-52, 54, 57*
Kojève, Alexandre *164, 171*
Kubrick, Stanley *109, 126*
Lebenswelten 60
Leitmotif 28
Lemmon, Jack *110, 115*
Living in Denial (Kari Norgaard) *42*
Local *29, 44, 59, 60-62, 191*
London Times 84
Luhmann, Niklas *7, 16, 163, 166-168*
MaddAddam (Margaret Atwood) *23*
McClure's Magazine 83, 90-91
Media *30, 43-44, 47, 50-51, 102, 122, 201*; and advertising *49, 86-89*; American film *181-200*; American newspapers *81-100*; cinematic power *110;* film *115;* mass media *82;* technologies *212*; television *109*
Meeker, Joseph *34*
Melodrama *114*
Melting Ice (Ilija Trojanow), see *EisTau*
Merwin, W.S. *15, 141, 143, 147-148*
Migration *15, 47, 139-159*; of animals *148-151*; and environment *142*; global *144*; human *143, 148-149, 157*; in nature *147*; process *140*; return *140*; and risk *151, 155*; seasonal *140*
Migration (W.S. Merwin) *141*
Mizruchi, Susan *122-123*
Mobility *73, 139, 154, 156*
Modernization *62, 104*
Mohun, Arwen *8-10*
Morton, William James *94*
Nash, Michael *140*
Narrative, of anticipation *24, 26-27, 30-31, 33, 36*; of catastrophe *24, 26*; of conversion *46*; of risk, see Risk narrative
National Radium Institute *84*
Nature *41, 54, 62, 68, 149, 151, 153, 157, 171-172*; control over *156-157, 191, 197, 214*; crimes against 205; destruction of *143*; and disaster *188-191*; domination of *156*; exploitation of *144-145*; as feminized *145*; and human *153*; man's incompatibility with *49*; love of *50*; maltreated *146*; potential agency *146*; revenge of *143-147*; subjugation of *145-146*; vengeful *143*
New York Times 83, 88, 90, 95, 115
Nichols, Mike *15, 102, 112*
Nixon, Rob *10*
Non-place *64, 72-73, 76*
Norgaard, Kari *13-14, 42, 50, 52, 56*
Novel *33*; domestic *33-34*; picaresque *33-35, 66*
Nuclear contamination *108, 110, 112-113*
Nuclear risk, see Risk
Nuclear power *101-102, 109*
O'Neill, Saffron *22, 126*
The Open (Giorgio Agamben) *166*
Oryx and Crake (Margaret Atwood) *16, 23, 161-180*
Ozone depletion *140*
Parable of the Sower (Octavia Butler) *23*
Parable of the Talents (Octavia Butler) *23*
Pastoral *30, 45-46, 48, 69, 71, 122, 149, 151*; "disrupted" (Heise) *48, 192*
Picaro 34-35, 66
Place *60-61, 65, 67, 69-77, 140, 143, 146, 148*; attachment to *63, 76*
Planet *49, 209, 213*; impact on *49*; earth *116, 212, 214*
Plutonium *103, 114*
Plutonium Files (Eileen Welsome) *119-120*
Politics, see Environment and politics
Pollution *26, 121, 192, 201-207, 211*
Postapocalyptic *16, 110, 164-166, 171-172, 184*; environment *173*
Posthuman *13, 16, 161-173, 175-178*; and human *147, 172*; narrative *177*
Radiation *15 101-103, 109, 121*; effect of *113, 119*; experiments with *119-120, 127, 132, 131*; exposure to *113;* invisibility of *103*; nuclear *112*; and plutonium *113, 116;* and radium *14, 81-100, 85*; and uranium *116*; visceral *110*
Radium Girls *14, 81-83, 81, 83*
Reflexive modernity *24*
The Revenge of the Radioactive Lady (Elizabeth Stuckey-French) *15, 119-135*
Risk *32, 41, 45, 57, 156, 169, 171, 196*; atmosphere of *151*; aversion to *171*; awareness of *7, 15, 54, 59-60, 96, 154-155*; calculation of *8, 177, 181, 208*; of climate change *31-35, 39, 48, 51, 59, 61, 68, 70*; of collective death *147*-151; and comedy *121*; communication of *12, 24, 26, 45, 96-97, 157*; consciousness of *97, 156*; as controversial reality *27, 32*; criticism of *124, 133*; denial of *56*; and disaster 181-200; and discipline *121, 204-207*; ecological *204*; environmental, see Environmental risk; erasure of *193*; experience of *12, 31, 35, 76*; evaluation of *75*; exposure to *74*; and fiction *134*; global *32, 60, 62-63, 68, 76, 121*; of human-nature relationship *141*; individual *148*; of infection *195*; literary exploration of *123*; logic of *163, 165, 167-168, 171, 177*; management of *16, 162, 167, 181, 186-187, 190-191, 196*; metamorphosis of *123*; and migration, see Migration and risk;

negotiation of *73*; notion of *142*; nuclear *13-14, 91-92, 102-103, 111, 114-115*; objective *175*; perception of *7, 10-11, 15, 22, 25, 39-42, 45, 56, 60, 97, 103, 105, 108, 110, 112, 124, 153*; physical *175*; and politics *121*; rhetoric of *164*; representation of *16*; and responsibility *127*; semantics of *165*; sense of *144, 155-156*; shifting notions of *141*; spectrum of *140*; staging of *25*; technological, see Technological risk; and uncertainty *129*; victims of *124*
Risk and Culture (Mary Douglas and Aaron Wildavsky) *41, 139*
Risk assessment *7, 10, 22, 25, 35, 41, 82, 166, 169-170*
Risk culture (Anthony Giddens) *10*
Risk narrative *13, 16, 24, 26-27, 30-31, 33, 35-36, 66-67, 123, 126, 133, 186, 193*
Risk research *7, 10, 25-26*
Risk scenario *11, 25-26, 29, 31, 46, 63, 66, 97, 106, 122, 143, 182, 184-188, 191-193, 196-197*
Risk society *9, 11, 15, 24, 60, 76, 82, 103-105, 120-122-126, 128-130, 133, 163, 165, 169*
Risk theory *7, 10, 24, 39-42, 44-46, 121, 123, 133*
Riskscape *14, 61, 64-65, 67, 69-70, 72-76, 120, 122, 133-134*; survival in *71*
The Road (John Hillcoat) *110*
Robinson, Kim Stanley *13, 24, 27, 31, 33-34, 36*
Saenger, Eugene *119*
Science *35, 44, 168, 197*; and authority *132*; and community *120, 130*; and control *208*; and development *119;* and evidence *39*; and knowledge *10, 30, 167, 169*; language of *124*; legitimacy of *50*; modelling *25*; and news *83*; in *Oryx and Crake 167*; and projection *59;* and radium *88*; and rationality *33*; and responsibility *214*; and scenario *35, 59-60*
Scientist *29-32, 49, 52, 54, 96, 130-131, 170-171, 174, 213-214*
Sea level, rise in *39, 140*
Security *9, 87, 109, 111, 113, 140, 165, 167, 169, 171, 197*
Sense of Place and Sense of Planet (Ursula Heise) *12, 40, 60, 63*
Shadow of the Colossus 214-217
Silent Spring (Rachel Carson) *9*
Silkwood (Mike Nichols) *15, 102-103, 106, 112, 114-115*
Sixty Days and Counting (Kim Stanley Robinson) *13, 24, 27, 31*
Slovic, Paul *10-11, 105, 182, 187, 190*
Slovic, Scott *11*
Slow Violence and the Environmentalism of the Poor (Rob Nixon) *10*
Soderbergh, Steven *17, 193*
Sontag, Susan *191*
Soziologie des Risikos (Niklas Luhmann) *166*
Space *62-64, 67-68, 74, 146, 148, 157*; of criminality *210*; empty *177*; of transit *73*
Species extinction *26, 48, 140, 148, 150, 177, 201-202, 215*
Staging of risk *25, 184, 197*
Stuckey-French, Elizabeth *15, 120, 127-129, 131-133*
Sublime *46, 48, 191;* of the mushroom *109*
Surveillance *33, 110, 205, 208, 211*
Survival *166, 174*
Survivor *45, 168, 192*
Tasty Planet 212-214
Technology *182, 189-190*; innovation in *10*; and science *188*
Technological risk *9, 68*
Temperature *39, 47, 54, 59, 208*
Things We Didn't See Coming (Steven Amsterdam) *14, 23, 59-78*
Threat *10, 17, 125, 146-147, 151, 153, 157, 164, 170, 203, 205*
Three Mile Island *103, 112*
Tragedy *45, 122, 127*
Trans-corporeality *104*
Trojanow, Ilija *13, 40, 42, 50, 54, 57*
Trope *45-46, 144, 147-148, 151, 153, 157, 163*; of ending *162*; multidimensional *143*
Tropical cyclone *59*
Uncertainty *28, 30-31, 33, 39, 121, 124-125, 127, 130, 133-134, 151, 153, 156, 168*; age of *126*; and environmental sensitivity *152*; and migration *152*; of risk, see Risk and uncertainty
Utopia *34, 162-164*
Video games *17, 201-219*; of environmental control *207-212*; of environmental discipline *204-207, 210, 212*; of environmental responsibility *212-217*
Weather *28, 30, 39-40, 51, 59, 65*; and anomaly *31, 33*; extreme *63, 72, 140*; irregularity of *31*; patterns of *31, 47*
White Noise (Don DeLillo) *122*
Wildavsky, Aaron *11, 41*
Wood, James *124-125*
When People Could Fly (Morton Marcus) *143-144*
When Species Meet (Donna Haraway) *212*
World at Risk (Ulrich Beck) *7, 12, 25, 102, 108, 123, 139*
World risk society (Ulrich Beck) *10, 16, 24-25, 27, 29, 31-32, 33, 35, 76, 122, 147*
Writing for an Endangered World (Lawrence Buell) *11*
The Year of the Flood (Margaret Atwood) *23*

List of Contributors

CHRISTINE GERHARDT is Professor of American literature and culture at the University of Bamberg, Germany. Her research and teaching focus on ecocriticism, migration literature, African American literature, regional literatures, and the poetry of Walt Whitman and Emily Dickinson. She has written a book on representations of the Reconstruction era in American fiction, *Rituale des Scheiterns: Die Reconstruction-Periode im US-amerikanischen Roman* (2002), and coedited the volume *Religion in the USA* (2011); her book *A Place for Humility: Whitman, Dickinson and the Natural World* will come out with the University of Iowa Press in the Fall of 2014. Her articles have appeared in *Profession, Forum for Modern Language Studies, Mississippi Quarterly, Poroi: An Interdiciplinary Journal of Rhetorical Analysis and Intervention,* and *The Emily Dickinson Journal.* She is currently working on an analysis of the intersections between migratory movements and environmental perspectives in American poetry.

AXEL GOODBODY is Professor of German and European Culture at the University of Bath, England. After graduating from Trinity College Dublin he lived for ten years in Germany, teaching and studying at the University of Kiel, before moving to Bath in 1983. His thesis on German Romantic and 20th century nature poetry was published as *Natursprache* (1984), and he has since written, edited books and organised conferences on aspects of modern German literature including exile studies, GDR studies, and cultural memory. His main research area is, however, German environmental literature. Heimat literature, German climate change fiction, and nature writing are focuses of his current work. He was a founding member of the European Association for the Study of Literature, Culture and Environment (EASLCE), served as its first President 2004-6, and is currently Associate Editor of EASLCE's journal *ECOZON@: European Journal of Literature, Culture and Environment.* He is currently engaged on a three-year project funded by the UK Arts & Humanities Research Council, "Stories of Change: Exploring Energy and Community in the Past, Present and Future."

KARIN HÖPKER is Assistant Professor of North American Studies at the Friedrich-Alexander University Erlangen-Nuremberg, Germany. She was a fellow of the interdisciplinary research training group "Cultural Hermeneutics: Reflections of Difference and Transdifference" (funded by the German Federal Research Council) at the University of Erlangen-Nuremberg and was awarded her PhD in 2008. She is currently part of the interdisciplinary Emerging Field Initiative "Bio-Objects and Bio-Subjects." Her research interests include architecture and urban studies, science and technology studies, contemporary American TV series, and 19th century economic history. Her book *No Maps for these Territories: Cities, Spaces, and Archaeologies of the Future in William Gibson* was published in 2011. She is currently working on her second book project on the topic "The Edge of Reason: Fiction, Risk, and Probability in American Antebellum Literature."

HOLGER KERSTEN is Professor of American Literature and Culture at the University of Magdeburg, Germany. He was executive director of the German Association for American Studies (2005-2008) and now serves on its advisory board. He is a member of various national and international academic associations (German Association for American Studies, Mark Twain Circle of America, Stephen Crane Society, Jack London Society, American Humor Studies Association, International Society for Humor Studies). He has published on Mark Twain, Jack London, Stephen Crane, the Lewis and Clark expedition, and humor in American literature. In addition to 19th-century American literature, his research interests include the use of nonstandard language in literature, national images, and environmental studies.

NICOLE MARUO-SCHRÖDER is Professor of Cultural Studies at the University of Koblenz-Landau, Germany. She has published on Native American and African American literature, concepts of culture and narrative identity, contemporary American film, ecocriticism as well as gender studies and intersectionality. Her books include *Spaces and Places in Motion: Spatial Concepts in Contemporary American Literature* (2006) as well as the edited volumes *Literature and Consumption in Nineteenth-Century America* (with Christoph Ribbat, 2014) and *Rereading the Machine in the Garden: Nature and Technology in American Culture* (with Eric Erbacher and Florian Sedlmeier, 2014). She is currently working on a monograph on commerce and consumption in antebellum American literature.

SYLVIA MAYER is Chair of American Studies and Anglophone Literatures and Cultures at the University of Bayreuth, Germany, and director of the Bayreuth Institute for American Studies (BIFAS). Her major fields of research are ecocriticism and African American literature. Her publications include monographs on Toni Morrison's novels and on the environmental ethical dimension of 19th century New England regionalist writing. She has edited and coedited several volumes of criticism, among them *Restoring the Connection to the Natural World: Essays on the African American Environmental Imagination* (2003), *Literature, Culture, Environment: Positioning Ecocriticism* (with Catrin Gersdorf, 2005) and *American Environments. Climate – Culture – Catastrophe* (with Christof Mauch, 2012). Her current research focuses on the Anglophone climate change novel and on environmental risk fiction across media.

ANTONIA MEHNERT is a PhD candidate in the Environment and Society program at the Rachel Carson Center and in American Studies at the University of Munich, Germany. Her dissertation project, entitled "Climate Change Fictions," focuses on future scenarios of climate change in American literature. She received her M.A. degree in American Studies, Latin-American studies and Economics at the University of Potsdam and the Free University Berlin. Her research interests include ecocriticism and climate change, risk theory, Chicana/o studies, the postcolonial Caribbean. She is the co-founder of EASLCE's postgraduate forum "Environment, Literature, Culture" (ELC).

COLIN MILBURN holds the Gary Snyder Chair in Science and the Humanities at the University of California, Davis, USA. His research focuses on the relations of literature, science, and media technologies. He is the author of *Nanovision: Engineering the Future* (2008) and *Mondo Nano: Fun and Games in the World of Digital Matter* (2014). He has published extensively on issues relating to the cultural dimensions of science and technology, and he is currently completing a new book called *All Your Base Are*

Belong to Us: Video Games and Technopolitics. Since 2009, he has been serving as the director of the UC Davis Humanities Innovation Lab.

ANNA THIEMANN obtained her M.Ed. (*Erstes Staatsexamen*) and M.A. (*Magistra Artium*) in English, German, Philosophy, and Communication Studies from Westfälische Wilhelms-Universität Münster, Germany. Since then, she has been a research and teaching assistant at WWU Münster, focusing on American literature and culture, literature and science, visual culture, African American studies, and gender studies. In 2013, she finished her Ph.D. thesis about trauma, neuroscience, and the contemporary literary imagination, which she developed at WWU Münster and Duke University, USA.

ALEXA WEIK VON MOSSNER is Assistant Professor of American Studies at the University of Klagenfurt, Austria, and International Curatorial Fellow at the Rachel Carson Center for Environment and Society at the University of Munich, Germany. She earned her Ph.D. in Literature at the University of California, San Diego in 2008. Her articles on cosmopolitanism, affective narratology, and various ecocritical issues in American literature and film have been published in journals such as *ISLE: Interdisciplinary Studies in Literature and Environment*, *Environmental Communication*, and the *Journal of Commonwealth and Postcolonial Studies*. She is the author of *Cosmopolitan Minds: Literature, Emotion, and the Transnational Imagination* (2014), the co-editor (with Christoph Irmscher) of a special issue of the *European Journal of English Studies* on "Dislocations and Ecologies" (2012), and the editor of *Moving Environments: Affect, Emotion, Ecology, and Film* (2014). Her current book project explores our affective engagements with environmental literature and visual culture from the perspective of cognitive ecocriticism.